No Fret Cooking

Something for Everyone

A blending of
Simple, Healthy, Yummy Recipes,
Community
and
Music

"Let food be thy medicine and medicine be thy food"
- *Hippocrates*

Dedicated with Love and Light:

To my husband Steve, and our daughters Sheri and Wendy

 INFINITY PUBLISHING

ISBN 978-0-7414-7449-0

Printed in the United States of America

Published May 2012

INFINITY PUBLISHING
1094 New DeHaven Street, Suite 100
West Conshohocken, PA 19428-2713
Toll-free (877) BUY BOOK
Local Phone (610) 941-9999
Fax (610) 941-9959
Info@buybooksontheweb.com
www.buybooksontheweb.com

Author:
Marilynn Carter | www.manypathsforhealth.com

Music and Creative Consultant:
Stephen Carter | www.frogstoryrecords.com

Content Layout and Consulting:
Sheri Santo, Graphic Designer | www.sherisanto.com

Book Title:
Wendy Carter

Cover Artwork and Layout:
Jo-el Gavel Cookman | www.indigoinferno.com

Forward:
Emily Loghmani, Registered Dietitian

Recipe Editor:
Toni McFarland

Content Editor:
Erica Hunter | elifeskills63@gmail.com

Reviewed Seasons Content:
Diana Ward, Acupuncturist | www.acuwerx.com | acuwerx@gmail.com

Contents

Dessert

Main Dishes – Fish and Seafood

Main Dishes – Meat

" If music be the food of love, play on...**"**

– William Shakespeare

FOREWORD

by Emily Loghmani, Registered Dietitian

Why buy this book? Glossy, colorful cookbooks with attractive pictures are in every bookstore and on every grocery shelf. Some end up as conversation pieces on coffee tables; some are forgotten on bookshelves. Others get pulled off the shelf for 1 or 2 special recipes. But the best ones end up in the kitchen splattered with grease, stained with fingerprints, well-worn and turned-down pages... and most importantly... used!

The creator of this cookbook, Marilynn Carter, wants this book to be used! She hopes it will become a resource for your everyday cooking, baking, and meal planning needs. This cookbook caters to all eating styles. There are recipes made with whole wheat and other alternative flours; ancient and modern grains; gluten-free recipes; recipes with sugar and natural alternatives; dairy-free recipes; meat dishes; vegetarian dishes; as well as simple, everyday, and fancy dishes. The variety of ingredients in this cookbook allows people to follow basic nutrition principles for healthy eating, a varied diet, moderation, and balance.

In No Fret Cooking, the author uses traditional as well as alternative ingredients in her recipes, so there is something for everyone, which eliminates the need for multiple cookbooks. The recipes here have been tested and you can use them with confidence, knowing that the end product will look attractive, be flavorful, and will contribute significantly to a healthy eating plan.

AUTHOR'S PHILOSOPHY

My goal when starting this project was to focus on presenting a broad and inclusive plan for healthy, nutritious and satisfying eating, that was also simple and tasty rather than focusing on one particular narrow path. We live in a world with many available resources for individual preferences and I hope that through awareness and the joy of exploration and experimentation, you will be inspired to try new ingredients and discover healthy foods and recipes that are creative, visually appealing, and easy to prepare while at the same time tantalize your taste buds. Although I emphasize and fully support the use of organic, grass fed, free-range, local, fresh food, which is prepared without preservatives, colorings or artificial ingredients, it is my hope that you will be encouraged to make healthy choices, there are no hard and fast rules. It is not my intention to persuade you to embrace all suggestions or change your eating habits in ways that are not right for you or are impractical for your lifestyle, but rather to bring awareness to other possibilities. For what is more important is that you continue to enjoy your meals and look forward to mealtime as one of life's daily pleasures.

For many years, I have been fortunate to have my husband play music while I prepare dinner. It is like receiving a beautiful gift that elevates me to another place as I cook. This year, my friend Beth and I started a new tradition. We attend a Zumba class, shop at Philbrick's Fresh Market, and then head to our house to cook and be serenaded by Steve's music. Together we've cooked several recipes from this book, and I can say the whole experience has been the highlight of our day and evening. This got me thinking that I wanted to pass on our experience to others. So to help make meal preparation more enjoyable, you will find a CD of original music composed by my husband, Steve Carter, to listen to while cooking, and then another CD, to be enjoyed once the meal is complete as you sit down to eat and enjoy the fresh, healthy, food you have prepared.

You will find that many recipes note "Cook's choice" which indicates ingredients I have used followed by suggested alternates. In this way, it is your choice whether you try something new or not. For the most part, the recipes can easily be adapted to make with ingredients you have on hand or prefer to use. I know change doesn't come easily or instantly, so I suggest you keep an open mind to think about trying some alternate suggestions at some point.

Wishing you all happy, healthy, simple eating as you use *No Fret Cooking*!

- Marilynn

INTRODUCTION - HOW THIS BOOK CAME TO BE

As I'm always curious how people get started on their path, I thought I'd satisfy my readers' curiosity too. And so it begins. There I was standing in my kitchen several years ago and I heard this voice say, "Do a cookbook." I thought, how strange. So I asked the question, "really - do a cookbook?" And immediately I got a YES. This wasn't anything I had ever thought about doing and certainly was not one of my life-long ambitions, but after a few minutes of mulling the idea over, I came to the conclusion—Why not! I liked to cook, had tried many different food approaches for health issues, including what was popular at the time, and this would be a great time to begin a project since I was just completing an eleven-month rotational food program. The timing did seem great to begin a cookbook and I was looking forward to getting back to cooking some old favorite recipes and trying some new ones.

So now you know how the book came to be, but I want to bring you back to an earlier time so you can more easily see how my cooking, food choices, and philosophy have changed and continues to change, as I make healthier changes for myself and my family.

Ever since I can remember, cooking has been part of my life. Both my parents worked and I remember coming home from school to watch my brother, Joey, and start preparing the evening meal. My training came from watching my dad who liked to cook but enjoyed eating even more. In those days there wasn't research like there is today about the benefits of healthy eating. Our meals were simple and I learned basic cooking skills. Growing up, I remember not liking many of the foods, but we had to try everything that was cooked by taking a "no thank you helping." Fortunately for me, we had a dog that was only too eager to be fed my "no thank you helpings" under the table. Looking back, I now understand that even at a young age I knew that brisket, tongue, white bread, iceberg lettuce, Jell-o, and canned vegetables weren't the most nutritious. Rarely did we have fresh vegetables and never did I get to experience lentils, legumes, whole wheat flour or any grains except for kasha, also known as buckwheat groats, which was an all-time favorite of mine.

Growing up, I developed allergies, though in those days they weren't referred to as allergies. It wasn't until I was married with children of my own that I was told I had allergies and food sensitivities. To lessen my sensitivity load, it was suggested I try different food programs, including yeast-free and candida-free, vegetarian, vegan, sugar-free, wheat-free, and finally a rotation diet. I learned a lot from these approaches and what eventually made sense to me was a diet that included a variety of ingredients, more fresh food, less processed food, no artificial colors or flavors, no genetically modified food, and eating organic and local when possible. I started to slowly incorporate these changes into my life and was able to tolerate most foods. This is when I began to understand there was a connection between what we eat and our health.

Back then, there weren't a lot of cookbooks I could refer to and not the alternative choices there are now, so it took some trial and error to figure out which products had the best taste and were the easiest to work with to create healthy, nutritious, and yummy meals. I believe because I had to try whatever was cooked for me as a child, I have not been afraid to try new foods and today enjoy a wide variety of foods and continue to be open to exploring, and finding healthier ways of eating and living. While my cooking style is different from my dad's, I too, love, to eat. I also enjoy the cooking aromas that fill our house, and seeing our plates filled with nutritious and colorful food.

One day while in a bookstore, I gazed at the rows of cookbooks and each seemed to have a particular theme. There were books dedicated to just about every health issue imaginable, books from every foreign country, and all types including vegetarian, raw foods, vegan, meat, and grilling. On and on they went. This got me thinking about what kind of cookbook I would like to create. It was at that point, I decided on a book that would have no main focus so if a person could have just one cookbook, this would be that ONE book. I wanted a book that would have something in it that would appeal to everyone.

In my health and wellness practice, Many Paths for Health, among other things, I am also a Jin Shin Jyutsu® practitioner and what I like about that practice is their approach to health issues. One JSJ philosophy is to not give an illness a label like heart disease, diabetes, arthritis, etc. as these labels are kind of scary and having a label gives an illness more power. So instead of labeling an illness, each label is called a project. Projects are fun to work on, gives us hope, and helps us to take control of our life. So with that philosophy in mind, I wanted a book that would appeal to everyone, and give readers an opportunity to make their own healthy choices, and yet be fun to cook with.

As a way to vary the diet, I created and am including recipes that use some alternative ingredients, like different flours, grains, and sweeteners, and have included informational chapters so you can learn more about ingredients used before giving them a try. Many of the alternatives used can be found at your local supermarket or health food store. My personal preferences are for organic, free-range and grass-fed chickens and cows, fresh and local food when available, less processed food, and cooking from scratch as much as possible. I am also supportive of local farms, farmers markets, and home-grown gardens if one is fortunate enough to have a bit of land or even a deck.

"It is also important to consider varying the foods you eat so you are not always eating the same food; eating in season; feeding your taste buds with all the various flavors of salty, sweet, spicy, sour and tart; as well as introducing lots of healthy greens and colorful fruits and vegetables."

An interesting occurrence developed from the process of writing this book as I received guidance and inspiration that music should accompany the book. Over the past few years, my husband and I have worked together on various projects so it wasn't surprising to me that music should be part of healthy eating. For as long as I can remember, while cooking dinner, my husband would play music for me. His style is very calming but at the same time uplifting. He would play my favorite songs as well as new songs he was composing, and before I knew it, dinner was ready. I mentioned to my husband that I felt we should include a CD with the book. He took it in stride and agreed to start composing the music. As more time passed and the book began to take shape, I realized that we needed to have two CDs so when you use this book you too can enjoy music while you cook and music while you dine.

Another focus of the book is about community and the opportunity for people to come together, supporting each other in the completion of a project. Being able to offer a book with something for everyone meant that I would need help from others to round out the recipe offerings. I put this idea out to family and friends to see if they would like to be part of this project and received many offers to help. My guidelines for recipe inclusion were very specific in that recipes should not include any products that contained preservatives, chemicals, or artificial colors. I was gifted with many favorite recipe contributions including some that had been passed down from other generations, some had won prizes, many were gluten-free, and some had fabulous new twists. I wondered how I could convey my gratitude for everyone's support, time, and effort. I decided to list each contributor's name, city and state, as well as their talent and contact information in the hope that you may be curious or interested in some of their services. Each is very gifted, and I highly recommend their services.

So with the spirit of healthy eating and the possibility of expanding your current choices, I entrust this book to you in the hope that you will explore some of the healthy alternatives, discover your favorites and begin to make creative changes that may appeal more to you. In the spirit of health, wellness, wisdom, and the joy of cooking and dining with music, we hope you enjoy *No Fret Cooking*!

WHY ORGANIC?

What Is Organic?

Organic refers to the way agricultural products, food, and fiber are grown and processed. Organic food production is based on a system of farming that maintains and replenishes soil fertility without the use of toxic and persistent pesticides and fertilizers. Organic foods are minimally processed without artificial ingredients, preservatives, or irradiation to maintain the integrity of the food.

Why Buy Organic?

Current law mandates that the U.S. Department of Agriculture (USDA) products labeled organic be free of pesticides, hormones, and genetically modified organisms (GMOs), and that animals be given access to the outdoors. Health Note: The National Institute of Health (NIH) and the Mount Sinai Medical Center Children's Environmental Health Center suggest links between agricultural antibiotic use and the rise in drug-resistant staph infections in humans and links between a rise in cancer and diabetes with the use of pesticides in food.

Is There an Official Definition of Organic?

The following excerpt is from the definition of organic that the National Organic Standards Board adopted in April 1995: "Organic agriculture is an ecological production management system that promotes and enhances biodiversity, biological cycles, and soil biological activity. It is based on minimal use of off-farm inputs and on management practices that restore, maintain, and enhance ecological harmony."

Is Organic Food Better for You?

There is mounting evidence at this time to suggest that organically produced foods may be more nutritious, less toxic, and taste better. In growing organic foods, farmers do not use toxic insecticides, herbicides, fungicides, fertilizers, and pesticides that are no longer approved by the Environmental Protection Agency (EPA). Extensive research now links these chemicals to cancer and other diseases. Researchers at Washington State University conducted taste trials that revealed organic berries were consistently judged to taste sweeter. Other research has verified that some organic produce is lower in nitrates and higher in antioxidants than conventional food. Ultimately, organic farming techniques provide a safer, more sustainable environment for everyone.

Who Regulates the Certified Organic Claims?

The federal government sets standards for the production, processing, and certification of organic food through the Organic Food Production Act of 1990 (OFPA). Any food labeled organic must meet national organic standards, and the USDA's National Organic program oversees these standards.

Are All Organic Products Completely Free of Pesticide Residues?

Certified organic products have been grown and handled according to strict standards without toxic and persistent chemical inputs. However, organic crops may be inadvertently exposed to agricultural chemicals that are now pervasive in rain and groundwater due to their overuse during the past fifty years in North America, and due to drift via wind and rain.

The following information was gathered from the following resources:

http://www.ota.comeorganic.html

http://www.ams.usda.gov/AMSv1.0/nop

The Environmental Working Group put together a guide for fruits and vegetables based on data collected from thousands of tests conducted between 2000 and 2008 by the U.S. Department of Agriculture and the U.S. Food and Drug Administration. Their findings suggest eating a varied diet, rinsing all produce, and buying organic when possible. The EWG put together "The Shopper's Guide to Pesticides" to help consumers make informed food purchasing choices to help lower their dietary pesticide load. The Guide includes a list of the Dirty Dozen foods grown with the highest levels of pesticides and recommends that foods on this list be bought organic. As well, the guide also suggests 15 Clean foods that are grown with the lowest amounts of pesticides.

Dirty Dozen

Highest amounts of pesticides used in order: apples, celery, strawberries followed by peaches, spinach, nectarines (imported), grapes (imported), sweet bell peppers, potatoes, blueberries, domestic lettuce, kale, and collard greens.

Clean 15

Least amounts of pesticides used in order: onions, sweet corn, pineapple followed by avocado, asparagus, sweet peas, mangos, eggplant, cantaloupe domestic, kiwi, cabbage, watermelon, sweet potato, grapefruit, and mushrooms.

For more information from the Environmental Working Group, The Power of Information: 202-667-6982: www.ewg.org

SEASONAL EATING

A few reasons why you might want to try to eat food within its harvest season: you get the freshest, most wholesome food when it is grown close to home and in season; you will be supporting your community; and you get to know the people who grow your food and their farming practices. Many rewards await you as you become aware of the pattern of the seasons attuning to the bounties of Mother Nature. When you eat seasonally you are assured the freshest and most nutritious foods.

One of the Reiki ideals or principles of life is Gratitude. Through the preparation and eating of food we bring gratitude into our lives each and every day. Being grateful to the earth and its changing seasons brings us an abundance of food that nourishes, harmonizes, and energizes us through the natural cycle of the seasons.

The Seasons

Chinese medicine follows the law of the 5-element theory and how we relate to the changing seasons of summer, late summer, fall, winter, and spring. And like the seasons, we, too, are constantly changing. As the body needs variety nutritionally to function optimally, it is suggested one try to stay in harmony with the seasons and the shifts of light and temperature. The accuracy of the 5-element theory has been verified over hundreds of years by countless numbers of successful practitioners of Chinese Medicine who maintain that a balance of the 5 flavors in our diet helps keep the body in harmony, builds strong bones and tender muscles, and allows the breath and blood to circulate freely through the body filling it with life essence.

Summer

Seasonal flavor: Bitter
Organs: Heart and Small Intestine

The perfect time of year to enjoy more laughter and the joy of life while spending more time being physically active out in the sunshine. A time to eat lighter with less cooked food and more fresh, raw foods will help one feel lighter and at the same time will have a cooling effect on the body. Eat less of the heavier foods of dairy and meat and add more bitter foods to strengthen digestion and drink lots of fresh water to reduce excess heat. Some suggestions include papaya, cucumber, endive, escarole, watercress, romaine, most lettuces, parsley, chicory coffee, tea, and unsweetened dark chocolate. Flower and leaf teas, including mint, chrysanthemum, and chamomile are a wonderful addition. You'll find two cooling refreshing drinks, watermelon juice and citrus fruit-smoothies in the drink chapter. Eat a variety of multicolored good food like corn, tomatoes, basil, zucchini, melons, garlic, ginger, raspberries, peaches, and watermelon. When we eat lightly, drink plenty of fresh water, have adequate fiber, and a variety of seasonal fresh foods, our internal cooling system will help keep us cool and comfortable during the warm season of summer.

Late Summer

Seasonal flavor: Sweet
Organs: Spleen and Stomach

The fifth season is an extra season that begins around the third week of August and continues until the Fall solstice. It marks the transition from the growing and abundant phases of spring and summer to the more inward cooking and mysterious fall and winter seasons. Also known as Indian Summer when we often experience a "hot spell." This is a short season in which we may experience wider temperature changes. Due to fluctuations in the weather during this time of transition, it is especially important to make adjustments in our lives and remain as centered and grounded to the Earth as possible. When one has a firm connection to the earth, it is easier to create and manifest what one wants most in life; whether it be more income, recognition, a new job, creative ideas, good health, or a healthier lifestyle. This is a great time of year to plant the seeds to make things happen.

Continue with a lighter diet on warm days but begin to move toward building a diet in which you add a little more fat when cooking and adding some fish, poultry, a little meat, and grains to provide more fuel. At this time, try to increase exercise so you produce some sweating which helps with elimination and cleansing of the body. As harvest begins to grow plump and ripen, food is plentiful with an abundance of apples, grapes, tomatoes, beans, zucchini, and corn. Also whole grains, millet, some beans, sprouts, seeds, nuts, dairy, eggs, dates, and green herbs: especially parsley and pumpkin seeds. Making nut or seed milks will also help build the body.

Fall

Seasonal flavor: Pungent or Spicy
Organs: Lungs and Large Intestine

A time of maturity, harvest, transition, letting go, and a time to be open to experience inner growth and reflection and adapt to the changes of life more easily let us process our food, thoughts, and emotions. Harvest is now gathered in preparation for winter. This is an important time to relax mentally, express emotions in a healthy way, limit stressful situations, get proper rest, and keep warm. Next to Spring, this is the second best season to cleanse the body.

To help with cleansing and harmonizing the body, try some organic grape juice or lemonade and vegetable juice recipes in this book. Increasing exercise for what feels right for you and maintaining some quiet relaxed time also will help maintain balance through the seasonal changes.

At this time of year we begin to eat less cold, uncooked food and more warm, cooked foods to help the body better adapt to the damp and cooler weather. Try to incorporate some pungent or spicy foods into your diet such as Roquefort, brie and Camembert cheese, peppers, and mustard, which help to open up the sinuses and stimulate the lungs. Begin to increase cooked soups, stews, steamed vegetables, and cooked fruits. Add some rose-hip tea and sour plum to your daily diet. Some warming foods this season include winter squash, winter peas, broccoli, cauliflower, sweet potatoes, yams, onions, beets, cabbage, leeks, chili peppers, pumpkin, carrots, turnips, celery, garlic, Brussel sprouts, spinach, apple, banana, cranberries, rice, and oatmeal. Eat more foods that help build the body for winter, including meat, fish, dairy, nuts, beans, seeds, and grains, as well as mushrooms and avocados. Good time of year to eat fermented foods. Recipes for miso soup and fermented cucumbers can be found in the Medicinal chapter. Also helpful to include kale, spinach, sea vegetables, as well as red and yellow foods and the herbs cinnamon, thyme, sage, cayenne, ginger, and garlic.

Winter

Seasonal flavor: Salty
Organs: Kidney and Bladder

Kidneys rule the emotions and control life force energy, our vitality, and longevity. A quiet season when Mother Nature is in her resting phase in preparation for Spring. Due to the holidays, this is a busy time of year so it is important to take time to strengthen your life force by getting adequate rest and relaxation. Take time to reflect and dream to help you gather and strengthen your energy for future use and warm the body's core. As this is the darkest and coldest season, it is important to stay warm and dry. It will be helpful to add more warm and substantial foods to the diet, like hearty soups, dahl, curry, casseroles, cooked apples, steamed and baked vegetables, and incorporate a variety of the root vegetables including carrots, turnips, onions, and potatoes into your meals. Also helpful to add some pungent and fermented foods like Kimchee, sourdough bread, sauerkraut. Add grains like rice, wheat, barley, oats, buckwheat, aduki and kidney beans, a variety of sea weeds, miso, and gomasio. Nuts and nut milk, feta cheese (from sheep's milk which is easier for the body to digest), halibut fish, and some chicken are good this time of year. You can also include some red meat occasionally to brighten up the blood, heart, and complexion. Note that too much meat at this time can damage kidneys. Try adding some warming spices of cayenne, ginger, turmeric, curry, and hot sauce to your food. This is a great season to enjoy a nice cup of warming tea made from herbs, seeds, and their roots like ginger root, ginseng, burdock, comfrey, marshmallow, peppermint, flax, and fenugreek.

Spring

Seasonal flavor: Sour
Organs: Liver and Gall Bladder

This is the greening season when seeds are being planted; it is a time of rebirth, renewal, and a good time of year to clear out the old to make way for new beginnings and create a personal spring within. This is the best season for cleansing the body (see Medicinal chapter for "Lemonade", and "Carrots and Friends'" recipes), and for fasting, drinking nourishing fruit and vegetable juices, and dancing. Also, it is important to make time to play, exercise, and try new things. In addition to making changes in diet, take time to create through self expression, awareness, meditation, and add in more laughter. Eating sweet tasting herbs, which is not the same as eating sweet foods, can help soften the liver if it has become rigid due to daily stress. Eating a grapefruit is a great way to begin the day as it supports the sour flavor of Spring and its sweet taste helps soften the liver. Also helpful are lemons and limes, fermented foods, pickles, and vinegar. Foods plentiful at this time include strawberries, cherries, plums, asparagus, local honey, lettuce, edible flowers, spearmint, parsley, chives, pears, apples, beets, sweet potato, cabbage, carrots, leeks, celery, spinach, and sprouts. Include in the diet some sunflower and sesame seeds, almonds, walnuts, pecans, and whole grains including brown rice, millet, wheat, rye, oats, as well as lentils, garbanzos, and other beans. Additionally, the sweet herb astragalus is known to boost qi (Life Force Energy) and will help give you a boost if feeling tired or run down. Adding astragalus root to soups and stocks is a great way to add this powerful herb to your diet. Other helpful herbs of the season include dandelion, milk thistle, chicory root, and peppermint.

"A jazz musician can improvise based on his knowledge of music. He understands how things go together. For a chef, once you have that basis, that's when cuisine is truly exciting."

– Charlie Trotter

FABULOUS MUSSELS - page 26

Appetizers and Snacks

Baba Zunouj

Buffalo Wings

Carob Orange Halavah Bites

Chocolate No Bake Snack Bars

Fabulous Mussels

Fancy Bean Dip

Fruit and Nut Truffles

Guac Out

Mexican Chocolate Chip Fudge

Mexican Shrimp Cocktail

Mexican Salsa/Salad Dip

Pepper Poppers

Sam Endive

Spinach Balls

Tis Zucchi

Baba Zunouj ("Baba Zunoosh")

Yields approximately 1 1/2 cups

A summer slant on a traditional Middle Eastern eggplant dip. During the New England summers, zucchini is so plentiful that one is always looking for ways to use it. So I took the opportunity to merge together eggplant with a bountiful supply of zucchini to make this delicious summer dip or spread.

Ingredients:

3 small eggplants

1 1/2 small zucchinis

1/4 cup onion, sliced

3 garlic cloves, 1 thinly sliced and 2 minced

2 teaspoons extra virgin olive oil

1/2 lemon, freshly squeezed

1/4 teaspoon salt or to taste

1/4 cup sesame tahini

3 shakes cayenne pepper (optional)

Tip:

If you prefer a spread rather than a dip, puree only about 1/4 of the mixture, mash remaining ingredients and stir all together until well blended. Spread on crackers or bread.

Note:

If tahini not a favorite or you prefer a lighter dip, tahini can be eliminated and you will still have a delicious dip.

Directions:

Preheat oven to 375 degrees. Thinly slice one large garlic clove. Wash eggplant and zucchini. Make a small slit on each side of each eggplant and stuff a slice of garlic into each slit. Place eggplant and zucchini on roasting pan. Mix 1 teaspoon oil into onions and place in roasting pan with vegetables. Roast eggplant and zucchini in oven for 1 hour (30 minutes on each side) or until tender. Check onions after 30 minutes to make sure they don't burn. They take less time to cook and will be a bit caramelized, so remove early if necessary. When vegetables are cooked, remove from oven and let cool. Peel skin off eggplant and place pulp in blender. Remove seeds from zucchini, scrape out soft pulp, and add to blender. Add onions, lemon juice, 1 teaspoon olive oil, 2 minced garlic cloves, salt and pepper. Blend until all pureed. Lastly, add tahini slowly until all blended. Sample and adjust spices to your taste.

Song: Baba Zunouj - Disc 1 - Song 1 - Funk - Medium Tempo
This funky little tune is based on the rhythm of the phrase "Baba Ghanosh."

Buffalo Wings

Serves 4 - 6

Ingredients:

24 chicken wings, drummettes

3 tablespoons vinegar

1/4 cup hot pepper sauce, or less according to taste

1/2 cup butter, melted

2 tablespoons dried parsley flakes

1/2 teaspoon pepper

1 tablespoon onion powder

1/2 teaspoon garlic powder

1/2 teaspoon salt

paprika (optional)

Alternative Directions:
(Cook's Choice)

Marinate wings in mixture of vinegar and hot pepper sauce in a plastic zip-lock bag in the refrigerator overnight. When ready to bake, place wings and sauce in a 9" x 13" pan. Pour butter over wings and toss well. Sprinkle with 1/2 the dry ingredients and continue with recipe above.

Alternate Cooking Method:

To cook in crock pot, combine all ingredients, cover, and cook on low 4-5 hours.

Directions:

Preheat oven to 350 degrees. For sauce, mix together vinegar, hot pepper sauce, and melted butter. Place chicken wings in a 9" x 13" baking dish or jelly roll pan in a single layer. Pour sauce over wings. Mix together all dry spice ingredients except paprika. Sprinkle with 1/2 the dry spices. Bake 25-30 minutes or until browned. Remove from oven and sprinkle remainder of dry ingredients over wings. Place under broiler for a few minutes until browned further for personal taste. Remove from oven and sprinkle with paprika.

Submitted by:

Debbi Merlin - Stafford, TX
Jewelry designer, author and animal lover | www.designsbydesu.com

Carob Orange Halavah Bites

Halavah is a flour or nut butter candy-like snack which is spelled many different ways and dates back 3,000 years. It refers to a wide range of confections found in Romania, Russia, Greece, Egypt, Israel, Lebanon, Turkey, and Algeria. As a young girl, I remember enjoying this nut butter snack which had a slightly sweet nutty flavor and a dry, dense slightly chewy texture. Of interest, Food timeline.org adds: "Halavah is of Turkish origin and was first sold in America at the turn of the century by Turkish, Syrian, and Armenian street vendors. The candy soon became a favorite of Jewish immigrants in New York, and today Halavah is still associated with Jewish delicatessens." The addition of Triple Sec or orange juice which is optional, lends a subtle flavor to the snack.

Ingredients:

1 cup raw organic sesame seeds

1-2 tablespoons raw carob powder

1/4 teaspoon ground cinnamon

1/8 teaspoon celtic sea salt

1/4 cup raw honey

2 tablespoons raw tahini

1 teaspoon Triple Sec, freshly squeezed orange juice, or Madagascar vanilla

additional raw carob powder (optional)

Note:

Dough will be slightly sticky. If you prefer a drier snack with more carob flavor, roll the balls in a little extra carob powder until fully coated. Store bites in a tightly sealed container in refrigerator up to 3 weeks or in the freezer for 4 months. It is best to keep bites cool until ready to eat so they do not soften too much. Bites can also be eaten right out of the freezer. We hope you enjoy this delicious raw food snack.

Directions:

Grind sesame seeds in a food processor or coffee grinder until fine. Place ground seeds in a medium size bowl with carob powder, cinnamon, and salt and stir to blend. Add honey, tahini, triple sec, orange juice or vanilla to dry ingredients and mix well. With your hands, knead all ingredients until dough forms a stiff ball. Pull off a small amount of dough and roll between your hands to form 1" balls for a perfect little snack of a bite or two.

Chocolate No Bake Snack Bars

Ingredients:

1/2 cup organic rice krispies

1 cup chocolate rice or whey protein powder

1/2 cup oats, plus an additional tablespoon

1/4 cup wheat germ

1/3 cup organic peanut butter or other nut butter

1/2 cup honey

Directions:

Combine rice krispies or whey protein powder with oats, wheat germ, and rice krispies. Stir until well blended. Add peanut or nut butter and honey and blend together with a pastry blender or by hand until well mixed. Pour into an 8" x 8" pan, press mixture down, and place in refrigerator. When cool, cut into 16 squares and store in a covered container in the refrigerator.

Submitted by:

Laura Melisi - Acton, ME
Flautist

Fabulous Mussels

Serves 6

Ingredients:

3 tablespoons olive oil

2 shallots, chopped

2 garlic cloves, chopped

1/2 teaspoon dried crushed red pepper

1/2 teaspoon sea salt, plus more for seasoning

3/4 cup dry white wine

1/4 cup chicken broth

1 tablespoon lemon juice, freshly squeezed

1 tablespoon fresh parsley leaves, chopped

2 pounds fresh mussels, scrubbed and de-bearded

1/2 cup tomatoes, chopped and seeded

2 tablespoon Parmesan cheese, grated

Directions:

Heat oil on medium heat in deep skillet that has a cover. Add shallots and cook until soft. Add garlic, crushed red pepper, and salt; cook for 1 minute. Add wine, chicken broth, lemon juice and Parmesan cheese; bring to boil. Add mussels. Cover pot and cook over medium-high heat for about 6 minutes or until mussel shells open. Discard any mussels that do not open. Stir in tomatoes and parsley. Transfer mussels to a large bowl and pour broth over mussels.

Submitted by:

Sheri Santo - Dover, NH
Graphic Designer | www.sherisanto.com

Fancy Bean Dip

Ingredients:

2 cups cooked or can beans, cannellini, pinto, or great northern
1 1/2 tablespoons extra virgin olive oil
3 shakes red pepper
1/4 teaspoon ground pepper
1/4 teaspoon ground mustard
2 tablespoons prepared horseradish
2 scallions, chopped
1 small tomato, chopped
2 tablespoons capers
sea salt to taste

Directions:

Combine beans and olive oil in blender or food processor and blend until smooth. Add spices, horseradish, and scallions and blend again until everything is completely mixed. Spoon mixture into serving bowl. Mix tomatoes and capers together and sprinkle over top of dip. Serve with a variety of crackers or small pieces of fresh bread.

Fruit and Nut Truffles or Brownies

Soooooooo easy! The combinations are endless. Have fun creating your own favorite treats.

Ingredients:

1 cup macadamia nuts

1 cup dates

    or

1 cup almonds

1 cup apricots

    or

1 cup walnuts

1 cup dates

Options: shaved coconut, ground nuts, cocoa powder

1/2 cup raw chocolate (cocoa powder) – for brownies

pinch of sea salt – for brownies

Directions:

For each 1 cup of nuts use 1 cup fruit and process in food processor. If fruit seems dry, soak it for 10 to 15 minutes in filtered water. Drain water from fruit (reserve a few tablespoons) before placing in food processor and process until well blended. If mixture seems too crumbly add reserved water until desired consistency is achieved. Get fancy by dressing up truffles by rolling in finely shaved coconut, ground nuts, or cocoa powder.

For brownies add 1/2 cup raw chocolate (cocoa powder) with a pinch of sea salt to mixture. Spread in a square pan, chill, and cut into squares when nicely chilled.

Guac Out

Great for parties or enjoy as an afternoon or evening snack.

Ingredients:

2 ripe medium size avocados

1 lime, freshly squeezed

1 teaspoon chili powder

1 teaspoon cumin

1/4 cup onion, finely chopped

1 medium tomato, chopped

1 teaspoon cilantro, finely chopped

2 cloves garlic, chopped

sprinkle of sea salt

few shakes of ground red pepper

1/8-1/4 teaspoon Tabasco or to taste (optional)

1 teaspoon tequila (optional)

Directions:

Slice avocado in half and scoop out pulp from skin. Place in a mini food processor, squeeze lime juice over avocado, and process until fairly smooth. Add chili powder and cumin and blend 30 seconds until well mixed. Spoon into a bowl, add onion, tomato, and cilantro. Adjust spices to taste. Place 1 avocado pit on top guacamole to help retain nice green color of the dip. Chill and remove pit just prior to serving.

Song: Guac Out! - Disc 1 - Song 7 - Rock - Medium Tempo
"Guac Out!" is an improvised funk-rock jam.

Mexican Chocolate Chip Fudge

Makes approximately 20 squares

This easy to make snack is healthy, delicious, and provides a quick energy boost - a bittersweet treat to fulfill all your snack cravings.

Ingredients:

1/2 cup coconut oil (*Cook's choice – organic unrefined*)

1 cup cocoa powder (*Cook's choice – organic*)

1/4 cup mini dark chocolate chips

1/2 cup almond butter (*Cook's choice – raw almond butter*)

1 tablespoon maple syrup

1 teaspoon chili powder

1 teaspoon ground cinnamon

1/2 teaspoon cayenne pepper

1/2 teaspoon sea salt

Tip:

If left at room temperature too long, fudge will become very soft and you will have messy fingers.

Notes:

The use of raw products, such as raw almond butter, provides additional nutritional benefits as raw ingredients have not been processed or refined in any way and will retain their natural occurring enzymes. However, raw ingredients are more costly and sometimes hard to find so their use is optional. But organic oil and cocoa can easily be found and are highly recommended.

This recipe is Gluten Free!

Directions:

Measure out coconut oil and if solid, place in a bowl of hot water until liquified. Place cocoa, chocolate chips, almond butter, maple syrup, chili powder, cinnamon, cayenne pepper, and salt in a large bowl and stir until well mixed. Line a 6 1/2" glass pan with wax paper. Spread fudge mixture in pan. Cover with a piece of parchment paper and place in freezer for about an hour until very firm. Remove from freezer and allow to soften slightly for about 20 minutes or until easily cut into squares. Store in a tightly sealed container in refrigerator or freezer. When stored in the freezer, snack will last up to 6 months, but trust me... it will be gone in no time!

Mexican Shrimp Cocktail

Serves 4 - 6

This is a wonderful recipe my sister-in-law likes to make for parties and for quick meals at home. She likes to add fresh salsa, lime juice, stewed tomatoes, and even a little black pepper, and suggests you omit the jalepeno if you don't like it too spicy. This is a delicious and non fattening treat you'll want to have again and again!!!

Ingredients:

1 large can V-8 or Clamato juice (spicy if desired)

2 avocados, chopped

2 cucumbers, seeded and chopped

1 medium red onion, chopped

1/2 bunch cilantro, chopped

1 pound large shrimp, peeled, de-veined and steamed

limes, quartered

Tabasco sauce

1 jalapeno, seeded and chopped, (optional)

Tip:
Do not over-cook the shrimp, as they become tough! Serve in a Margarita glass with a lime wheel... so good!!!!

Directions:

Prepare and cook shrimp and set aside. Mix all ingredients in a large non-reactive container. Let sit for a few hours in refrigerator, or overnight. Serve with limes and Tabasco sauce.

Submitted by:

Rose Santo - Las Vegas, NV
Hair Stylist

Mexican Salsa Salad/Dip

Serves 6 - 8

A super easy, delicious, healthy, and quick dip for vegetables or chips!
Great as a salad or a side! Cook recommends you add more of your favorite
ingredients and use less of your not so favorites.

Ingredients:

1 pint fresh salsa, good quality

1 16-ounce can of black beans

1 12-ounce can of corn or 1 frozen bag

1 4-ounce can of jalapenos (optional)

1 small onion, chopped (optional)

1 small green pepper, chopped (optional)

salt and pepper (optional)

Directions:

Open can of beans, drain, and rinse in a colander. If using frozen corn,
rinse, and cook according to package directions. Drain can of jalapenos if
using. In a large non-metal bowl, mix all ingredients together. Refrigerate
at least 3 hours to allow flavors to meld. Serve as a dip or a delicious side
salad.

Submitted by:

Susan Sirois

Black Bird Designs & Blue Moon Gifts | www.bluemoondover.com

Pepper Poppers

Yields 18

Like the song on CD #1, these peppers really sizzle and pop as they lightly blacken in the broiler. They are then stuffed with a zippy filling that blends well with the sweetness of the peppers. These make great little appetizers, snacks, or side dishes with Mexican food. They blend so well with the music you cannot help but smile and bop while cooking and eating!

Ingredients:

1 10-ounce package of mini peppers

3 cups yellow yukon gold potatoes or
potato of choice, peeled and chopped

3 garlic cloves, minced

1 tablespoon extra virgin olive oil

1 tablespoon butter

1/4 cup cheddar or cheese of choice, grated

1/3 cup corn, frozen niblets or fresh if
in season

1/2 cup scallions, thinly sliced

3 shakes cayenne

1/4 teaspoon sea salt

1/4 teaspoon ground cumin

1/4 teaspoon chili powder or to taste

sprinkle of paprika

1 chili pepper, finely diced (optional)

Directions:

Boil potatoes and garlic until tender. While potatoes boil cut off tops of peppers, remove seeds, wash but do not dry, and brush all around outside of each pepper with oil, and broil, until peppers are slightly blackened on both sides. Allow to cool a bit. While peppers blacken and cool, mash potatoes with butter, stir in cheese, and mix until well blended. Add corn, scallions, spices, and chili pepper. Stir until everything is well blended and adjust seasoning for personal taste. Use a small spoon to fill mini peppers with potato and vegetable mixture, mound a bit, and sprinkle lightly with paprika. Place in a shallow casserole and heat until warm.

Song: Pepper Poppers - Disc 1 - Song 2 - Mexican Style - Fast Tempo

This song is inspired by Mexican Mariachi music. I spiced it with percussion to make it sizzle and pop just like the appetizer does as it cooks.

Sam Endive

These simple, quick, and delicious little bites make perfect finger appetizers to serve on warm summer evenings. The title comes from a blending of smoked salmon and the bitter, green endive. Be sure and listen to the awesome song with this title on CD #1.

Ingredients:

1 endive bulb

1, 3-ounce package organic cream cheese

1, 4-ounce package of smoked wild salmon, cut in thin strips

1/4 teaspoon mustard powder

2 tablespoons capers

2 tablespoons red onion, shallot or scallion, thinly sliced

2 tablespoons fresh dill (optional)

Notes:

This recipe is Gluten Free!

Directions:

Separate, wash, and dry endive. Mix powdered mustard into cream cheese and stir until well blended. Spread cream cheese mixture along the inside of each endive leaf. Sprinkle capers on top of cream cheese layer, then add onions, some fresh dill, and top off with slices of salmon strips. Slice endive boats into 1" pieces and chill until served.

Song: Sam Endive - Disc 1 - Song 5 - Rock - Medium Tempo

Beth was over for dinner and said we need a cool title with the word endive in it and Marilynn said but let's not forget the salmon and that's when I laughed and said how about Sam Endive as the name. Somehow the name made me think of a TV detective. I remembered the old Peter Gunn theme, which featured a bass line, so I wrote a tune where the bass line is the melody.

Spinach Balls

Makes about 5 dozen

These make great appetizers for parties or an anytime snack. To make party preparations easier, no fret these can be prepared in advance and stored in a tightly sealed container or bag in the freezer. Prior to serving, place frozen spinach balls in oven to cook. When ready, place a toothpick in each one and serve.

Ingredients:

2 packages frozen chopped spinach

4 organic eggs

2 teaspoons fresh thyme, chopped

1/4 teaspoon sea salt

1/4 teaspoon pepper

2/3 cup Parmesan or Romano cheese, grated

3/4 cup butter, melted

1 cup onion, finely diced

3 cloves garlic, minced

2 cups organic corn flakes, crushed (Cook's Choice - Natures Path cereal)

3 shakes cayenne pepper (optional)

Tip:

As so much of our corn supply is now genetically modified, it is recommended to use organic corn whenever possible.

Note:

The use of corn flakes instead of traditional bread crumbs makes this recipe Gluten Free!

Directions:

Preheat oven to 300 degrees. Cook spinach according to directions, drain and squeeze out all liquid. In a separate bowl, beat eggs and mix in thyme, salt, pepper, cheese, butter, onion, garlic, cayenne, corn flakes, and spinach. Stir until ingredients are well blended. Roll into 1" balls and place on a cookie sheet in refrigerator to chill. Bake about 30 minutes.

'Tis Zucchi

Yields about 1 1/2 cups

The title is a play on words for Tzaztiki, the classic Greek dish made with cucumber and dill. This one is sure to become a summer favorite. If seeking new and delicious ways to prepare zucchini from your garden, try this quick, easy, light dip that can be enjoyed as a snack, as a lunch, or as a great addition to your party buffet. Serve with some cut fresh vegetables, sourdough or pita bread, pretzels, or crackers.

Ingredients:

3/4 cup zucchini, finely shredded

1 cup plain yogurt, whole fat (*Cook's choice* - Greek God's)

1 tablespoon freshly squeezed lemon juice or a bit more for personal preference

1 tablespoon fresh cilantro, finely chopped or 1 teaspoon, dried

3 shakes cayenne pepper

1/2 teaspoon Himalayan salt

Notes:

This recipe is Gluten Free!

Directions:

Place all ingredients in a bowl, stir to blend, and allow to chill for several hours. 'Tis Yummy!

Breads and Muffins

Almost Brown Bread

Apple Bread Times 3

Banana Date Bread

Banana-Pear-Orange Muffins

Banana Walnut Muffins

Blueberry Blues Bread

Butternut Squash Molasses Muffins

Chickpea Mushroom Biscuits

Coconut-Pumpkin Muffins

Cran Orange Ginger Bread

Gluten Free Blueberry Muffins

Scallion Corn Bread

Scallion Oat Cakes

Three Fruits Bread

Almost Brown Bread

Yields 1 loaf

Ingredients:

1/4 cup butter, softened

1/4 cup brown sugar

1/4 cup molasses

1 1/2 cups whole organic milk

1 teaspoon apple cider vinegar

1 egg

3 cups dark rye flour (*Cook's choice* - Bob's Red Mill)

1 teaspoon baking powder

1 teaspoon baking soda

1/2 teaspoon sea salt

1/4 cup raisins

Directions:

Preheat oven to 350 degrees. Cream butter, sugar, and molasses together. Add vinegar to milk and let sit for 5 minutes. Add milk mixture and egg to creamed butter and sugar mixture and beat until well blended. Measure flour, baking powder, baking soda, and salt and add to liquid ingredients and beat all until blended. Batter will be very thick, so scrape beaters occasionally, and finish stirring by hand until ingredients are well blended. Stir in raisins and spoon into a greased 9" x 5" x 3" glass or ceramic loaf pan. Alternatively instead of greasing pan, line it with a piece of parchment paper before adding batter. Bake 1 hour or until done and toothpick inserted in middle of bread comes out clean. Allow to cool 15 minutes before removing from pan to slice.

Apple Bread Times 3

Makes 1 - 9" x 5" loaf

Ingredients:

1 1/2 cups spelt flour

1/2 cup whole wheat flour

1 teaspoon baking powder

1 teaspoon baking soda

1/2 teaspoon ground cinnamon

1/4 teaspoon ground nutmeg

1/2 teaspoon sea salt

2 large organic eggs

1/4 cup extra virgin olive oil

1/4 cup applesauce

1/4 cup light brown sugar, firmly packed

1/4 cup apple juice (*Cook's choice* - Granny Smith)

2 cups apples, peeled & finely chopped

1/2 cup raisins (optional)

1 teaspoon sugar, for topping (optional)

> **Note:**
>
> If top of bread starts to darken before done, cover with a sheet of parchment paper to protect it from browning too much.

Directions:

Preheat oven to 350 degrees. Butter and flour a 9 x 5" loaf pan or line with parchment paper. In medium bowl combine flours, baking powder, baking soda, cinnamon, nutmeg, and salt, and stir until completely mixed. Beat eggs in a large bowl, add oil, applesauce, brown sugar and juice. Add flour mixture, raisins, and apples, and stir until evenly coated. Sprinkle one teaspoon of sugar over top to give a more finished, glazed look. Bake 70 minutes or until toothpick inserted in center of loaf comes out clean. Let cool on rack 10 minutes before removing from pan. Cool completely before slicing.

Banana Date Bread

Makes 1 - 9" x 5" loaf

This versatile bread works well with brown rice flour for a gluten-free version and the addition of natural fruits make it a tasty choice for anyone looking for a bread without the need for additional sugar.

Ingredients:

2 cups brown rice flour, oat flour or a combination of both

1 teaspoon baking soda

1/2 teaspoon baking powder

1/4 teaspoon sea salt

1/2 teaspoon ground cinnamon

1/4 teaspoon ground cloves

1/4 teaspoon ground nutmeg

1/4 cup walnut oil, olive oil, or your choice

1/4 cup applesauce

2 organic eggs

1 cup bananas, mashed (about 3 small)

1/2 cup organic milk, apple juice, or cider

1 teaspoon vanilla extract

7–10 pitted dates, chopped or 2–3 tablespoons maple syrup (*Cook's choice* - dates)

1/2 cup walnuts, chopped (optional)

Note:

The use of brown rice or oat flour makes this recipe Gluten Free!

Tips:

Use apple juice or cider instead of milk to make this recipe Dairy Free!

Omit walnuts to make this recipe Nut Free!

Directions:

Preheat oven to 350 degrees. Butter and flour 1 1/2 quart glass loaf pan or line pan with parchment paper. Combine all dry ingredients. In another bowl add oil, applesauce, eggs, banana, milk or juice, maple syrup if using, and vanilla, and beat until well mixed. Stir in dates and walnuts. Pour into flour mixture and stir until evenly moistened. Pour batter into a prepared pan and bake 60-70 minutes depending on oven or until knife inserted in center of loaf comes out clean. Let cool on wire rack 10 minutes before removing from pan. Cool 2 hours before slicing or bread will crumble a bit. Tastes so yummy!

Banana-Pear-Orange Muffins

Makes 1 dozen

Ingredients:

1 ripe banana, sliced

2 pears, chopped

1 egg

1 tablespoon extra virgin olive oil

1 cup oat flour

3/4 cup brown rice flour

3/4 cup organic oats

2 teaspoon baking powder

1/2 cup freshly squeezed orange juice

1/2 teaspoon orange rind, finely grated

Notes:

The use of brown rice flour makes this recipe Gluten Free!

When cooking Gluten Free, be sure to check your oats to see if they were packaged in a facility that also processes wheat.

Directions:

Place banana, pears, egg, and oil in a blender, and process on low until smooth or use an electric mixer. Add orange juice and orange rind to banana mixture and blend. In medium bowl combine flours, oats, baking powder, and stir to thoroughly blend. Pour liquid mixture into flour mixture and stir until well blended. Preheat oven to 400 degrees, place paper parchment muffin cups in muffin pans, pour batter into cups, and bake for 15 minutes.

Banana Walnut Muffins

Muffin Ingredients:

1 cup Gluten Free baking flour or organic white spelt flour

1/2 cup coconut flour

1 teaspoon baking soda

1 teaspoon baking powder

1/4 teaspoon sea salt

2 ripe bananas

3 tablespoons honey

2 tablespoons canola oil

1 egg

1/2 cup milk

1 teaspoon vanilla

1/3 cup unsalted butter, softened

1/4 cup chopped walnuts

1/4 cup sugar

> **Tips:**
> Use Gluten Free baking flour to make this recipe Gluten Free! (*Cooks choice* - Bob's Red Mill)
>
> Omit walnuts to make this recipe Nut Free!

Topping Ingredients:

1/4 cup brown sugar

1/4 teaspoon cinnamon

1 tablespoon butter

Directions:

Preheat oven to 375 degrees. Combine flours, baking soda, baking powder, and salt. Set aside. In large bowl combine bananas, sugar, egg, honey, oil, milk, vanilla, and butter. Slowly and in stages mix in dry ingredients and blend until smooth. Add chopped walnuts. Pour into greased or paper-lined muffin tins. In a separate bowl combine brown sugar and cinnamon and cut in butter until mixture forms small crumbles. Sprinkle over top of muffins. Bake for 18 minutes.

Submitted by:

Sheri Santo, *Graphic Designer* | www.sherisanto.com

Blueberry Blues Bread

Yields 1 bread, 2 small breads or 20 muffins

Ingredients:

2 1/2 cups brown rice, whole wheat, or
spelt flour (*Cook's choice* – brown rice flour)

1 heaping teaspoon baking soda

1/2 teaspoon sea salt

1/2 teaspoon ground cloves

1/2 teaspoon ground cinnamon

3/4 teaspoon ground ginger

1/4 cup maple syrup

1/4 cup molasses

2 eggs

1/4 cup extra virgin olive oil

1/4 cup applesauce

2/3 cup green tea, steeped 15 minutes

1 cup blueberries

butter or parchment paper

1 tablespoon of sugar (optional)

> **Tip:**
> Use brown rice to make this recipe Gluten Free!

Directions:

Preheat oven to 350 degrees. Measure flour and dry ingredients into large mixing bowl. Stir until well blended. Add eggs, maple syrup, molasses, oil, applesauce, and green tea. Beat on low speed until all blended. Gently fold in blueberries. Lightly grease pans or line with parchment paper. For muffin pans, recommend using unbleached paper baking cups. Pour batter into a 9" x 13" pan, small bread pans, or muffin pans. Sprinkle small amount of sugar over batter prior to baking to give a more finished look to bread. Bake 15-20 minutes for muffin pans, 30-35 minutes for small bread pans, or about 1 hour for a 9" x 13" pan. To avoid over-cooking and make sure bread is done, insert a toothpick into bread before stated time. Bread is done when toothpick comes out clean. Remove from oven, let sit 15 minutes before removing from pans, and place on a cooling rack until cool enough to slice.

> **Song: Blueberry Blues** - Disc 2 - Song 3 - Swing Style - Medium Tempo
>
> If you have a craving for Marilynn's blueberry bread, and there are no blueberries in the fridge, you just might get the "Blueberry Blues."

Butternut Squash Molasses Muffins

Yields 12 Muffins

Ingredients:

1 cup spelt or all purpose flour

2 teaspoon baking powder

1/4 teaspoon baking soda

1 teaspoon ground ginger

1/2 teaspoon ground cloves

1/4 teaspoon ground cinnamon

1/4 teaspoon ground allspice

1/4 teaspoon sea salt

1/3 cup butter, softened or melted

1 cup baked butternut squash, mashed and cooled

1/8 cup sugar

2 organic eggs

1/2 cup dark molasses

Tip:
Sprinkle a little sugar on top of each muffin before baking, no more than 1 teaspoon in total.

Directions:

Preheat oven to 350 degrees. Stir together flour, baking powder, baking soda, ginger, cloves, cinnamon, allspice, and salt and set aside. In a separate bowl, combine butter, squash and sugar and blend well. Beat eggs adding one at a time to squash mixture. Add flour mixture with spices, alternating with molasses until well mixed. Pour batter into muffin pans that have been lined with paper baking cups or lightly greased. Bake 20 minutes or until done when a toothpick inserted comes out clean.

Chickpea Mushroom Biscuits

Yields 8

Ingredients:

3/4 cup chickpea (garbanzo) flour

1/4 teaspoon sea salt

1/4 teaspoon garlic granules

1/8 teaspoon baking powder

1 large egg

1 tablespoon extra virgin olive oil

1 tablespoon water

3 mushrooms, thinly sliced

Note:

These are a variation on scallion oat cakes.

This recipe is Gluten Free!

Directions:

Mix together flour, sea salt, garlic and baking powder. Blend well. Beat egg, oil, and water, and pour in flour spice mixture. Mixture will be very sticky but continue to mix until all blended. Add mushrooms and stir well. Divide into 8 equal pieces. Roll each piece into a ball, flatten each a bit with a spatula, and place in a lightly oiled cast iron skillet. Flatten again and lightly fry one side at a time until both sides are lightly browned. Serve with a little dab of butter.

Coconut Pumpkin Muffins

Makes 10

Ingredients:

1/4 cup butter, softened

1/4 cup organic, grade B maple syrup

1/8 cup granulated sugar

1 large egg

1/3 cup of coconut milk, nut milk, oat milk, or regular milk

1 teaspoon apple cider vinegar

1/2 cup freshly mashed pumpkin

1/2 cup spelt flour

1/2 cup oat flour

1 1/2 teaspoons baking powder

1/8 teaspoon baking soda

1/4 teaspoon sea salt

1/2 teaspoon ground cinnamon

1/4 teaspoon ground ginger

> **Tips:**
> To make coconut milk: Boil water and add coconut cream. For each cup water, use 1 teaspoon cream. Alternatively you can use fresh coconut milk or a small can.
>
> To make fresh oat flour: Place raw oats in a clean coffee grinder and grind until oats are ground to a flour consistency.

Directions:

Heat oven to 375 degrees. Mix butter, maple syrup, sugar, egg, coconut milk, vinegar, and pumpkin in large bowl. In another bowl, mix flours, baking powder, baking soda, salt, cinnamon, and ginger. Combine all ingredients and stir until completely moistened. Spoon batter into paper lined or greased muffin cups, filling cups about 2/3 full. Bake about 20 minutes or until toothpick inserted in center comes out clean.

Cran Orange Ginger Bread

Yields 1 loaf

Freshly squeezed orange juice and freshly made ginger tea enhance the flavors in this cranberry bread. The result is a yummy, moist bread that can be enjoyed for breakfast, brunch, tea time, or with Thanksgiving or Christmas dinner.

Ingredients:

1 tablespoon fresh ginger

2 cups organic flour (*Cook's choice* - combination of whole wheat and spelt)

1 1/2 teaspoons baking powder

1 teaspoon sea salt

1/2 teaspoon baking soda

1/4 cup maple syrup

1/4 cup walnut or extra virgin olive oil

1 teaspoon freshly grated orange peel

1/2 cup freshly squeezed orange juice, 1 large orange

1/4 cup freshly brewed ginger tea

1 large egg, beaten

1 cup organic cranberries, coarsely chopped

1/2 cup chopped nuts (optional)

1-2 teaspoons organic sugar (optional)

> **Note:**
> The ginger tea is delicious on its own so enjoy the remaining tea while bread bakes.

Directions:

Preheat oven to 350 degrees. Make ginger tea by washing, peeling, and chopping ginger into small pieces until one tablespoon is yielded. Pour 3/4 cup boiling water over ginger, cover and steep for 15 minutes. While tea steeps, measure all dry ingredients together. Mix together maple syrup, oil, orange peel, orange juice, and 1/4 cup of steeped ginger tea along with the pieces of ginger. Stir egg until well beaten, add liquid ingredients, mix, and add to dry ingredients. Add cranberries and stir until all ingredients are blended and moistened. Add chopped nuts if desired. Grease a 9" x 5" x 3" loaf pan or line pan with parchment paper. Turn batter into pan. Sprinkle a thin coating of sugar over top of bread. Bake 1 hour. Allow bread to cool before slicing.

Gluten-Free Blueberry Muffins

Makes 6 good sized muffins

Ingredients:

1/4 cup and 2 tablespoons coconut flour

1/4 cup gluten free all purpose flour

1/2 teaspoon baking powder

1/4 teaspoon salt

1 teaspoon sugar

3 eggs

3 tablespoons honey

1 teaspoon vanilla

1 teaspoon lemon juice

4 tablespoon milk

3 tablespoons olive oil

2 tablespoons butter melted

1 small container blueberries

> **Note:**
> This recipe is Gluten Free!

Crumble Topping Ingredients:

1 tablespoon butter melted

1/4 cup walnut pieces

1 tablespoon brown sugar

Directions:

Preheat oven to 400 degrees. Combine eggs, milk, oil, melted butter, honey, and vanilla. Mix in sugar. In a separate bowl, sift together flours, salt, and baking powder. Combine dry ingredients with wet ingredients and stir well, breaking up lumps until smooth. Add blueberries to batter. Spray muffin pan with non-stick spray or use baking cups. Pour batter into pan. In a food processor combine walnuts, 1 tablespoon melted butter, and brown sugar. Chop or pulse until blended but not completely ground. Sprinkle crumble topping on top of batter in muffin pan. Bake 20-25 minutes until done.

Submitted by:

Sheri Santo, *Graphic Designer* | www.sherisanto.com

Scallion Corn Bread

Yields 8 triangles or 16 squares

A delicious, moist corn bread that has a multitude of flavors from blending a variety of flours and the addition of yogurt.

Ingredients:

1 cup cornmeal

1/2 cup spelt flour

1/4 cup millet flour

1/4 cup coconut flour

2 teaspoons baking powder

1/2 teaspoon baking soda

1/2 teaspoon sea salt

6 ounces coconut or vanilla yogurt
(*Cook's choice* - coconut)

2 ounces water or plain yogurt

1 egg

2 tablespoons maple syrup or honey

2 tablespoons butter, melted

4 scallions, thinly sliced

1 1/2 tablespoons extra virgin olive or coconut oil

Options:

You can eliminate the millet and coconut flour by increasing the spelt or substitute with whole wheat flour.

Sour cream can be used instead of yogurt.

Directions:

Preheat oven to 350 degrees. Grease a 9" round cast iron pan or an 8" square baking pan with butter. In a bowl combine dry ingredients. In another bowl combine wet ingredients including sweetener. Mix wet ingredients into dry and stir until completely blended. Add 1 to 2 additional ounces of water until perfect consistency. Batter will be a little stiff. Stir in scallions and spread into prepared pan. Bake 20 minutes or until center is firm to touch. You might want to check bread sooner since ovens vary.

Scallion Oat Cakes

Yields 6

Serve these little cakes with soup or stew on a cool winter evening.

Ingredients:

3/4 cup oats, freshly ground or oat flour

1/8 teaspoon sea salt

1/4 teaspoon garlic granules

1/8 teaspoon baking powder

1 large egg

1 tablespoon extra virgin olive oil

1 tablespoon water

2 teaspoons coconut oil

1/8 cup scallions, thinly sliced

Notes:

The use of oat flour makes this recipe Gluten Free!

When cooking Gluten Free, be sure to check your oats to see if they were packaged in a facility that also processes wheat.

Directions:

Grind oats in small batches in a coffee grinder or food processor until they measure 3/4 cup. Add flour, salt, garlic granules, and baking powder, and mix until all blended. In small bowl beat egg with oil and water, and stir until well mixed. Add flour mixture to egg mixture and stir together until all blended. Stir in scallions and knead until a soft dough is formed. Place dough on wax paper and roll out or pat into a circle. Cut circle into 6 triangles. Heat coconut oil and when pan is hot add the triangles. Cook on medium heat about 4 minutes on each side or until lightly browned.

Three Fruits Bread

Makes 1 large loaf or 2 or 3 small loaves

No need for any sugar in this bread as the combination of fruits lends a natural sweetness to satisfy any sweet tooth.

Ingredients:

1 1/2 cups spelt flour

1/2 cup brown rice flour or buckwheat flour

2 teaspoons baking power

1/2 teaspoon baking soda

1/4 teaspoon sea salt

1/4 teaspoon ground cinnamon

1/4 cup extra virgin olive oil or oil of choice

1 large egg

1 8-ounce can crushed pineapple with its juice

1 ripe pear, grated

2 small ripe bananas, mashed

few walnuts or pecans (optional)

1 teaspoon sugar (optional)

Options:

Use 1 cup cranberries, chopped small instead of banana.

Use 1 cup freshly squeezed orange juice with pulp instead of juice from can of pineapple.

Use 1/2 tablespoon grated orange peel instead of pear.

Directions:

Preheat oven to 350 degrees. Line a bread pan with parchment paper or prepare pan with oil. Set aside. Mix together in a large bowl flours, baking powder, baking soda, cinnamon, and salt. Set aside. Put oil, egg, and pineapple juice in a separate bowl and mix until well blended. Add flour mixture to liquid ingredients and mix well. Add bananas, pear, and pineapple and stir again until well blended. Turn batter into a prepared loaf pan and smooth out evenly. For a nice finishing touch, place some whole walnuts or pecans down center of bread and either brush a bit of the pineapple juice over batter or sprinkle with 1 teaspoon of sugar to give the nuts a slightly glazed look. Bake 60 minutes until bread is golden or toothpick inserted comes out clean. Let cool 15 minutes, remove from pan, and place on a rack until completely cool. To store, wrap and place in refrigerator or freezer.

" Food is music to the body, music is food to the heart."

– Gregory David Roberts

BUCKWHEAT AND BROWN RICE PANCAKES - page 56

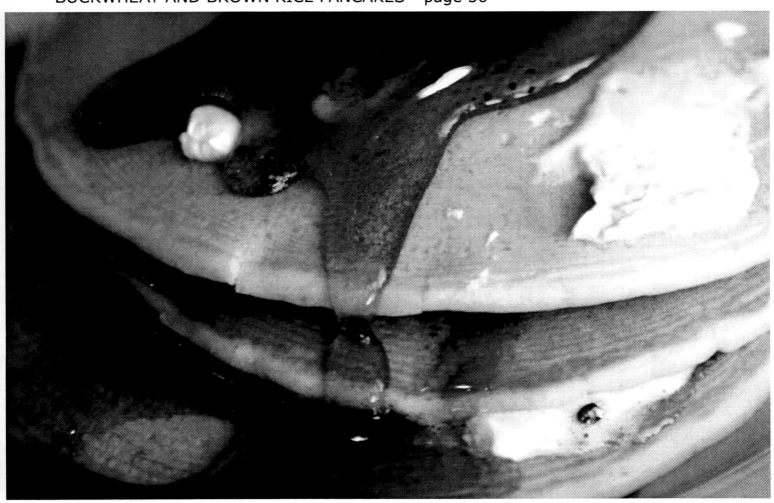

Breakfast or Brunch

Apple, Macadamia Spiced Oatmeal

Beach Cottage Granola

Buckwheat and Brown Rice Pancakes

Buckwheat Pancakes or Waffles

Cinnamon Date Scones

Christmas Fritatta

Colada-Nog Coffee Cake

Confetti Scrambled Eggs

Cornmeal Pancakes

Inside out Stuffed Spinach Goat Cheese Omelet

Nut Milk French Toast

Pumpkin Pancakes

Quinoa Waffles with Fruit Sauce

Special Brunch Fruit Plate

Zucchini, Egg, Provolone Bake

Apple, Macadamia Spiced Oatmeal

Serves 2

A great breakfast to warm you up on cold winter mornings which is rich in fiber, iron and B vitamins.

Ingredients:

1 2/3 cup water

1/3 cup macadamia nuts (to make nut milk)

1/2 teaspoon ground cinnamon

1/4 teaspoon ground nutmeg

1/2 cup apple, chopped

2/3 cup organic whole grain rolled oats

Tip:

Depending on personal preference, use any nut milk or regular whole milk.

Notes:

This recipe is Gluten Free!

When cooking Gluten Free, be sure to check your oats to see if they were packaged in a facility that also processes wheat.

Directions:

Place nuts in a blender and blend until fine powder. Add water to nuts and whirl until well blended. Place macadamia milk and spices in medium size saucepan and bring to boil. Reduce heat, stir in apples and oats and simmer for 20 minutes. Stir a few times and cook until oatmeal is desired consistency. Remove from heat and allow to sit for a few minutes before serving. Add additional milk if desired or drizzle on a bit of maple syrup.

Beach Cottage Granola

While raising a vegetarian son in our little York Beach, Maine apartment, I always tried to maximize protein and healthy fat in my cooking. This recipe was a big hit with him and I got much satisfaction watching him gobble it up!

Ingredients:

4 cups of Old Fashioned (slow cooking) oats

1/2 cup raw sunflower seeds

1/3 cup raw sesame seeds

1/3 cup raw walnuts, chopped or sliced

1/3 cup raw pecans, chopped or sliced

1/3 cup raw almonds, chopped or sliced

1/2 cup vegetable oil (*Cook's choice* – mix in a couple drops of sesame seed oil)

1/2 cup honey or real maple syrup (*Cook's choice* – combination of both)

3 tablespoons water

1/2 cup raisins

1/2 cup unsweetened coconut

> **Tip:**
> Can be kept in a sealed container for quite a while at room temperature or in refrigerator or freezer.

Directions:

Preheat oven to 300 degrees. In a large bowl mix together oats, sunflower seeds, sesame seeds, and nuts. Pour in oil, honey or maple syrup, and water, and mix all until well blended.

Spread out on cookie sheet and bake for 10-12 minutes. Remove from oven, add raisins and unsweetened coconut, and blend. Let cool.

Submitted by:

Beth Boynton, RN - NH/ME Seacoast
www.bethboynton.com | www.confidentvoices.com

Buckwheat and Brown Rice Pancakes

Serves 4

These flours blend well together to make light, delicious, gluten and dairy-free pancakes and will be naturally delicious if sweetened only with fresh fruit and eliminating the maple syrup.

Ingredients:

1/3 cup walnuts or nuts of choice

1 1/2 cups water or a bit more or milk

1 teaspoon apple cider vinegar

1 cup light buckwheat flour

1/2 cup brown rice flour

1 1/2 teaspoons baking powder

1/2 teaspoon baking soda

1/2 teaspoon ground cinnamon

1/4 teaspoon ground nutmeg

1 banana, mashed or 1 ripe pear, chopped or 2 tablespoons maple syrup

1 teaspoon Madagascar vanilla

1 tablespoon flax seeds, ground (optional)

butter (optional)

2 tablespoons walnut oil or oil of choice

Tip:

If batter is too thick, add a little more water to desired consistency. Use cider vinegar only if making milk. If using banana or pear as binder, eliminate flax. Pancakes will still be very tasty but not as good in consistency if you use fruit and flax seeds.

Serving Suggestions:

Top with warm sautéed apples, a fruit sauce, or with the traditional butter and maple syrup.

Note:

This recipe is Gluten and Dairy Free!

Directions:

Place walnuts in a blender and whirl until completely crushed. Add water and blend until mixed. Presto! You have some fresh made walnut milk. Add cider vinegar to milk and let sit 5 minutes while measuring the flours, baking powder, soda, flax, and spices. Add maple syrup or fruit, vanilla, and oil to milk mixture and whir until blended. Pour flour into blender a little at a time, blend, scrape sides, and continue to blend until well mixed. Add a little oil to cast iron skillet and heat until hot. Drop in batter by tablespoons. Once bubbles start to form, turn over and heat other side.

Buckwheat Pancakes or Waffles

Serves 5

These are tasty and hearty pancakes.

Pancakes Ingredients:

2 1/4 cups flour, a combination of 1/2 dark and 1/2 light buckwheat or 1/2 spelt

3 teaspoons baking powder

dash of sea salt

1 1/2 cups organic raw whole milk, coconut or almond milk

3 tablespoons extra virgin olive or walnut oil

2 large eggs

1/2 teaspoon ground cinnamon

1/4 teaspoon ground nutmeg

2-3 tablespoons maple syrup or other sweetener (optional)

> **Tips:**
>
> Using 1/2 light buckwheat flour with 1/2 spelt flour yields a lighter, less dense pancake.
>
> Leftover pancakes freeze nicely. Wrap in parchment paper, then store in freezer bag.

Pancake Directions:

Stir flour, baking powder, spices, and salt together in mixing bowl. With hand mixer, blend together milk, oil and sweetener. Add egg to liquid ingredients, mix and add to flour mixture. Mix well. If batter is too stiff, add a little more liquid. If eggs are omitted, you will need 2–3 tablespoons more liquid for each egg. Drop by spoonfuls into hot cast iron skillet. As buckwheat browns quickly, make sure pan isn't too hot. Serve with maple syrup, applesauce or fruit puree.

Waffle Directions:

As above but you need to double amount of oil used. Waffles are good, very crisp and work well without egg or sweetener.

Cinnamon Date Scones

Makes 15–18

Ingredients:

1 1/2 cups spelt flour

1 1/2 cups oat flour

1 tablespoon baking powder

1/4 teaspoon sea salt

1/2 teaspoon baking soda

1 cup organic apple juice or
freshly juice some apples

1/3 cup sunflower or choice of oil

1/2 cup dates, chopped (about 7 - 9)

1 teaspoon ground cinnamon

> **Tip:**
> *Cook's Choice*, make your own fresh flour by grinding oats in a coffee grinder.

Directions:

Preheat oven to 350 degrees. Combine ingredients in large bowl. Lightly oil cookie sheet or cover baking tray with parchment paper. With a tablespoon, drop batter onto cookie sheet leaving 1" space between each. Bake 15 minutes. Allow to cool before serving.

Christmas Frittata

Serves 2 - 3

Although filled with festive holidays colors, this simple and delicious dish can be enjoyed anytime.

Ingredients:

1 tablespoon extra virgin olive oil

1 small onion, chopped

1/2 yellow pepper, chopped

1 ripe avocado

1 small tomato, chopped

3 large eggs

2 tablespoons water

salt and pepper to taste

1/4 teaspoon cumin

1/4 cup feta or goat cheese, crumbled

1 teaspoon dried hot chili peppers

1 tablespoon fresh cilantro, minced

Directions:

In a cast iron skillet, saute onion and pepper in oil over medium heat until onions are limp. Add tomato, stir and cook 1 minute, then stir in avocado. Whisk eggs with water and pour over vegetables in skillet. Tilt skillet so egg covers bottom of pan. Sprinkle on cheese and cilantro and cook over medium heat until eggs are set around edge. Place pan on top shelf of oven and broil on high for a few minutes or until center is set. Cut fritatta into 4 or 6 wedges and slide onto serving plates.

Colada-Nog Coffee Cake or Muffins

Yields 1 coffee cake or 12 - 14 muffins

A very moist, yummy coffee cake nice enough to serve at a brunch. If in a hurry, use batter to make muffins.

Batter Ingredients:

1/4 cup butter

1/4 cup sugar

1 large egg or 1 tablespoon ground flax seed

3/4 cup banana, mashed

1/4 cup applesauce

6 ounces coconut milk or coconut yogurt

2 cups whole wheat, spelt or gluten free -
all purpose flour

1 teaspoon baking powder

1 teaspoon baking soda

1/4 teaspoon sea salt

1/3 cup fresh pineapple, finely chopped or
canned without liquid

Tips:

For an egg-free version, substitute egg with ground flax seed. For variety, layer ingredients. First layer a little less than half the topping, then half the batter, evenly spread pineapple over batter, spread remaining batter over pineapple and top batter with rest of nut topping. Freeze remaining pineapple or use in a fruit smoothie.

Topping Ingredients:

1/2 teaspoon ground cinnamon

1/2 teaspoon ground nutmeg

1/2 cup nuts, chopped

1/8 cup sugar

Directions:

Preheat oven to 350 degrees. In a small bowl combine topping ingredients and stir until well blended. Set bowl aside. In a large bowl cream butter. Add sugar to creamed butter and beat until well mixed. Add egg or flax to butter, sugar mixture and beat until fluffy. Add mashed banana, applesauce, coconut milk or yogurt, and beat with a mixer until well mixed. In separate bowl add flour, baking powder, baking soda, and salt and stir until blended. Fold flour mixture into liquid ingredients and mix until well blended. Add pineapple and stir until well blended. Sprinkle half the nut and spice mixture on the bottom of a bundt or spring form pan that has either been greased or lined with parchment paper. Spread batter evenly in pan over nut mixture and sprinkle remaining topping over top of batter. Bake coffee cake for 45 minutes or until done or 20-25 minutes for muffins.

Confetti Scrambled Eggs

Serves 2 - 3

Ingredients:

4 large eggs

4 tablespoons water

1/3 cup orange and yellow peppers, chopped

1 large tomato, chopped

1/4 cup scallions, thinly sliced

2 cloves garlic, minced

Himalayan salt and pepper to taste

dash or more tabasco sauce

1 tablespoon extra virgin olive oil, coconut oil, or a little of each

1/4 cup cheese of choice (optional)

Tips:

To retain all the healthy benefits in the garlic, add at the end, stir and cook 30 seconds.

Directions:

Saute peppers in oil until tender. In a medium bowl, whisk eggs with water until blended. Add salt, pepper, and tabasco. When peppers are soft and slightly golden, add egg mixture, and stir gently. Add tomato, 1 tablespoon scallions, half the garlic and stir until eggs are completely cooked and tomato has softened. If using cheese, stir into eggs with remaining garlic, and 1 tablespoon scallions, and cook 30 seconds. To serve, sprinkle last tablespoon scallions on top eggs as a garnish.

Cornmeal Pancakes

Makes 12 pancakes

Ingredients:

2 cups organic cornmeal

1/4 cup sugar

1/2 teaspoon sea salt

2 teaspoon baking powder

1 large egg

1 1/2 cup organic whole milk

1/4 cup extra virgin olive oil

Directions:

Mix dry ingredients together. Mix liquid ingredients together. Pour liquids into dry ingredients and mix well. Heat griddle to medium high. Pour batter onto pan. Use about 1/4 cup batter for each pancake. Turn pancakes over when bubbles appear.

Inside Out Stuffed Spinach Goat Cheese Omelet

Serves 2

Ingredients:

1 tablespoon butter

1 tablespoon extra virgin olive oil or olive oil spray

1/4 cup onion, chopped

2 cups fresh organic baby spinach, chopped

4 large organic eggs

4 tablespoons water

salt and pepper to taste

1/2 cup goat or feta cheese, crumbled (*Cook's choice* - goat)

1 fresh orange, thinly sliced for garnish, optional

Directions:

Oil cast iron pan and heat to medium. In a separate pan, melt 1 tablespoon butter and sauté onion and spinach until onion is soft and spinach is limp and dark green. Mix eggs, water, and spices together and add to cast iron pan. Tilt the pan in several directions until all egg is set. Place spinach and onion mixture on top of egg, sprinkle crumbled cheese evenly over egg, and cook until cheese begins to melt. To serve two people, cut egg in half and fold each half in half again. Garnish with orange slices.

Nut Milk French Toast

Serves 3

Ingredients:

1/3 cup walnuts, crushed or nuts of your choice

1 cup water, filtered

3 large eggs

1/2 teaspoon Madagascar vanilla

1 teaspoon coconut oil

7-8 slices bread (*Cook's choice - sourdough or raisin spelt*)

Serving Options:

Top with butter and maple syrup, powdered sugar, jam, warm applesauce or sauteed fruit.

Tip:

To cut recipe in half, use half the milk and 2 eggs.

Directions:

Blend walnuts in blender until crushed. Add water and blend again for quick fresh walnut milk. Add eggs and vanilla to milk mixture and whirl until completely blended. In a cast iron skillet add coconut oil. When pan is hot, dip each side of bread into batter and place in pan. Cook one side, turn over and cook other side. Depending on size of pan, cook two to three slices of toast at a time. Serve with a variety of toppings.

Pumpkin Pancakes

Makes about 20 pancakes

These hearty and delicious pancakes are great served during holidays as their aromas will fill your home with warmth and holiday cheer.

Ingredients:

1/3 cup pecans, ground

1 1/2 cups water or whole milk

2 tablespoons coconut oil, olive or oil of choice

3 tablespoons maple syrup

2/3 cup fresh pumpkin, roasted and mashed, or canned

2 cups brown rice flour, wheat, spelt, or a combination, or your favorite

2 teaspoons baking powder

1 1/4 teaspoon ground cinnamon

1/2 teaspoon ground ginger

1/2 teaspoon ground nutmeg

Note:
The use of water and brown rice flour make this recipe Gluten and Dairy Free. Use regular milk and all purpose flour for anyone without gluten or dairy sensitivities.

Directions:

If making your own milk, grind pecans and place in a blender with water and whirl until well mixed. Combine milk, oil, maple syrup, and pumpkin in blender or use a mixer and mix until well blended. Measure out flour and baking powder. Add spices and stir. Combine liquid ingredients with flour and blend until well mixed. If batter seems too thick, add a bit more water. Add a little oil or butter to a cast iron skillet or griddle pan. When pan is hot, spoon in a large tablespoon of batter and cook until bubbles form on top, turn and cook until lightly golden. Oil or grease pan as needed and repeat until batter is used up. Serve with sauce below, additional maple syrup and butter, powdered sugar, or warm applesauce.

Continued on the next page...

Pumpkin Pancakes (continued)

Quick and Easy Sauce Ingredients:

1 tablespoon maple syrup

1/4 cup dark rum

1/2 cup water

3 tablespoons butter

1/4 teaspoon ground ginger

1/2 teaspoon arrowroot, cornstarch
or kudzu

Tip:

Depending on which thickener is used and whether you like a thin or thicker sauce you may want to adjust thickener.

Sauce Directions:

Melt butter, add maple syrup and stir until blended. Add water and ginger, stir and bring to a boil. Reduce heat and slowly add rum. Cook over medium heat until mixture reduces by about half. In a little bowl add water to arrowroot and stir to blend. Add to sauce and stir until well blended and sauce has thickened a bit.

Quinoa Waffles With Fruit Sauce

Makes 8-10 waffles. Quantity depends on waffle maker. I use a Belgium waffle maker.

I recommend quinoa flour which does not have a lot of flavor on its own. But, adding juice and spices makes these the tastiest and lightest waffles I ever ate without the need for added sugar or sweeteners. The use of ginger in the batter and in the fruit sauce creates a wonderful zing. If not a fan of ginger, reduce amount by half or eliminate it.

Waffle Ingredients:

1 1/2 cups quinoa flour

2 teaspoons baking powder

2 teaspoons ground cinnamon

1/2 teaspoon ground ginger

1 1/4 cups organic apple juice

2 tablespoons walnut oil or oil of choice

2 large eggs (optional)

1-2 tablespoons maple syrup (optional)

Tip:

The use of Quinoa flour makes this recipe Gluten Free!

Serve with fresh home made whip cream.

Waffle Directions:

Stir flour, baking powder, and spices together in a medium bowl until blended. In a separate bowl, add juice, oil, eggs (if not using eggs add 1/4 cup water), maple syrup if using, and stir or whisk together. When completely blended, add liquid ingredients to dry ingredients. Batter should be light rather than heavy, so add more water if batter is too thick. Oil waffle iron and heat until hot. Add batter and close iron. As batter heats, steam will escape from iron. When steaming stops, waffles are done.

Continued on next page...

Quinoa Waffles With Fruit Sauce (continued)

Fruit Sauce Ingredients:

3 large strawberries

1/2 cup blueberries

1 peach

1/2 cup water

1/2 teaspoon ground ginger

1 teaspoon arrowroot

Fruit Sauce Directions:

Wash fruit and slice. Fruit yields about 1 cup. Amounts can be varied depending on personal preference. Place all ingredients except arrowroot in a small sauce pan. Bring to boil and simmer until sauce is colored and fruit has softened. Remove about 2 tablespoons of liquid from pan and place in small bowl. Stir arrowroot into liquid until blended. Pour back into sauce-pan and stir until blended and sauce has thickened.

Fresh Home Made Whip Cream:

Place a metal bowl and beaters in the freezer to chill for at least 15 minutes. Remove bowl from freezer, add whipping or heavy cream, and a bit more ginger which is optional. Whip until almost thickened, add about 1 teaspoon of powdered sugar or to taste, and whip until sugar is mixed in, and cream is ready. ENJOY!

Special Brunch Fruit Plate

Serves 6

A beautiful perfect fruit presentation is accompanied with a little bowl of fresh fruit juice sauce to drizzle over. This dish is so versatile it can easily be changed by serving in a bowl, placing a dollop of plain Greek yogurt over fruit, and finishing with a drizzle of the light sauce. Either way it will delight your senses and tickle your palate!

Ingredients:

2 tablespoons orange juice, freshly squeezed

1 tablespoon lime juice, freshly squeezed

3/4 teaspoon sugar

1 teaspoon kudzu

1/2 fresh pineapple

1 orange, thinly sliced

1 kiwi, thinly sliced

1 tablespoon triple sec (optional)

Directions:

To make sauce squeeze orange and lime juices into a bowl, add triple sec, sugar, and kudzu, and stir until well blended. This makes a slightly thickened sauce without the need to cook. For a thicker sauce mix a little of the fruit juices with kudzu, heat it a bit, and return to the rest of the mixture. You may want to adjust the kudzu by adding a bit more or less for a thicker or thinner sauce. Set sauce aside. For a nice presentation, keep leaves attached to pineapple as you slice fruit in half. Slice through the leaves and pineapple half you are serving so you now have 2 quarters. Use a long knife to slice pineapple all along the rind so you have one large piece of pineapple without rind. The rind serves as a boat for the fruit. Cut off the top hard core, slice pineapple into crosswise pieces, and return pineapple slices to each quarter of the pineapple boat. Place a few orange slices on top of each pineapple boat and a few kiwi slices on top of the oranges. Arrange pineapple boats on a rectangle or oval platter with leaves of one quarter pineapple going to left and leaves of the other boat going to the right. You can also place more sliced fruit around the boat and at each end. Place sauce in a little bowl to drizzle over fruit if desired.

Zucchini Egg Provolone Bake

Serves 4

Ingredients:

1 cup onion, chopped

1/2 red pepper, chopped

4 cups zucchini, quartered and thinly sliced

2 tablespoons fresh basil, minced or 2 teaspoons dried

1/4 teaspoon sea salt

1/4 teaspoon black pepper

4 large eggs, beaten

1 1/2 cups provolone cheese, shredded

3/4 cup whole ricotta cheese

2-3 garlic cloves, or to taste

1 tablespoon coconut or extra virgin olive oil

paprika

> **Tip:**
> Serve hot or at room temperature.

Directions:

Preheat oven to 350 degrees. Add oil, onion, and pepper to skillet and cook 5 minutes or until tender. Stir occasionally so evenly cooked. Add zucchini to vegetables, stir so all are evenly blended, and cook stirring off and on until zucchini is crisp tender. Remove from heat and add basil, salt, and pepper. Beat eggs. Add cheeses to eggs and stir until all are well blended. Add chopped garlic and spoon mixture into a glass baking dish coated with a light film of oil or cooking spray. Shake some paprika over top and bake 35-40 minutes or until top is lightly brown.

Dessert

Apple Cake

Baked Pumpkin Custard

Carob Mint Cookies

Chocolate Chip Raspberry Brownies

Choco-molay Pudding and Carob-molay Pudding

Chocolate Surprise Cake

Melon Sunset

Modern Day Bread Pudding

Oatmeal Apple Pie Cookies

Oatmeal Banookies

Oatmeal Chocolate Chip Cookies

Parsnip Spice Cake

Quartet of Fruit Crisps

Raspberry Cream Cheese Coffeecake

Squash Cheesecake

Strawberry Rhubarb Crisp

Toasted Oatmeal Cookies

Apple Cake

This makes a delicious cake for everyone, gluten free or not.

Ingredients:
1 stick butter
2/3 cup sugar
1/3 cup honey
1/4 cup safflower oil
1 egg
1/2 cup flour (*Cook's choice* – All purpose Gluten free baking flour)
1/2 cup coconut flour
1/2 teaspoon baking soda
1/2 teaspoon cinnamon
1/4 teaspoon nutmeg
1/8 teaspoon ginger
3 cup diced apples
1/2 cup chopped walnuts

Directions:
Preheat oven to 350 degrees. Cream together butter and sugar. Add remaining ingredients. Pour into greased and floured 8" square pan. Bake 1 hour. Great served warm or cold.

Submitted by:
Sheri Santo, *Graphic Designer* | www.sherisanto.com

Baked Pumpkin Custard

Serves 4

This recipe is so simple and delicious. For easy preparation simply place all ingredients into a blender and blend on medium speed until well mixed. Pour into a prepared casserole pan, bake, and enjoy the wonderful aromas filling your kitchen.

Ingredients:

1 cup fresh pumpkin puree from one small sugar pumpkin, or if fresh pumpkins are out of season, use 1 cup organic canned pumpkin

2 large eggs

3/4 cup organic whole milk or raw milk if available

1/3 cup organic maple syrup

2 tablespoons butter, melted

1 tablespoon spelt flour or flour of choice

1 teaspoon ground ginger

1 teaspoon ground nutmeg

1 teaspoon ground cinnamon

1/8 teaspoon salt

ginger cream topping, optional (see below)

> **Note:**
> Recipe can be easily doubled using 1 1/2 quart casserole.

Directions:

Preheat oven to 350 degrees. Wash pumpkin, pierce it a few times, and place in a glass baking dish. Bake whole pumpkin for about one hour, turning a few times. When pumpkin is soft, remove from oven, cut in half, and scoop out pumpkin seeds. If desired, set aside seeds to roast later in oven. Scoop out pumpkin pulp and mash. Add eggs, milk, pumpkin, maple syrup, butter, flour, and all spices. Place in a blender and blend on medium speed until thoroughly mixed. A hand mixer can be used to blend all ingredients if you prefer. Pour into a greased 1-quart casserole and place in a shallow baking pan containing about 1"-2" hot water. Place on bottom rack in oven and bake one hour and 10 minutes or until knife inserted in center comes out clean. Serve warm or cool, with or without ginger cream topping.

Continued on next page...

Baked Pumpkin Custard (continued)

Ginger Cream Topping Ingredients:

1/4 teaspoon ground ginger

1 cup organic heavy cream or whipping cream

1 teaspoon confection sugar

Ginger Cream Topping Directions:

Beat cream, ginger, and sugar until cream thickens.

Carob Mint Cookies

Makes about 32 cookies

It is a good idea to wash hands before getting started, so you can enjoy licking any batter that sticks to your fingers. Children will love helping with this one.

Ingredients:

1 cup kamut, spelt, or amaranth flour

3/4 cup garbanzo flour

1/2 cup carob powder

1 tablespoon flax seeds, ground

1 1/2 teaspoon baking powder

1/4 teaspoon sea salt

1/2 cup walnuts, pecans or macadamia nuts, ground

1/3 cup walnut or olive oil

1/4 cup maple syrup

3/4 cup peppermint tea

> **Note:**
> This recipe is Vegan and can be Gluten Free if using an alternative flour.

Directions:

Preheat oven to 350 degrees. Place a hefty teaspoon of peppermint tea in a paper tea bag or tea ball, add 3/4 cup of boiling water and let steep 15 minutes. While tea steeps, mix flours, carob powder, ground flax seeds, baking powder, salt, and ground nuts. Stir until well blended. Mix together oil, maple syrup, and tea and add slowly to flour mixture. Stir until well blended. Batter will be sticky. Place one teaspoon of batter at a time on a cookie sheet lined with parchment paper. Flatten cookies a little and bake about 12 minutes until toothpick comes out clean and bottom is a tiny bit brown.

Chocolate Chip Raspberry Brownies

Makes 20 small brownies

Delicious, moist, easy to make brownies with a hint of raspberry, and hard to believe they are gluten free.

Ingredients:

3/4 cup applesauce

1/4 cup walnut or sunflower oil
or your choice of oil

1 large egg

1 tablespoon Chambord liquor

1/3 cup unsweetened cocoa (*Cook's choice* - Ghiradelli)

1 cup and 2 tablespoons gluten-free all purpose baking flour (or your own combo)

1 cup organic sugar

1/2 teaspoon baking powder

1/4 teaspoon sea salt

1 cup small chocolate chips (Ghiradelli)

Note:

As these are so fudgey and rich, you may need to wipe off the knife repeatedly while cutting into squares.

This recipe is Gluten Free!

Directions:

Preheat oven to 350 degrees. Mix all ingredients together except for chips. Blend for one to two minutes until all ingredients are well blended. Stir in chocolate chips until well mixed. Pour batter into a lightly greased 8" x 8" glass baking pan. Bake 40 minutes depending on oven or until a toothpick inserted comes out clean. Allow to cool completely before cutting into small squares.

Choco-Molay Pudding

Serves 2

These delicious desserts feature the healthy avocado which is nutritionally rich in mono-unsaturated fat, potassium, and folate.

Ingredients:

2 avocados, chopped

3 teaspoons white crème de menthe or peppermint extract

7 tablespoons nut milk of your choice (*Cook's choice* – walnut, see below to make your own)

2 tablespoons organic maple syrup

1/3 cup powdered Dagoba organic chocolate

> **Tip:**
> If using crème de menthe, make sure it is white so you do not ingest any artificial color.

Directions:

Make nut milk or use store bought. Place half milk in blender with crème de menthe and one chopped avocado. Blend until well mixed. Add second chopped avocado, rest of nut milk, maple syrup, chocolate, and blend well until thick. Serve in 4-ounce fancy glasses or custard cups.

Alternative Ingredients:

2 avocados, chopped

5 teaspoons white crème de menthe or peppermint extract

3/4 cup macadamia nut milk or your choice of milk

3 tablespoons organic maple syrup

1/3 cup carob powder

> **Tip:**
> If making almond milk, you will want to strain the milk prior to use to assure creamy texture to your pudding.

Alternative Directions:

Prepare according to directions above, using the alternative ingredients.

Make your own nut milk:

Place 1/4 cup nuts of choice into a blender and blend until well ground. Add 3/4 cup water and blend until thoroughly blended.

Chocolate Surprise Cake

The batter is very red but when baked becomes a beautiful, moist, dark chocolate cake. If you add a little beet juice, the icing almost looks like cotton candy without any artificial color or flavoring. This healthier version will delight children as well adults.

Ingredients:

1 3/4 cup spelt flour

1 1/2 teaspoon baking soda

1/4 teaspoon sea salt

1/4 cup cocoa powder, organic if possible

2 cups beet puree (2 large or 3 small)

1/2 cup extra virgin olive oil

1/2 cup organic apple sauce

3 large eggs

1 teaspoon Madagascar vanilla

1/2 cup sugar

2 ounces organic chocolate (*Cook's choice - a 73% dark chocolate organic candy bar*)

1/2 cup chocolate chips (optional)

> **Tip:**
> Steep peppermint tea in a covered container for 15 minutes to enhance the flavor of the tea. Enjoy the rest of the tea while the cake cooks.

Directions for Beet Puree:

Wash beets, cut off ends, peel or leave unpeeled, place in a saucepan, and cover with water. Bring to boil, lower heat, and simmer about 40 minutes until beets are easily pierced with a fork. Let beets cool. Put in blender with about 1/4 cup cooking liquid from the beets and blend until pureed. Puree can be made one to two days ahead and stored in refrigerator.

Continued on next page...

Directions for Cake:

Preheat oven to 350 degrees. In a 2-cup measure, add flour, baking soda, salt, and cocoa, and stir until blended. Put chocolate squares in a coffee mug and place in small pan containing 1-2 inches of water. Simmer on low until chocolate has melted. Set aside to cool. Mix together beet puree, oil, applesauce, eggs, vanilla, and sugar until well blended. Fold chocolate into beet mixture, add dry ingredients, and combine. Mix until completely blended. Stir in chips if using. Pour batter into a greased 9" x 13" pan so evenly distributed. Bake for 35-40 minutes until a toothpick inserted into cake comes out clean. If making cupcakes, bake 15-20 minutes depending on how full you fill cupcake papers. Cool completely before icing.

Ingredients for Icing:

1 stick butter

1/4 cup peppermint tea or a tad less or for an added surprise use peppermint schnapps

1 teaspoon beet liquid or beet puree, colors icing naturally

1 1/3 cups confection sugar

Directions for Icing:

Let butter soften while cake cools. When softened, alternate adding confection sugar, peppermint tea, beet juice or puree, and blend. Continue until all ingredients have been added and icing is creamy and well blended. You may want to add a little more tea or beet juice depending on desired consistency. Add additional liquid a little at a time.

Melon Sunset

Serves 4

Simple, Nutritious, Delicious, and Elegant!

Ingredients:

3 cups honeydew melon

1 avocado

1 teaspoon shaved 70% dark chocolate

mini dark chocolate chips to decorate

fresh mint, for garnish (optional)

Directions:

Cube melon and blend until smooth. Peel and chop avocado and add to melon mixture. Blend until all mixed. Grate chocolate. Put some melon and avocado mixture in a parfait glass. Sprinkle with some shaved chocolate. Pour another layer of melon and avocado mixture over chocolate and sprinkle a little more chocolate on top. Decorate with some mini dark chocolate chips and garnish with a piece of fresh mint if desired.

Modern Day Bread Pudding

Serves 4 - 6

This makes a delicious, nutritious and not too sweet dessert.

Ingredients:

4 cups raisin spelt or sourdough bread,
cut in 1" pieces or smaller (about 6 slices)

1/4 cup butter, melted

3 large eggs

2 cups organic whole milk

1 tablespoon organic maple syrup

2 teaspoons vanilla

1/2 teaspoon ground cinnamon

1/2 teaspoon ground nutmeg

1/2 teaspoon sea salt

1/4 cup raisins (optional)

Tip:

Can use sourdough or any bread of your choice and add 1/4 cup of raisins which is optional.

Directions:

Preheat oven to 375 degrees. Place bread cubes in a 2-quart greased casserole, pour butter over, and toss to coat. Place eggs, milk, maple syrup, vanilla, and spices in a blender and blend. If using bread without raisins and you want to include raisins, sprinkle them over bread. Pour batter over bread and stir to coat. Bake uncovered 40 minutes or until knife inserted near center comes out clean.

Oatmeal Apple Pie Cookies

Yields 2 1/2 dozen

Ingredients:

1/3 cup butter, softened

1/4 cup brown sugar

1/4 cup sugar

1 egg

1 teaspoon vanilla extract

1 1/4 teaspoon cinnamon

1/4 teaspoon nutmeg

1/2 teaspoon baking soda

1/2 teaspoon salt

1 cup peeled, diced apples

1 1/2 cup oats, not instant

3/4 cup chopped walnuts (optional)

Note:

This recipe is Gluten Free!

Directions:

Preheat oven to 375 degrees. Lightly grease baking sheet. Cream butter, sugars, egg, and vanilla at medium speed for 1 1/2 minutes. Combine cinnamon, nutmeg, baking soda, and salt. Stir into creamed mixture until well blended. Stir in apples, nuts, and oats. Drop rounded tablespoons of dough on cookie sheet. Bake 13 minutes.

Submitted by:

Sheri Santo - Dover, NH

Graphic Designer | www.sherisanto.com

Oatmeal Banookies

Ingredients:

3 ripe bananas

2 cups rolled oats

3/4 cup semi-sweet chocolate chips

1/3 cup vegetable oil

3 tablespoons brown sugar

1 tablespoon honey or molasses

1 teaspoon vanilla extract

Note:

This recipe is Gluten Free!

Directions:

Preheat oven to 350 degrees. Mash bananas in a large bowl. Stir in oats, chocolate chips, oil, brown sugar, honey, and vanilla. Mix well and refrigerate for 15 minutes. Drop by teaspoonfuls onto an ungreased cookie sheet. Bake 20 minutes or until lightly browned.

Submitted by:

Sheri Santo - Dover, NH

Graphic Designer | www.sherisanto.com

Oatmeal, Coconut, Chocolate Chip Cookies

Yields approximately 3 1/2 dozen cookies

Ingredients:

1/2 cup oats

1 cup spelt flour

1/2 cup coconut flour

1/2 teaspoon sea salt, little less

1/2 teaspoon baking soda

2 large eggs

1/2 cup maple syrup

4 tablespoons coconut or extra virgin olive oil

2 tablespoons butter, melted

2 tablespoons water

1/3 cup mini chocolate chips

1/4 cup raisins (optional)

Directions:

Preheat oven to 350 degrees. Measure oats, flours, salt, and baking soda, and stir until well mixed. Mix eggs, maple syrup, oil, butter, and water together. Add liquid ingredients to dry ingredients and stir until well blended. Stir in chocolate chips and raisins if using. With a tablespoon scoop up batter and drop onto cookie sheets that have been lined with parchment paper or lightly grease pans. Bake about 15 minutes or until done.

Parsnip Spice Cake

Yields 12 - 16 pieces

Here is a great alternative to the standard favorite carrot cake. This one is always a hit when I bring it to events and share it with company at home.

Ingredients for Cake:

3/4 cup quinoa flour

3/4 cup spelt flour

1 teaspoon baking powder

1 teaspoon baking soda

1 teaspoon ground cinnamon

1/2 teaspoon ground nutmeg

1/8 teaspoon ground cloves

2 teaspoon flax seeds, freshly ground

1 large egg

1/3 cup extra virgin olive oil

1/3 cup applesauce

1/2 cup crushed pineapple

1 teaspoon ginger, freshly grated

1 teaspoon Madagascar vanilla

1 cup parsnips, finely shredded

Directions:

Preheat oven to 350 degrees. Mix flours together in a large bowl with baking powder, baking soda, ground spices, flax seeds, and stir all together. In a 2-cup measure add egg, oil, applesauce, pineapple, grated ginger, vanilla and parsnips. Stir to blend. Add to flour mixture and beat all together until batter is thoroughly blended and smooth. Grease a 9" x 9" square pan and bake 35 minutes. To make sure cake is done, insert tooth-pick in center and when toothpick comes out clean, cake is done. Remove cake from oven and let cool. When cool, frost with frosting below.

Continued on next page...

Parsnip Spice Cake (continued)

Ingredients for Frosting:

3 tablespoons butter

1/3 cup cream cheese

1 teaspoon ground ginger

1 cup powdered confection sugar

Directions for Frosting:

Put butter and cream cheese in a bowl on the counter to soften. Measure sugar, ginger, and confection sugar, and stir to blend. When butter and cream cheese are soft, add to sugar mixture, and blend with a hand mixer until creamy and smooth. When cake is completely cooled, use a small spatula to frost top of cake.

Raspberry Cream Cheese Coffee Cake

Serves 16

This recipe is a bit labor intensive but so delicious it's worth the work!
Every time I serve it or bring it as a house gift, it is a hit.

Ingredients:

2 1/4 cups spelt or all purpose flour

3/4 cup sugar

3/4 cup butter

1/2 teaspoon baking powder

1/2 teaspoon baking soda

1/4 teaspoon sea salt

3/4 cup plain yogurt (*Cook's choice* - Greek Gods yogurt)

1 large egg

1 teaspoon vanilla extract

1/2 cup Polaner all fruit seedless raspberry fruit spread

1/2 cup macadamia nuts, finely chopped

Filling Ingredients:

8 ounces organic cream cheese, softened

1/4 cup sugar

1 large egg

Directions:

Preheat oven to 350 degrees. Grease and flour sides of 9" or 10" spring form pan. In large bowl combine flour and 3/4 cup sugar. Cut in butter until mixture resembles coarse crumbles. Set aside 1 cup crumble mixture to be used with macadamia nuts in the topping. For batter, combine baking powder, baking soda, salt, yogurt, egg, and vanilla, and blend well. Spread batter over bottom and 2" up sides of prepared pan. Batter should be 1/4" thick on sides. In small bowl combine filling ingredients of cream cheese, sugar, and egg, and blend well. Pour filling over batter and evenly spread over top. Carefully spread preserves evenly over cheese filling. In a small bowl, mix reserved crumb mixture with macadamias and sprinkle over top. Bake 45-55 minutes until cream cheese is set and crust is lightly golden. Cool 15 minutes before removing side from spring form pan. Cut in wedges when completely cool. Refrigerate any leftovers.

Squash Cheesecake

This variation on a traditional pumpkin cheesecake won for most delicious at my work's monthly potluck, an event known for fierce competition! Winter squash is a great replacement for sugar pumpkin because it is usually less expensive, and is available during more of the year. The use of yogurt in place of the typical second package of cream cheese makes it possible to make this delicious dessert on the spur of the moment. After all, who keeps 2 packets of cream cheese on hand in the fridge? Not me. Enjoy!

Ingredients:

1/2 cup pecans, walnuts, or macadamias

1 1/4 cups gingersnap cookie crumbs (approximately 28 cookies)

5 tablespoons butter, melted

1 cup winter squash, baked (Ambercup or Gold Nugget)

1 8-ounce package of cream cheese

1 1/2 cup plain yogurt

3/4 cup sugar

1 teaspoon vanilla

3 eggs

3/4 teaspoon ground cinnamon

1/4 teaspoon ground nutmeg

1/4 teaspoon ground cloves

Notes:

This recipe works very well without a crust.

Mi-Del gluten free ginger cookies are a good substitute for anyone eliminating gluten.

Directions:

Preheat oven to 325 degrees. For crust, place nuts and ginger cookies in grinder, food processor, or blender and process until fine crumbs for crust. Add butter to mixture and stir until well blended. Press blended mixture firmly into a 10" pie pan or a spring form pan. Bake crust 10 minutes, remove from oven and set aside to cool. While crust is cooling, make filling. Turn oven up to 425 degrees. Pierce squash several times with fork and place in glass baking dish. Bake squash for about 1 hour. Remove from oven and cool. When cool, mash and set aside 1 cup in a bowl. Mix cream cheese, yogurt, sugar, and vanilla, and blend until smooth. Mix in eggs one at a time and blend in spices. Spread filling into crust and bake another 50 minutes or until set.

Submitted by:

Wendy Carter

Strawberry Rhubarb Crisp

Serves 6

This has always been one of our family's favorite summer desserts combining the sweetness and tartness of these two delicious summer fruits.

Ingredients:

1/4 cup sugar

3 tablespoons oat flour

1/3 cup butter

1/2 cup oat flour (Cook's choice - freshly ground)

1/2 cup oats

1/4 cup brown sugar

3 large stalks rhubarb, sliced

1 quart fresh strawberries, sliced

Tips:

Grind oats in a coffee grinder or food processor makes for nice, fresh oat flour.

You may want to add a little more or less sugar or butter depending on personal taste.

Directions:

Preheat oven to 350 degrees. Wash strawberries, remove leaves, cut off ends, and put in a bowl. Wash rhubarb, peel, slice, and add to bowl with strawberries. Toss fruit with sugar and flour until well coated. Allow fruit to sit for 15 minutes for flavors to meld together. Mix together butter, flour, oats, and brown sugar until crumbly and well blended for the topping and set aside. Grease an 8" glass baking pan. Stir fruit again, place in pan, and cover with crumbled topping. Bake 30-40 minutes until top is lightly browned and bubbly.

Toasted Oatmeal Cookies

Yields about 4 dozen

Ingredients:

3/4 cup butter

2 1/2 cups raw rolled oats

1/2 cup oat flour or flour of choice

1 teaspoon ground cinnamon

3/4 teaspoon ground allspice

1/2 teaspoon sea salt

1/2 teaspoon baking soda

1/2 cup brown sugar

1 large egg

1 teaspoon vanilla extract

Optional add ins

1/4 mini chocolate chips

1/4 cup cranberries

Notes:

To make fresh oatmeal flour, place small amounts of oats into a coffee grinder and grind until oats have turned into flour.

Directions:

Preheat oven to 375 degrees. In skillet, over medium heat melt butter making sure butter doesn't burn. Add oats and continue to stir and sauté for about 5 minutes until oats are golden. Remove from heat and let cool. In a bowl combine flour, spices, salt, and baking soda. Stir until all mixed and set aside. In another bowl combine sugar, egg, and vanilla. Beat or stir with a wooden spoon until batter is blended. Add buttered oats and flour and stir until well combined. If using optional add ins, stir into batter until well blended. Drop slightly rounded teaspoons of batter, about 3 inches apart, onto a cookie sheet lined with parchment paper. Bake 10-12 minutes until nicely golden. Remove and cool completely.

Quartet of Fruit Crisps

Serves 6 - Choose your favorite fruit dessert!

Apple Oat Crisp

Ingredients:

8 apples, peeled and chopped (Cook's choice - Cortland)

1/4 teaspoon sea salt

1 tablespoon maple syrup

1/4 cup water

Topping:

1 cup oat flour (Cook's choice - freshly ground oats)

1/4 cup rolled oats, not quick cooking or ground

1/4 cup sugar (little less)

3/4 teaspoon ground cinnamon

1/3 cup butter, softened

Directions:

Preheat oven to 350 degrees. Grease a 10" x 6" x 2" glass baking dish. In a bowl add apples, 1/2 teaspoon cinnamon, salt, maple syrup, and water, and stir until apples are evenly coated. Place apple mixture in baking dish. For topping, combine flour, oats, sugar, 1/4 teaspoon cinnamon, and butter, and rub together until crumbly. Sprinkle topping over apples. Bake 40 minutes.

Apple, Pear, Cranberry Oat Crisp

Ingredients:

4 apples, chopped

4 pears, chopped

1/4 cup cranberries, chopped

1/2 teaspoon ground ginger

Directions:

Follow recipe as above

Fruit Sweetened Blueberry Oat Crisp

Ingredients:

2 cups fresh blueberries or frozen
and thawed

5 dates, chopped small

Topping Ingredients:

3/4 cup oat flour or a combination of oat,
barley, and teff flour

1 1/4 cup rolled oats, not quick cooking

1/2 teaspoon ground cinnamon

5 tablespoon cold butter

1/2 teaspoon sea salt (optional)

Note:
Recipe uses only natural sugar from blueberries and dates.

Directions:

Preheat oven to 350 degrees. Mix blueberries and dates together and place in greased glass baking dish. Mix flour or combination of flours with oats, cinnamon, and salt. Measure out one cup topping and store in freezer for future use. For topping, cut butter into flour mixture and rub until mixture is crumbly. Drop topping over fruit. Bake 30 minutes or until done and topping lightly browned.

Peach Alternative Crisp

Ingredients:

3 cups fresh or frozen peaches, sliced
(about 3 pounds)

1/2 cup barley or oatmeal flour

1/2 cup barley flakes or rolled oatmeal

1/4 teaspoon ground cinnamon

1/4 teaspoon ground nutmeg

2 tablespoons butter

2 tablespoons sunflower or extra virgin
olive oil

1/4 teaspoon ground ginger (optional)

Note:
Oatmeal flour can be substituted for barley flour and rolled oatmeal for barley flakes.

Directions:

Preheat oven to 375 degrees. Peel and slice peaches and place in a lightly buttered 8" x 8" baking dish. In small bowl combine flour, barley flakes or oatmeal, and all spices, and stir until well blended. For topping, add butter and oil and mix with hands until crumbly. Sprinkle crumb mixture over peaches and bake 30 minutes or until peaches are tender.

Serving Suggestions:

Serve alone or with a wedge of sharp cheddar cheese or top with vanilla yogurt, vanilla or ginger ice cream.

Song: Fruit Quartet - Disc 2 - Song 5 - Swing - Medium-Slow Tempo

The Fruit Quartet recipe features four fruits, so I composed a piece that features four guitars -- one of them an electric bass guitar.

" To give life to beauty, the painter uses a whole range of colours, musicians of sounds, the cook of tastes — and it is indeed remarkable that there are seven colours, seven musical notes and seven tastes."

– Lucien Tendret (1825-1896) 'La Table au pays de Brillat-Savarin'

GRILLED SWORDFISH SALAD - page 100

Main Dishes – Fish and Seafood

Baked Tilapia - Too Easy to Be Legal

Beer Battered

Catfish Parmesan Fillets

Flounder with Avocado Mango Salsa

Grilled Swordfish Salad

Haddock with Crabmeat Stuffing

Pan Seared Scallops

Parmesan Crusted Sea Bass

Salmon Cakes

Salmon Teriyaki with Nori

Smoked Salmon and Pasta Salad

Snapdragon Salmon

Stoned Crab and Pasta

Stuffed Flounder or Haddock

Tilapia Creole

Baked Tilapia – Too Easy to be Legal

Serves 2 - 4

This recipe is foolproof and delicious every time.

Ingredients:

4 tilapia fillets

4 tablespoons butter, melted

bread crumbs for topping, unseasoned

salt or lemon pepper to taste

Serving Suggestion:

As the fillets are small, hungry diners may want two.

Directions:

Heat oven to 500 degrees. Sprinkle fillets with spices. Pour butter over top of fillets. Top with light layer of bread crumbs for approximately 15 minutes until cooked through, piping hot, bubbly, and browned to your liking. A couple extra minutes under broiler can brown a little more if preferred.

Submitted by:

Toni McFarland

Beer Battered

Serves 4 - 6

Chickpea flour used in this dish, also known as garbanzo flour is made by grinding chickpeas, which are legumes, into flour. For vegan dishes, it can be used as a replacement for egg batter by mixing equal amounts of flour and water together. Chickpea flour is also gluten free and a good substitute for anyone sensitive to wheat. Chickpeas are a great choice for vegetarians as they are high in protein. Check out the music for this song on CD #1.

Ingredients:

1 1/2 pounds wild caught flounder or cod

1/2 cup organic rice krispies, crushed

1/2 teaspoon pepper

1/2 teaspoon Himalayan salt

1 teaspoon ground turmeric

1/2 teaspoon paprika

1 cup chickpea flour

1 large egg, beaten

1/2 cup dark beer (*Cook's choice* - Guinness)

1 tablespoon extra virgin olive oil

1-2 tablespoons butter

additional butter, melted

Directions:

Preheat oven to 400 degrees. Add rice krispies and spices to chickpea flour and set aside. Mix egg and beer together. Cut fish into serving pieces, dip into egg and beer mixture, and dredge both sides in flour mixture. Place fish in a glass or ceramic baking dish coated with oil and butter. Bake 10 minutes, turn fish, drizzle additional melted butter over fish, and bake for about 10 more minutes depending on thickness of fish.

Song: Beer Battered - Disc 1 - Song 3 - Funk - Medium Tempo

The melody of this funky tune is based on the rhythm of the phrase "beer battered."

Catfish Parmesan Fillets

Serves 4

This recipe is from my cousin who borrowed it from a friend reported to be an excellent cook. My cousin praises this recipe as one of the very best dishes she has ever had the pleasure of being served, and one of the most delicious fish recipes EVER! Hence, it wins a blue ribbon award.

Ingredients:

2/3 cup Parmesan cheese, freshly grated

1/4 cup all-purpose flour

1/2 teaspoon salt

1/4 teaspoon black pepper

1 teaspoon paprika

1 egg, beaten

1/4 cup milk

4 catfish fillets, about 1 1/2 pounds

1/3 cup sliced almonds

1/4 to 1/2 cup butter, melted

Directions:

Preheat oven to 350 degrees. Combine Parmesan cheese, flour, salt, pepper, and paprika; stir and set aside. Combine egg and milk and mix well. Dip fillets in egg mixture and dredge in Parmesan mixture. Arrange fillets on a foil-lined baking pan sprayed with nonstick cooking spray. Sprinkle almonds over fillets and drizzle with melted butter. Bake 35 to 40 minutes or until fish flakes easily with a fork.

Submitted by:

Toni McFarland

Flounder With Mango-Avocado Salsa

Serves 5

Fish Ingredients:

1 pound wild flounder fillets

1 tablespoon extra virgin olive oil

1 tablespoon lime juice

1 1/2 teaspoons cilantro, minced

1/2 garlic clove, chopped

1/4-1/2 teaspoon pepper flakes or to taste

dash cayenne pepper

1/4 teaspoon salt or to taste

1 star fruit, thinly sliced (optional)

Serving Suggestion:

Cook 1 cup quinoa according to directions. When done, place in middle of plate, lay a fish fillet on top and top fish with the fruit and avocado salsa. If you like, place a few slices of star fruit around the quinoa just before serving.

Salsa Ingredients:

1 mango, chopped

1 yellow pepper, chopped

1/2 red onion, finely chopped

1 avocado, chopped

1/2 garlic clove, minced

12 cherry or grape tomatoes, chopped

1/4 cup fresh cilantro, finely chopped

1 teaspoon fresh mint, finely chopped

1 1/2 tablespoon fresh ginger, finely chopped

1 tablespoon rice vinegar

1 tablespoon freshly squeezed lime juice

1/4 teaspoon sea salt

Directions:

Preheat oven to 400 degrees. In shallow baking dish, combine oil, lime juice, cilantro, garlic, salt, pepper flakes, and cayenne pepper and stir until well mixed. Wash fish fillets, pat dry, and place in shallow baking dish. Turn fish a few times to coat with all seasonings. Bake 15-20 minutes, depending on thickness of fish. While fish cooks, make salsa. Combine mango, pepper, onion, avocado, garlic, tomatoes, cilantro, mint, ginger, vinegar, lime juice, and salt in a serving bowl. Stir well to blend all ingredients and leave on counter at room temperature so flavors meld together. Serve with fish.

Grilled Swordfish Salad

Makes 2 dinner size or 4 side dish servings

Marinade Ingredients:

1 pound swordfish steak (halibut or other firm fish)

3 tablespoons olive oil

1 tablespoon lemon juice

2 cloves garlic, minced

1 tablespoon fresh parsley, chopped

2 pinches sea salt

cracked black pepper to taste

Salad Ingredients:

2 cups romaine heart leaves, chopped

2 cups baby spinach

1 tomato, chopped

1/2 cup crimini mushrooms, sliced

1/3 cup black olives, sliced

Dressing Ingredients:

2 tablespoons olive oil

2 teaspoon white wine vinegar

1 tablespoon grated Parmesan cheese

1 teaspoon lemon juice

1 shallot, chopped

pinch sea salt

cracked black pepper to taste

Directions:

Whisk together marinade ingredients. Cut fish into 1" cubes and combine with marinade. Refrigerate at least 1 hour. Make dressing and set aside. Remove fish from marinade, put on skewers and discard marinade. Heat outdoor or indoor grill to medium low. Cook skewers, rotating until each side is lightly browned 12-15 minutes. Chop lettuce, tomato, mushrooms, and black olives and toss with baby spinach. Place cubes of fish on salad and drizzle with dressing.

Submitted by:

Sheri Santo | www.sherisanto.com

Haddock with Crabmeat Stuffing

Ingredients:

2 pounds haddock

2 tablespoons butter

3 scallions, sliced

8 ounces crabmeat

1/3 cup cheddar cheese, grated

3 tablespoons light cream or organic whole milk

1 tablespoon horseradish sauce

1 tablespoon fresh parsley, chopped

1/8 teaspoon cayenne pepper

1/8 teaspoon ground nutmeg

1/3 cup fine, plain breadcrumbs or crushed corn flakes

lemon wedges

salt and pepper to taste

Note:
Using corn flakes instead of breadcrumbs makes this recipe Gluten Free!

Directions:

Rinse the haddock in cold water and pat dry with paper towel. Cut into 4 pieces. Lightly salt and pepper both sides of each piece and squirt with lemon wedges. Spray glass baking dish with cooking spray and arrange haddock pieces in baking dish. Melt butter in saucepan and add remaining ingredients. Stir and cook over med-low heat for 5 minutes. Spoon mixture on top of haddock pieces and bake at 350 degrees for 15-20 minutes, depending on oven and thickness of fish.

Submitted by:

Sheri Santo | www.sherisanto.com

Pan Seared Scallops

Serves 2

Simple, delicious dinner that takes no time to prepare.

Ingredients:

10 large dry sea scallops

1 teaspoon organic coconut oil

1 teaspoon butter

garlic granules

sea salt and pepper to taste

Serving Suggestion:

Serve scallops on a bed of mashed potatoes, mashed parsnips, or rice with a side of steamed spinach, beet greens, or rainbow chard.

Tip:

What is a foot? It is a side muscle that looks like a small rectangular piece of tissue on the side of a scallop and feels tougher than the rest of the scallop. To remove, pinch between fingers and tear it off.

Directions:

Use a cast iron skillet, coat bottom of skillet with oil, and heat to medium high. While skillet gets hot, remove foot from scallop and discard. Place scallops on a plate, season one side with garlic granules, salt, and pepper. Add butter to hot skillet and place scallops seasoning side down in skillet. Make sure scallops do not touch each other. Sear scallops until they have a nice golden crust, about 2 minutes. Season tops of scallops and use a pair of tongs to turn scallops over. Sear another 1-2 minutes until second side has a golden crust. Remove immediately and serve.

Parmesan Crusted Sea Bass

Ingredients:

2 pounds sea bass

1/2 cup grated Parmesan cheese

2 tablespoons all purpose flour, regular or gluten free

2 tablespoons breadcrumbs or crushed corn flakes

1 teaspoon dried parsley

2 tablespoons butter, melted

olive oil for drizzling

lemon juice, freshly squeezed or bottled

sea salt

fresh ground pepper

Tip:

Use corn flakes instead of breadcrumbs and gluten free flour to make this recipe Gluten Free!

Directions:

Preheat oven to 350 degrees. Mix Parmesan cheese, flour, breadcrumbs or cornflake crumbs, and parsley together in small bowl. Melt butter and combine with Parmesan mixture until well blended. Remove skin from bass and cut into 4 equal pieces. Place pieces in lightly greased baking pan or use cooking spray. Drizzle pieces with olive oil and squeeze lemon juice over them. Season each piece with a bit of sea salt and freshly ground pepper. Spoon Parmesan topping on each piece, covering well by using your hands to pat the topping down. Drizzle olive oil over topping. Bake uncovered for 15 minutes. Broil for an additional 5 minutes so topping forms a crunchy crust.

Submitted by:

Sheri Santo | www.sherisanto.com

Salmon Cakes

Yields 4 cakes

I always keep a can of Alaskan salmon on hand for those times when there is nothing in the house, and I want a quick meal.

Ingredients:

2 shallots, chopped

3 garlic cloves, chopped

2 tablespoons fresh parsley, minced

3 tablespoons pine nuts, crushed or your favorite breadcrumbs

1 tablespoon prepared horseradish

1, 6-ounce can Alaskan salmon

1 large egg

2 teaspoons extra virgin olive oil

1/2 teaspoon butter

extra virgin olive oil

sea salt and pepper (optional)

Alternatives:
For a dairy-free dish, omit egg and replace with 1 tablespoon ground flax seeds and a little less than 1/4 cup water. For gluten free version, use pine nuts instead of bread crumbs.

Directions:

Saute shallots and garlic in oil until tender. Beat egg, add shallot garlic mixture, and rest of ingredients. Mix until thoroughly blended. Place mixture in freezer for 3 minutes to firm up a bit, then divide and form into 4 patties. Brush cast iron skillet with oil, add butter, and place salmon patties in pan. Cook on medium heat for about 6 minutes per side or until cooked through and lightly brown.

Salmon Teriyaki with Nori

Serves 4 - 6

Ingredients:

4 wild Alaskan salmon fillets, skinned and boned (6-8 ounces each)

1/8 cup extra virgin olive oil

1 tablespoon kudzu or arrowroot or cornstarch

2 tablespoons water

3/4 cup raw coconut aminos or tamari sauce

1 cup water

3 tablespoons brown rice vinegar

4-5 tablespoons honey or maple syrup, adjust to taste

1 teaspoon red pepper flakes

1 sheet toasted nori cut into 1 inch strips, or use packaged precut strips

1/4 cup scallions, thinly sliced

Directions:

Preheat oven to 350 degrees. To make marinade, mix coconut aminos or tamari, water, rice vinegar, honey, and red pepper flakes. Mix kudzu, arrowroot, or cornstarch with 2 tablespoons water until smoothly blended and add to marinade. Place salmon fillets in a glass baking dish with half the marinade for at least 30 minutes. Set aside remaining marinade and pour into a small saucepan to gently heat. Stir occasionally until thickened and add more water if sauce becomes too thick. Bake salmon for 5 minutes, then place strips of nori over salmon. Pour a little sauce over the nori, add half the chopped scallions, and bake for another 8-12 minutes depending on thickness of salmon. Baste at least once during baking. Sprinkle with remaining scallions and serve.

Complete Dinner Suggestion #1:

Place salmon on top of mashed parsnips or mashed celery root and drizzle a little sauce over fish and root vegetable and top with some chopped scallions. Serve with a combo of sauteed thinly sliced zucchini, red pepper, onions, garlic, and salt and pepper to taste.

Complete Dinner Suggestion #2:

Prepare salmon as above and serve on a bed of pasta. My favorite pastas are either kamut udon pasta, quinoa linguine, or buckwheat soba (an Oriental pasta that may or may not be wheat free) or use your favorite. Drizzle with a little sauce and sprinkle with scallions. Serve with some steamed beet greens mixed with a little melted butter, salt and pepper to complete the dinner.

Smoked Salmon Pasta Salad

Ingredients:

4 ounces Scottish smoked salmon, thinly sliced

1/2 cup green peas

8-ounces brown rice fusilli pasta

1/2 cup red pepper, chopped

2 tablespoons capers

1/4 cup fresh parsley, minced

1/2 lemon, freshly squeezed

3/4 teaspoon dry mustard

1 tablespoon extra virgin olive oil

1 tablespoon brown rice vinegar

1 tablespoon white wine

sea salt and cracked black pepper (optional)

Directions:

Cook green peas. Cook pasta according to package directions. Combine salmon, pasta, peas, and peppers in a bowl. Mix in capers and parsley. Whisk together lemon, mustard, oil, vinegar, and wine, and pour over pasta mixture, stirring until everything is well blended. Season with salt and pepper to taste.

Snapdragon Salmon

Ingredients:

1 -2 small jalapeno peppers

1/4 red onion, chopped

2 medium garlic cloves, minced

2 tablespoons fresh parsley, chopped

2 teaspoons red wine vinegar

1 teaspoon lime juice, freshly squeezed

3 teaspoons honey or agave nectar

1/4 cup olive oil

sea salt

cracked black pepper

1 1/2 pounds salmon

Tips:

If you want flavor but no heat, use 1 pepper with all seeds and veins removed.

If you like heat, use up to 2 peppers and leave in some of the seeds.

Directions:

Combine all ingredients except salmon in food processor and grind until a liquid/paste sauce forms. Brush sauce on one side of salmon and broil on top rack for 5 - 7 minutes. Turn salmon and brush sauce on other side. Broil for 5 - 7 minutes or until sauce slightly browns.

Submitted by:

Sheri Santo | www.sherisanto.com

Stoned Crab and Pasta

Serves 4

A great dish to serve for company but so delicious you might not want to wait, so enjoy it anytime whether you have company or not. Recipe can easily be doubled to serve 8.

Ingredients:

2 shallots or red onion, chopped

2 garlic cloves, minced

2 tablespoons extra virgin olive oil

2 1/2 cups fresh tomatoes, chopped or use a can or box of tomatoes

1 tablespoon fresh basil, minced or 1 teaspoon dried

1/4 cup fresh parsley, minced

1 dried bay leaf

1/4 teaspoon sea salt

1/4 teaspoon ground black pepper

1/4 teaspoon dried red hot peppers

1 8-ounce container of wild fresh crabmeat

1/3 cup vodka

1/4 cup heavy cream

1/4 cup Parmesan cheese, grated

pasta of your choice

Directions:

In saucepan heat oil, add onion and half the garlic and saute about 2 minutes. Add tomatoes, basil, 1/2 the parsley, bay leaf, salt, black pepper, and red hot peppers, and simmer covered for 1 hour. Remove bay leaf and adjust seasoning. Add vodka and rest of garlic and continue simmering for about 20 minutes or until mixture reduces a bit. Bring pot of water to a boil and cook pasta while sauce reduces. Stir crabmeat into sauce, cook a few minutes, add cream, and continue to simmer on low until sauce is heated through. Stir in cheese and heat until it is melted. Give sauce a final stir and spoon over pasta. Sprinkle a little remaining parsley over each plate and serve.

Stuffed Haddock or Flounder Fillets

Serves 2 - 3

The option uses flounder fillets which gives the dish a more delicate presentation.

Ingredients:

3/4 pound flounder or haddock

1 1/2 teaspoons extra virgin olive oil

2 small shallots or 1 large onion, chopped

3 garlic cloves, chopped

7 ounces fresh spinach, chopped or
1 medium zucchini, finely grated

1/4 cup feta or Gorgonzola cheese, crumbled

1/2 teaspoon dried basil

1/2 teaspoon dried oregano

1 teaspoon butter

4 tablespoons dry white wine, lemon juice, or water

black pepper to taste

1 tomato, chopped

fresh parsley or watercress for garnish

4 black olives for garnish

8 large mushrooms, sliced (optional)

Option:

If using flounder fillets, substitute spinach for zucchini in filling. Place one fourth of filling on one end of each fish fillet and roll up. Place seam side down or secure with a natural toothpick. Place fillets in a shallow baking dish. Pour wine, water, or lemon juice over fish and add a twist of black pepper or use ingredients added in last 5 minutes above. Follow and adjust baking directions above.

Serving Suggestion:

Jasmine rice cooked with 1/2 of a freshly squeezed lemon and the rind, thinly sliced. Place fish on top of rice and finish with a sprinkling of freshly minced parsley or watercress.

Directions:

Preheat oven to 350 degrees. Heat oil in medium size skillet. Add mushrooms, shallots or onions, and 2 garlic cloves, stirring over low heat until lightly browned. Stir in spinach and cook until spinach is wilted and any liquid has evaporated. Add cheese, basil and oregano, and stir until thoroughly blended. Place mixture in refrigerator for 20 minutes to firm up. Melt butter in baking pan. Cut fish in half and place one half in pan. Evenly spread filling over fish and place remaining fish over filling. Pour wine, water, or lemon juice over fish, add black pepper, and cover with parchment paper. Bake until fish is flaky and opaque throughout, about 30-40 minutes. basting a few times during baking. Time will vary depending on which cut of fish is used. While fish bakes, briefly sauté a tomato, remaining garlic clove, and a few sprigs of fresh parsley or watercress. Five minutes before fish is done, pour tomato mixture over fish and top with a few sliced pitted black olives.

Tilapia Creole

Serves 6

Ingredients:

1 1/2 pounds tilapia steaks or cod

1 medium red onion, chopped

3-4 garlic cloves, minced

1 small sweet red pepper, seeded and chopped

1 small green pepper, seeded and chopped

1 small red hot pepper, seeded and chopped

1 26-1/2 ounce box chopped Italian tomatoes, liquid drained and reserved

1/3 cup dry white wine

1/4 teaspoon cayenne pepper

1 teaspoon dried basil

1 teaspoon dried oregano

1/4 teaspoon sea salt

1/2 cup stuffed green olives, thinly sliced

1 cup mushrooms, sliced

1/2 teaspoon arrowroot powder

fresh parsley for garnish

> **Tip:**
> Based on your preference for heat you may want to omit or adjust amount of chili pepper used.

Directions:

Preheat oven to 350 degrees. Place onions, half the garlic, green and red peppers, hot peppers, and tomatoes in 11" x 13" glass baking dish. Stir in half of white wine and sprinkle with cayenne, basil, oregano, salt, chopped olives, and mushrooms. Stir to blend all and bake 20 minutes. While sauce bakes, cut fish into 1 1/2" pieces. Mix arrowroot with reserved tomato juice and stir until well blended. Add remaining wine to tomato juice, mix until well blended, and pour over tomato vegetable mixture already cooking. Add tilapia and stir to completely blend. Bake another 20 minutes or until fish flakes easily with a fork. Add remaining garlic just before serving and garnish with some fresh parsley.

Main Dishes – Meat

Grilled Bison & Roasted Vegetable Skewers

Herb Marinated Ostrich Steak

Lamb Curry

Laura's Slow Cooker Beef Stew

Moroccan Lamb

Pork Tenderloin in Mustard and Beer Sauce

Sausage and Zucchini Casserole

Steak, Prosciutto, and Provolone Roll-ups

Stuffed Buffalo Mounds

Stuffed Green Peppers

Veal Stew with Fennel

Grilled Bison and Roasted Vegetable Skewers

Serves 4

Bison is considered a heart-healthy red meat that is free of added chemicals including hormones, antibiotics, preservatives, and drug residues. It is a very flavorful meat similar to beef but with a sweeter and richer taste. It also contains more iron than beef and contains less fat, calories, and cholesterol.

Ingredients for Skewers:

1 pound lean bison, ground

1/4 cup crumbled crackers (about 6 small squares)

1/4 cup cilantro or Italian parsley, chopped

1 egg white, beaten

3 ounces feta cheese, crumbled

3 tablespoons Kalamata or black olives, chopped

3/4 teaspoon salt

1/2 teaspoon cinnamon, ground

1/2 teaspoon black pepper

2 cloves garlic, minced

16 2"-bell pepper squares

fresh cut vegetables: mushrooms, onions, zucchini, yellow squash, red and yellow peppers

flavored olive oil for basting

8 8"-wooden skewers, soaked in water for 20 minutes

Ingredients for Spicy Orange Barbecue Sauce:

1/4 cup orange marmalade

1 tablespoon chili powder

1 teaspoon dry mustard

1 teaspoon vinegar

Continued on next page...

Grilled Bison and Roasted Vegetable Skewers (continued)

Directions:

In a small bowl, mix together all ingredients for basting sauce. In medium bowl, combine bison, cracker crumbs, cilantro, egg white, feta, olives, salt, cinnamon, black pepper, and garlic. Mix until well blended. Shape into 8 large meatballs. To prepare skewers, alternate 2 meatballs with bell pepper squares on four of the eight skewers, and alternate assorted cut vegetables on remaining four skewers. Prepare barbecue grill and allow coals to burn down to ash gray. Barbecue all skewers for 5 minutes and turn. Baste meatball/pepper skewers with spicy barbecue sauce and grill 4-5 minutes longer or until done. Baste vegetable skewers with flavored oil and grill 5-7 minutes longer or until tender. Serve each guest a meatball/pepper skewer and an assorted vegetable skewer.

Permission to use granted by:

The Healthy Buffalo

Route 4, Chichester, NH 03258

www.healthybuffalo.com

Herb Marinated Ostrich Steak

Serves 8

According to The National Culinary Review, ostrich can be seen as "the premier red meat of the next century" because no other meat combines the flavor, versatility, and nutritional benefits of ostrich. It is similar in taste, texture, and appearance to beef and is comparable to beef in iron and protein content. Ostrich has less than half the fat of chicken and two-thirds less fat than beef and pork. Ostrich beats the competition with fewer calories too. For these reasons, ostrich is a great choice for health-conscious consumers without sacrificing flavor.

Ingredients:

2 pounds tender ostrich steaks (approximately 1-1/2 inches thick)

2/3 cup balsamic vinegar

1/4 cup olive oil

2 tablespoons garlic, finely chopped

1 tablespoon rosemary, crushed

1 tablespoon thyme leaves

1 teaspoon black pepper, freshly ground

Directions:

Combine marinade ingredients in a glass jar, shake until well blended, and pour into a bowl. Add meat to marinade in bowl and turn to coat both sides. Cover bowl securely and marinate in refrigerator one hour, turning occasionally. Remove meat from marinade and discard marinade. Place meat on rack in broiler pan so surface of meat is 3 to 4" from heat. Broil 26 to 31 minutes for medium-rare to medium doneness, turning once. Carve into slices.

Permission to use granted by:

The Healthy Buffalo

Route 4, Chichester, NH 03258

www.healthybuffalo.com

Lamb Curry

Serves 4

This is a very simple curry dish, not too spicy but with lots of flavor. If you don't have all the spices on hand you can easily leave out one or more and still have a delicious dish. Below is the fish version I created for my husband who is not a meat eater. This is one of those dishes that is quick and easy to make so everyone is happy.

Ingredients:

2/3 pound lamb, ground (*Cook's choice - organic, grass fed*)

1 cup onions, chopped

3 cloves garlic, minced

1 tablespoon butter or ghee (clarified butter)

1 tablespoon extra virgin olive oil

1/4 teaspoon ground cinnamon

1/2 teaspoon ground cumin

3/4 teaspoon ground turmeric

1/4 teaspoon ground curry

1/2 teaspoon sea salt

1/4 teaspoon red pepper, ground

1/8 teaspoon ground cloves

1 teaspoon ground coriander (optional)

1/2 teaspoon ground cardamon (optional)

15 ounces coconut milk

1 cup green peas, frozen

1/2 cup yellow raisins (optional)

1/4 cup cashews (optional)

1-2 tablespoons fresh ginger, minced or 1-2 teaspoons ground ginger

---

Serving Suggestion:

Serve over rice and accompany with your choice of yogurt, chutney, or pakoras.

Fish Alternative:

Use 2/3 pound of pollack cut into bite size pieces. Make sauce, add 1/2 of a fresh lemon, thinly sliced. Stir sauce until well blended and cook 15 minutes. Add fish and cook 5-10 minutes until done; depends on size of fish pieces.

Directions:

Make sauce by first browning onion and 1 clove of garlic in butter and oil until slightly caramelized. Add all spices and stir so onions are evenly coated. Add coconut milk, raisins and cashews if using, and stir all until well blended. Add peas. Cook about 10 minutes until peas are defrosted but don't loose their beautiful green color. While sauce, spices, vegetables, raisins, and nuts simmer, sauté lamb in a separate pan until thoroughly cooked. Add cooked lamb to simmering sauce with remaining garlic and ginger.

Laura's Slow Cooker Beef Stew

Serves 6

Ingredients:

2 pounds sirloin tips or stew beef

1 medium onion, chopped

4 carrots, peeled and sliced

2 ribs celery, sliced

1 medium green pepper, chopped

handful of string beans cut in half

4 medium potatoes, peeled and cubed

1 28-ounce can organic whole tomatoes undrained or use fresh

1 10 1/2-ounce can beef broth

1 tablespoon worcestershire sauce

1 bay leaf

1/2 cup fresh parsley, minced

1/4 teaspoon dried thyme

1/4 teaspoon black pepper

2 tablespoons quick cooking tapioca

1 teaspoon salt or less (optional)

Directions:

Brown beef cubes over medium heat. Transfer to a slow cooker. Add remaining ingredients and stir to blend. Cook either 2 hours on high and 6 hours on low, or 5 hours on high and 2 hours on low.

Submitted by:

Laura Melisi, Flautist

Moroccan Lamb

Serves 5 - 6

Ingredients:

2-3 pounds boneless lamb

2 tablespoons olive oil

1 medium or large onion, chopped

2 large garlic cloves, minced

1 tablespoon fresh ginger, grated

2 1/2 cups water

1 - 6-ounce package long grain and wild rice mix

1/2 teaspoon black pepper

1/4 teaspoon cinnamon or to taste

1/4 teaspoon cayenne pepper

dash of powder ginger

2 medium yellow squash, cut into 1" pieces (about 2 1/2 cups)

1 8-ounce package fresh mushrooms, sliced

1/2 cup dried tart cherries or dried cranberries

1/2 cup raisins

3/4 cup dried apricots

Directions:

Trim fat from lamb and cut into 1" pieces. Heat oil in large skillet or wok with a cover. Brown lamb on all sides. Remove from skillet and drain fat. Wipe out skillet and add a little oil, onion, garlic, and ginger. Sauté until soft. Return lamb to skillet and add water. Bring mixture to boil, reduce heat, and cover. Simmer 25 minutes. Add rice and seasoning mixture, black pepper, cinnamon, cayenne pepper, and dash of ginger. Return to boiling, reduce heat, cover, and simmer 20 minutes. Cook squash separately until just crisp tender and add to mixture along with mushrooms, cherries, raisins and apricots. Simmer covered about 10 minutes. Total preparation and cooking time from start to finish is 2 1/2–3 hrs.

Submitted by:

Laura Melisi, Flautist

Pork Tenderloin in Mustard and Beer Sauce

Serves 4

Ingredients:

1-2 pounds pork tenderloin

1 tablespoon olive oil

1/2 teaspoon black pepper

1/4 teaspoon salt

1 1/2 cups beer (*Cook's choice - white ale or wheat beer*)

1 tablespoon whole-grain mustard

2 tablespoons Dijon mustard

2 tablespoons water

2 teaspoons cornstarch

Tip:

Using 2 pounds of pork can easily serve more than 4 people. There will be plenty of sauce whether you use 1 or 2 pounds of pork.

Directions:

Trim the tenderloin of fat and cut crosswise into 12 (1" thick) slices. Heat oil in a large skillet over medium to medium-high heat. Sprinkle the pork slices with cracked pepper and sea salt on both sides. Place pork in pan; cook about 5 minutes on each side or until just browned.

While pork is browning, combine the beer and mustard. Once pork is browned, add beer mixture to pan. Cover, reduce heat, and simmer 10 minutes. Combine water and cornstarch in a small bowl. Stir cornstarch mixture into pan; bring to a boil, and cook 1 minute or until sauce thickens. Serve pork with sauce over mashed potatoes.

Submitted by:

Sheri Santo | www.sherisanto.com

Sausage and Zucchini Casserole

Serves 6 - 8

Ingredients:

1 pound turkey sausage, ground and cooked

2 zucchini's, thinly sliced

1/4 cup celery, chopped

1/2 cup onion, diced

1/2 cup green pepper, diced

1 14-ounce can Italian style crushed tomatoes or fresh tomatoes

1 8-ounce can tomato sauce or equivalent of homemade sauce

1 teaspoon dried oregano

1/2 teaspoon pepper or to taste

crushed red pepper flakes to taste

1 tablespoon parsley

1/2 cup sharp cheddar or mozzarella cheese, shredded

Directions:

Preheat oven to 350 degrees. Crumble sausage, brown, and drain. Remove from heat. Stir in celery, onion, green peppers, tomatoes, sauce, and seasonings. Place a layer of zucchini on bottom of casserole dish. Spoon sausage mixture on top. Repeat layers until all is used, ending with sauce. Cook 30-35 minutes. Top with cheese and cook an additional 15 minutes.

Submitted by:

Debbi Merlin - Stafford, TX

Jewelry designer, author and animal lover | www.designsbydesu.com

Steak, Prosciutto, and Provolone Roll-ups

Ingredients:

1 flank steak, 1-2 pounds

1 package or 6 deli slices prosciutto

1 package or 6 slices provolone cheese

1/2 stick butter, softened

1 tablespoon fresh basil, chopped

1 tablespoon fresh parsley, chopped

1/4 cup Parmesan cheese

6-8 Wooden skewers

olive oil

sea salt and cracked pepper

> **Tips:**
> The directions may sound a bit confusing, but once you get the hang of rolling and slicing the steak, it's really pretty easy.
>
> You will need a meat thermometer to check temperature of steak.

Directions:

Place wooden skewers in a glass of water for a few minutes so they don't burn in oven. Place steak between 2 sheets of cling wrap or wax paper on a board on a flat surface. Pound with a meat mallet until steak is approximately 1/4 to 1/2" thick. Remove wrap and season steak on both sides with sea salt and cracked pepper. Combine softened butter with chopped herbs and spread evenly over one side of the steak. Lay 4-6 slices of cheese and Prosciutto evenly over the herb buttered steak, leaving 1" uncovered at the top (of the wide end) for rolling. Start at bottom (wide end) of the layered steak and begin tightly rolling up towards the top end. As you roll up, use your hands to keep the cheese and Prosciutto tucked inside the steak. As you reach the top, stick skewers in through top flap and through center of the roll to secure the roll together. Place first skewer 2" from end of the roll and place each skewer about 2" apart. When done, slice the roll all the way through between each skewer. You should end up with 6-8 slices, each about 2" thick. Drizzle olive oil on each of the flat sides of the rolled up slices. Place slices, flat side down on broiler pan. Broil on one side for 5-7 minutes, then flip slices over and sprinkle Parmesan cheese and olive oil on the top of the slices. Place back in oven and broil for an additional 5-7 minutes or until cheese on top is slightly browned and center of steak reaches 135 degrees for medium rare.

Submitted by:

Sheri Santo | www.sherisanto.com

Stuffed Buffalo Mounds

Serves 4

Buffalo meat is considered a healthy red meat. It has a great texture, is very flavorful, and contains no antibiotics, hormones or preservatives. To learn more about it, see the alternatives section.

Ingredients:

1 pound buffalo meat, ground

4 tablespoons panko or breadcrumbs of choice

4 1" cubes of jalapeno cheese or cheese of choice

extra virgin olive oil

Directions:

Heat oven to 400 degrees. Place buffalo meat in a bowl and mix in bread-crumbs until evenly blended. Divide buffalo meat mixture into four equal sections. Flatten one section in palm of your hand and place a cube of cheese in center. Fold over meat and roll in your hands to form a ball, ensuring meat completely covers the cheese. Use same procedure for the remaining three sections of meat mixture. Lightly coat 4 sections of a muffin pan with oil and place a ball in each. Press down slightly so ball fills muffin tin. Lightly brush tops with oil. Place a little water in remaining muffin cups not used, so they don't burn. Bake about 25 minutes or until thoroughly cooked. Sometimes a small amount of cheese melts through like a volcano erupting. If that happens, just spoon up and place on top of round. When done, mounds almost resemble little mountains with some snow on top.

Stuffed Green Peppers

Serves 4

Really, they are delicious. I never liked stuffed peppers before discovering this wonderful recipe on a television cooking show. They looked so good I could almost smell them from watching. I used the roasting method the show suggested and made my own stuffing. Give this recipe a try, you will be glad you did!

Ingredients:

4 green peppers, whole

1 pound hamburger, coarsely crumbled

1/2 cup uncooked rice

1 teaspoon butter

1 small to medium onion, chopped

olive oil for roasting peppers

1 16-ounce can diced or crushed tomatoes

2-3 large garlic cloves, chopped

salt and pepper to taste

4 slices of cheese, your choice

Tip:

Roasting peppers on top of the stove makes all the difference. They will taste fresh and sweet. It is most important that peppers are not overcooked. Their al dente consistency adds to the fresh taste of the dish, and is a great contrast in texture to the soft centers.

Serving Suggestion:

Peppers are wonderful served on a bed of pasta or mashed potatoes topped with the tomato sauce.

Directions:

Cook hamburger and onion together on top of stove in fry pan until meat is brown through, drain grease and set aside. Cook rice with butter. Combine enough rice with hamburger mixture for a ratio of approximately 2/3 meat to 1/3 rice. Set aside. Season bottom of a fairly large pot with oil. Add garlic and heat at medium. Cut tops off peppers, core, and remove seeds. Place peppers on their sides in pot and roast until just beginning to soften and brown a tiny bit. Important to not overcook peppers, so remove them from pot while still bright green and set aside. Add tomatoes to pot with oil and garlic, and simmer. Stuff peppers with meat mixture until lightly packed to the top. Add a level teaspoon of sauce to each pepper and mix with meat mixture. Place peppers standing up in pot on top of sauce and cover with pepper tops. Cover pot and continue to cook peppers until just done, still bright green, and al dente. Check often to prevent overcooking. When done, remove pepper tops and melt a slice of cheese on top. It should take about 30 seconds to melt cheese. Serve with sauce according to suggestions above.

Submitted by:

Toni McFarland

Veal Stew with Fennel

Serves 4

Ingredients:

1 1/2 pounds veal stew

1-2 tablespoons ghee or cooking oil

paprika, salt, and pepper to taste

1/2 cup water

Braggs liquid aminos

1 shallot, diced

2 small fennel bulbs

3 peppers, 1 red, 1 green,
and 1 yellow or orange

1 zucchini, sliced (optional)

2 tablespoons Sunrise Lebany
premium yogurt spread or Greek yogurt (optional)

Tip:

Recipe suitable for anyone following a candida-free diet. You can also substitute veal with chicken thigh. Leftovers freeze very well.

Serving Suggestion:

Serve with rice or pasta.

Directions:

Wash meat, pat dry, and cut into bite size pieces. Lightly brown meat in ghee or oil. Add shallots near end of browning process. Dust meat with paprika, salt, and pepper. Add 1/2 cup boiling water and simmer for about 25-30 minutes. Check often to make sure there is enough water in pot. While meat simmers, wash vegetables. Trim tough parts of fennel bulbs, slice, and chop into small pieces. Reserve some of the fennel green for garnish. If necessary, add some water to meat and a couple squirts of Braggs liquid aminos to taste and simmer for about 10 minutes. Add trimmed, cut peppers and simmer for 12 more minutes or until desired tenderness. For extra vegetables in stew, add one zucchini 5 minutes before end of cooking process. Turn off heat and let cool a few minutes. There should be very little liquid left before adding yogurt. Stir in yogurt spread or yogurt if desired.

Submitted by:

Gerhilde Williams

" Give me book, fruit, French wine, and fine weather and a little music out of doors played by someone I do not know."

– John Keats

CHICKEN PICCATA - page 131

Main Dishes – Poultry

Chicken Balls With Vegetable Sauce

Chicken Breast Stuffed with Sausage

Chicken Cacciatore

Chicken Fricassee

Chicken Piccata

Hawaiian Chicken Skewers

Lemon Chicken

Rosemary Chicken with Marsala Mushroom Sauce

Turkey Meatloaf

Chicken Balls with Vegetable Sauce

Serves 4 - 6

This is a yummy gluten free recipe using organic rice krispies. The chicken has a nice delicate flavor and can be served with the sauce on the side, without sauce, or even with a light gravy. This recipe lends itself to many variations.

Ingredients for Chicken Balls:

1 pound organic chicken, ground (*Cook's choice* - Smart Chicken)

3/4 cup organic rice krispies, crushed or sourdough breadcrumbs

1/2 cup red onions, chopped

1/2 cup carrots, finely grated

1 egg, beaten

1/2 teaspoon dried oregano

1/2 teaspoon dried basil

1/2 teaspoon dried thyme

1/2 teaspoon sea salt

1/4 teaspoon black pepper

extra virgin olive oil

> **Note:**
> Use rice krispies instead of breadcrumbs to make this recipe Gluten Free!

Directions:

Preheat oven to 350 degrees. Combine chicken, rice krispies or bread crumbs, onion, carrot, spices, and egg. Form into balls. Oil a shallow baking pan, add balls, and bake 30 minutes. Turn occasionally to cook balls on all sides. While chicken balls bake, make vegetable sauce.

Continued on next page...

Chicken Balls with Vegetable Sauce (continued)

Ingredients for Vegetable Sauce:
1/2 cup yellow peppers, chopped
2 cups fresh tomatoes, chopped or 1 16-ounce can crushed tomatoes
2 1/2 cups zucchini, quartered and thinly sliced
1/2 cup summer squash, quartered and thinly sliced
1 small onion, chopped
1/2 cup mushrooms, chopped
3-4 garlic cloves, minced
1 tablespoon extra virgin olive oil
1 tablespoon fresh oregano, minced
1 tablespoon fresh basil, minced
1 tablespoon fresh parsley, minced
1 tablespoon arrowroot or cornstarch
3/4 cup vegetable or chicken broth
1/4 cup dry white wine (optional)
1/4 teaspoon red pepper to taste (optional)
1/4 teaspoon sea salt (optional)

Sauce Directions:
Sauté zucchini, summer squash, mushrooms, onions, peppers, and 2 garlic cloves in oil for about 10 minutes. Add tomatoes and spices and simmer for 10 more minutes. In a separate bowl, blend arrowroot or cornstarch into a little broth, and stir until well mixed. Gradually add remainder of broth, wine, red pepper, and salt, and stir until blended. Pour over chicken balls, add remaining garlic, and continue baking for 15 more minutes. Serve over rice, couscous, quinoa, or pasta of your choice.

Chicken Breast Stuffed with Sausage

Serves 4

One Sunday, my husband Steve, and Danny a long time friend, were asked to play music for the grand opening at Philbrick's Fresh Market in North Hampton, NH. Shoppers had the opportunity to hear music while checking out the store and sampling new and local products offered by the various food vendors present at the festivities. I was able to spend a few minutes at the event with Dean Strang, the Account Manager, who enthusiastically recommended a chicken product offered by one of the vendors and suggested I try a sample. The chicken was moist and delicious, I asked Dean if I could include a recipe from the vendor's website in a cookbook I was writing. He told me to choose a recipe I liked. I decided on the recipe below, and made a few changes so it was a bit more in line with my style of cooking. The website is noted below, and I invite you to visit it, and take a look at the company.

Ingredients:

1 package sweet or hot Smart Chicken Italian Sausage, removed from casings

1/2 cup walnuts, chopped or nuts of choice

1/3 cup celery, chopped

1/4 cup onion or shallots, chopped

1/2 cup bread crumbs

1 egg

8 organic boneless skinless chicken breasts

1/2 cup whole wheat, spelt, or all-purpose flour

3/4 teaspoon paprika

2 tablespoons walnut or olive oil

1 10 3/4-ounce can chicken broth

1 tablespoon arrowroot or cornstarch

2 tablespoons white wine

Directions:

Slowly cook sausage, nuts, celery, and onion in a large pan about 30 minutes. Remove from heat. Stir in bread crumbs and egg. Pound breasts very thin. Divide sausage mixture evenly among breasts, roll them up, and secure tightly with toothpicks. Combine flour and paprika, and coat chicken in mixture. Heat oil in same pan used to cook sausage. Brown chicken on all sides. Pour in broth, reduce heat, cover, and simmer 30 minutes. Remove chicken to a warm plate. Dissolve arrowroot or cornstarch in wine, add to pot, and stir until sauce thickens. Pour sauce over chicken.

Inspired from website: www.Smart Chicken.com

Chicken Cacciatore

Serves 3

Ingredients:

6 or more pieces chicken, cut in pieces with skin and bone for flavor

1 cup green peppers, coarsely chopped

1 cup red peppers, coarsely chopped

1 medium yellow onion, coarsely chopped

1 cup mushrooms, sliced

2-3 cloves fresh garlic, coarsely chopped

salt and pepper to taste

1 16-ounce can tomatoes (or more) or fresh organic tomatoes (*Cook's choice - canned Pastene tomatoes*)

1 teaspoon olive oil

Tip:

For quicker version, prepare a lightly oiled large frying pan and fry chicken in covered fry pan until tender and almost cooked through. Add vegetables and garlic and cook 15-30 minutes until tender. Add tomatoes, salt, and pepper to chicken, and cook another 15-20 minutes until everything is moist, soft, well blended, and tomatoes are hot. This version cooks in about half the time as recipe above.

Serving Suggestion:

Pasta, rice, or potatoes, and a nice salad.

Directions:

Preheat oven to 350 degrees. Wash and clean chicken and place in an oiled baking dish. Cover and bake chicken, stirring occasionally, for about 1-1 1/2 hours (depending on quantity) until chicken is brown and mostly cooked inside. Add vegetables and garlic to baking dish. Stir a few times and continue to bake for another 30 minutes or longer until vegetables are soft and coated with chicken juices. Add tomatoes, salt, and pepper after the chicken and vegetables are cooked and continue to bake for another 30 minutes or so. Take cover off baking dish during last 15 minutes so everything gets a bit brown.

Submitted by:

Pat Lepore, Reiki Practitioner

Chicken Fricassee

Serves 4 - 6

This recipe is very versatile and was inspired by Nana's mom. It actually can be considered as two recipes, as it makes plenty of chicken; enough for fricassee and enough to make her yummy chicken salad which you'll find in the salad chapter.

Ingredients:

4 very large chicken breasts (approximately 9 cups)

2 large onions, chopped

14 3" twigs of fresh lemon thyme or regular thyme

handful of fresh parsley, minced

1 teaspoon fresh dill weed, minced

1 teaspoon fresh cilantro, minced

salt and pepper to taste

flour or cornstarch to thicken (optional)

Tips:

Six pounds chicken yields enough for 2 recipes, Chicken Fricassee above and Chicken Salad in Salad Chapter. Any remaining chicken can be used in your favorite casserole, chicken pie, over biscuits, or any personal favorite.

Serving Suggestion:

Serve over mashed potatoes, rice, or grain of choice. For a light lunch, serve over lightly toasted bread with some cranberry sauce.

Directions:

Place chicken breasts in a large pot and add enough water to cover chicken. Add onions and all herbs and simmer until tender. Remove chicken from pot and set aside. Strain broth. Remove meat from 2 chicken breasts (approximately 3 1/2 cups chicken), and set aside. You will need 4-5 cups of the chicken broth to make the Fricassee sauce. Refrigerate or freeze remaining broth for future use. If you prefer a thicker sauce, add thickener to broth until you reach your preferred creamy consistency. If you prefer more chicken, use some from remaining 2 breasts.

Submitted by:

Nana of 5 hungry boys

Chicken Picatta

Serves 4

Ingredients:

1 package angel hair pasta or brown rice spaghetti

2 skinless and boneless organic chicken breasts, cut in half and butterflied

1/2 cup grated Parmesan cheese

1/4 cup organic white flour or gluten free baking flour

2 teaspoons lemon pepper seasoning or 1 teaspoon grated lemon zest and 1 teaspoon black pepper

3 tablespoons butter

3 tablespoons olive oil

1 cup organic chicken stock or broth

1/2 cup white wine

1/2 cup reserved water from pasta

2 tablespoons lemon juice

3 tablespoons capers

1/3 cup fresh parsley, chopped

1 large or 2 small shallots, diced

2 garlic cloves, minced

sea salt and fresh ground black pepper to taste

1 teaspoon cornstarch (optional)

> **Note:**
>
> Use brown rice spaghetti (*Cook's Choice* - Tinkyada Pasta Joy) to make this recipe Gluten Free!

Directions:

Combine Parmesan cheese, flour, and lemon pepper seasoning and reserve 3 tablespoons. Trim fat from chicken breasts. Add oil to large skillet and heat at medium. Rinse chicken in cold water, dredge in Parmesan mixture, and add to skillet. Cook chicken until golden brown on each side. While chicken cooks, boil pasta until al dente (firm) and add a few pinches of sea salt, and a drizzle of olive oil for flavor and to prevent pasta from sticking together. Remove chicken from skillet when done. Add butter, shallots, and garlic to skillet and sauté lightly. Add reserved 3 tablespoons of flour mixture to shallots and butter and cook for 2 minutes. Add remaining ingredients to skillet and cook at medium heat. If sauce seems too thin, combine 1 teaspoon corn starch with 1 tablespoon cold water. Add to sauce and stir. Place chicken on top of hot cooked pasta and pour sauce over entire dish. Top with shredded Parmesan cheese if desired.

Submitted by:

Sheri Santo | www.sherisanto.com

Hawaiian Chicken Skewers

Serves 6

Ingredients:

1/3 cup molasses

1/3 cup red wine vinegar

5 tablespoons Worcestershire sauce

2 tablespoons olive oil

2 tablespoons light brown sugar

2 chipotle peppers in adobo, chopped

3 pounds boneless skinless chicken breasts, cut in strips

2 cans pineapple chunks

1 package bacon

Wooden skewers

Directions:

Soak skewers in water for a few minutes before using so they don't burn in the oven. Combine everything except chicken, pineapple, and bacon in a large bowl and whisk to mix. Add chicken and toss to coat. Cover and marinate at least 45 minutes and up to 4 hours. When ready to cook, heat broiler and arrange a rack in the upper third of the oven. Remove chicken from marinade (reserving marinade) and thread the end of one piece of bacon on the skewer, alternating chicken and pineapple, threading the rest of the slice of bacon on skewer in between each piece. Heat reserved marinade to boiling and boil for 3 minutes. Cool a bit before using. Baste skewers with marinade. Broil 7-10 minutes, turn over and broil another 7-10 minutes or until chicken is cooked through.

Submitted by:

Sheri Santo | www.sherisanto.com

Lemon Chicken (with or without Shrimp)

Since my husband doesn't eat chicken and I don't eat shrimp, I keep us both happy by dividing the batter in half, using half for the chicken and half for the shrimp. You may prefer to make chicken one time and shrimp the next.

Ingredients for Marinade:

1 tablespoon extra virgin olive oil

1 large egg, lightly beaten

1 teaspoon arrowroot

1/4 teaspoon sea salt

1 teaspoon coconut aminos or tamari sauce

1/8 teaspoon black pepper

Ingredients for Battered Chicken:

4 boneless organic chicken breasts or see shrimp option below

1/4 cup chick pea/garbanzo flour

1/4 cup water

2 tablespoons arrowroot

2 tablespoons extra virgin olive oil

1/4 teaspoon baking soda

1/4 teaspoon Himalayan or sea salt

2 teaspoon coconut oil

1 teaspoon grapeseed oil or oil of choice

> **Option:**
> If making chicken and shrimp, use 2 chicken breasts and 1/2 pound large shrimp.

Continued on next page...

Lemon Chicken (with or without Shrimp) continued

Ingredients for Sauce:

1/4 cup water

2 tablespoons organic sugar, honey, or maple syrup

4 tablespoons lemon juice, freshly squeezed

1 tablespoon brown rice vinegar

1 tablespoon extra virgin olive oil

2 garlic cloves, finely chopped

1/4 teaspoon Himalayan or sea salt

dash red pepper

1/2 - 1 fresh tomato, depending on size, chopped

3/4 lemon, thinly sliced

1 tablespoon arrowroot

1 tablespoon cold water

2 scallions, thinly sliced for garnish

1/8 cup almonds, thinly sliced for garnish

Miscellaneous Ingredients:

white rice, brown rice, or quinoa

Directions for Marinade:

Mix egg and oil together. When well blended add arrowroot, aminos or tamari, salt, and pepper. Slice chicken into 1" strips and add to marinade. Stir to thoroughly coat chicken, cover and refrigerate for 30 minutes.

Directions for Batter:

While chicken is marinating, mix flour, water, arrowroot, oil, baking soda, and salt together. Remove chicken from marinade and add reserved marinade to batter, stirring until completely mixed. Coat chicken in marinated batter.

Lemon Chicken (with or without Shrimp) continued

Directions for Batter Dipped Chicken:

Preheat oven to 350 degrees. Heat a cast iron skillet and when warm add grapeseed and coconut oil. In hot pan, fry chicken on medium heat until batter is set and golden brown. When ready, turn and cook other side. Time depends on thickness of chicken. When chicken is done, remove to a cookie sheet lined with parchment paper and place in oven to keep warm.

Directions for Batter Dipped Shrimp:

Peel, clean, and devein shrimp. Coat in marinated batter. Use a separate skillet for cooking shrimp. Prepare skillet and heat following directions above for cooking chicken, cooking shrimp quickly on each side until batter is golden brown. Shrimp cooks quickly so do not overcook. Remove and place on cookie sheet as directed above.

Directions for Sauce:

Heat water, sweetener, lemon juice, vinegar, oil, half the garlic, salt, and pepper. Add tomato, rest of garlic, and lemon slices, and continue cooking for another 10 minutes. While sauce cooks, mix arrowroot and 1 tablespoon water together and slowly add to sauce until all arrowroot is blended and sauce has thickened.

Directions for Serving:

Place chicken and or shrimp on top of white rice, brown rice or quinoa, pour lemon sauce over all, and garnish with scallions and almonds.

Rosemary Chicken with Marsala Mushroom Sauce

This recipe is enhanced with the use of Marsala wine which is produced in the region surrounding the Italian city of Marsala in Sicily. Wikipedia, says it is similar to Port and was originally fortified with alcohol to ensure that it would last long ocean voyages, but now is made that way because of its popularity in foreign markets.

Ingredients:

1 pound organic chicken breasts

2 sprigs fresh rosemary, chopped

sea salt

cracked pepper

4 garlic cloves, crushed

2 tablespoons safflower or olive oil

1/3 cup Marsala wine

1/3 cup chicken broth

1/2 cup mushrooms, chopped (crimini or button)

1 tablespoon cornstarch

1/2 cup milk or milk substitute

Directions:

Preheat oven to 400 degrees. Trim fat and butterfly chicken breasts. Sprinkle on each side of breast rosemary, salt, pepper, and garlic. Heat oil in pan over medium heat. Place breasts in pan and lightly sear on each side until lightly browned. Remove chicken from pan and set aside. Add Marsala wine and chicken broth and de-glaze the pan. Add mushrooms. In separate bowl, combine cornstarch with cold milk, and add to pan. Continue to cook sauce over medium heat until sauce slightly thickens and mushrooms become soft. Return chicken breasts to pan, and coat all sides with sauce. Place pan in oven for 10 minutes or until chicken is cooked through. Serve with sauce poured over the chicken breasts.

Submitted by:

Sheri Santo | www.sherisanto.com

Turkey Meatloaf

Meatloaf Ingredients:

1 pound ground turkey

1 egg

1/3 cup milk

1 large shallot, chopped

1/2 teaspoon poultry seasoning

1/4 cup corn flakes, crushed

1 tablespoon ketchup

1 tablespoon barbecue sauce

sea salt and cracked pepper to taste

Tip:

Use organic ketchup and barbecue sauce to assure no artificial ingredients or colors.

Note:

The use of corn flakes instead of traditional bread-crumbs makes this recipe Gluten Free!

Glaze Ingredients:

3 tablespoons brown sugar

2 tablespoons barbecue sauce

1 tablespoon ketchup

1 teaspoon powdered mustard

Directions:

Preheat oven to 375 degrees. Beat egg and milk together in bowl, add shallot, seasoning, corn flakes, ketchup, and barbecue sauce. Mix well and spoon into loaf pan. Bake for 30 minutes. Combine glaze ingredients. After baking meatloaf for 30 minutes, remove from oven and spoon glaze over top. Bake for 10 minutes and then broil for 5 additional minutes to caramelize the glaze on top.

Submitted by:

Sheri Santo | www.sherisanto.com

" Next to jazz music, there is nothing that lifts the spirit and strengthens the soul more than a good bowl of chili."

– Harry James

CHILI - VEGETARIAN CASHEW OR MEXICAN - page 144

Main Dishes – Vegetarian

A Lighter Shade of Parm

Beans and Rice Simplified

Beso-dia

Carrot and Parsnip Mash

Cauliflower Curry

Chili - Vegetarian Cashew or Mexican

Dal with Greens

Grandma's Modern Potato Latkes

Laura's Zucchini Pie in Biscuit Crust

Lentil Burgers

Lentil Tortilla Bake

Macaroni Green Vegi Tart

Parsnip Burgers

Rice and Beans with Pineapple Salsa

Sweet and Spicy Beans and Veggies

Vegetable Cutlets

Zucchini Rice Pizza - Spicy Style

Zucchini Spaghetti

Zucchini and Summer Squash Boats

A Lighter Shade of Parm

Serves 6

Cook's choice is to use half green zucchini and half golden zucchini. You can also use a combination of zucchini and summer squash. This dish is a nice change from the traditional heavier, breaded, and fried zucchini Parmesan.

Ingredients:

3 medium size zucchini

1-2 tablespoons extra virgin olive oil

1 large onion, thinly sliced

1 medium green pepper, thinly sliced

4 ounces fresh mushrooms, thinly sliced

3 garlic cloves, chopped

3-3 1/2 cups fresh tomatoes, chopped

1 small jalapeno pepper, minced

2 tablespoons fresh parsley, chopped

1 tablespoon fresh oregano, chopped

1/3 cup Parmesan cheese, grated

1 1/4 cup fresh mozzarella cheese, grated

1/4 teaspoon Himalayan salt or to taste

Directions:

Preheat oven to 375 degrees. Saute onions, green pepper, and mushrooms in oil about 5 minutes. Add half the garlic and sauté until softened a bit. Add tomatoes, parsley, oregano, and jalapeno pepper to sautéed vegetables and simmer 20 minutes. While sauce simmers, cut zucchini in half and then slice lengthwise in 1/4" pieces and grate cheeses. Place a thin layer of sauce in 8 1/2 x 11" glass baking pan and cover with a layer of zucchini, 1/2 the Parmesan cheese, another layer of zucchini, top with remaining sauce, and sprinkle with remaining Parmesan cheese. Cover with parchment paper and bake 40 minutes. Lower heat to 350 degrees, remove parchment paper, and sprinkle Mozzarella on top. Bake another 5-10 minutes or until cheese melts.

Song: A Lighter Shade of Parm - Disc 2 - Song 1 - Rock Style - Slow Tempo

This song is a riff on the well-known rock tune. (Can you guess the tune?)

Beans and Rice Simplified

Serves 4 - 6

So simple, quick and nutritious!

Ingredients:

1 1/2 cups onion, chopped

2 tablespoons extra virgin olive oil

2 cups fresh tomatoes, chopped

1 can red kidney beans

1 can pinto beans

1 teaspoon ground cumin

1 tablespoon ground chili pepper or to taste

3 garlic cloves, minced

1 jalapeno pepper or a green pepper, seeded and minced

1 cup of Texmati rice or rice of choice

Directions:

Chop onions and sauté in oil until tender. Add tomatoes and simmer 10 minutes. Rinse and drain beans. Add beans, cumin, and chili pepper to onion and tomato mixture and simmer another 10 minutes. Add garlic and jalapeno, and simmer another 10 minutes until heated through. While mixture is simmering, prepare rice according to directions. Place a mound of rice on plate and top with bean mixture.

Beso-dia

Serves 6

This recipe is similar to a Mexican lasagna and is a great way to use any leftover rice and any vegetables taking up space in the refrigerator. The vegetables lend different flavors and nutrients to the dish but are hardly visible, so it's a great meal for those who don't like to eat their veggies!

Ingredients:

1 cup cooked rice
1 tablespoon extra virgin olive oil
1 cup onion, chopped
1/2 cup beet or Swiss chard stems, chopped
1 cup beet greens, spinach, or Swiss chard, thinly sliced
2 cups canned black or pinto beans or a combination
1 1/2 cups Monteray Jack or cheddar cheese, shredded
1 11-ounce package of corn tortillas (*Cook's choice* - Maria and Ricardos)
2 garlic cloves, chopped
3 cups fresh tomatoes, chopped or canned
1 jalapeno pepper, seeded and minced
2 mangos, chopped
1/2 cup red pepper, chopped
1/4 teaspoon ground cumin
sea salt and pepper to taste
1/2-1 lime, freshly squeezed
2 cups zucchini (optional)

Directions:

Preheat oven to 350 degrees. In oil, sauté onion, pepper, and beet or chard stems in oil until slightly caramelized. Stir in greens, zucchini if using, one garlic clove, and sauté briefly until vegetables are wilted. To make sauce, combine tomatoes, jalapeno, mango, red pepper, and remaining garlic. Stir in cumin, salt, and lime juice until well blended. Place 1 cup or more of sauce on bottom of an 8 1/2" x 13" glass or ceramic baking pan. Cut each corn tortilla into 3 strips and lay half the strips covering the bottom of the pan and begin layering ingredients. First place a layer of rice over tortilla strips, next spread layer of beans over rice, then spread vegetables over the beans, sprinkle cheese over beans, and place remaining tortilla strips over cheese. Top with remaining tomato mango sauce. Bake about 30 minutes or until heated through and bubbly.

Song: Beso Dia - Disc 2 - Song 2 - Beguine - Medium Tempo

"Beso" means kiss in Spanish, and "Dia" means day in Portuguese. So this song celebrates "the kiss of the day." Just as the title mixes languages, the music mixes the rhythms of various countries.

Colorful Curry

Serves 6

Ingredients:

2 potatoes, chopped in small cubes

1-2 tablespoons coconut oil or oil of choice

1 cup onions, chopped

1 head of cauliflower, chopped in 1" pieces

2 carrots, thinly sliced

2 tablespoons fresh ginger, minced

1 tablespoon mustard seeds

1 teaspoon turmeric

1/2 teaspoon ground allspice or cloves

1/8 teaspoon cayenne pepper

4 garlic cloves, chopped

1/4-1/2 cup water, as needed for pureeing

1/4 cup raisins

1/2 cup cashew nuts, lightly toasted

1 cup peas or chick peas or combo of each

1/2 teaspoon sea salt or to taste

1/2 cup coconut milk or water

2 tablespoons lemon juice, freshly squeezed

> **Serving Suggestion:**
> Serve curry over cooked millet, quinoa or rice.

Directions:

Boil potatoes until just tender, drain and set aside. In skillet add coconut oil and sauté onions, cauliflower, carrot, and fresh ginger over medium heat for 5 minutes. Cover skillet and continue to cook for another 10 to 15 minutes until vegetables are desired tenderness. Check to see if extra water is needed to prevent vegetables sticking to pan. While vegetables cook, place ground spices, mustard seeds, and garlic in blender with a little water and blend until a smooth puree. Once vegetables are desired tenderness, add potatoes, spice puree, raisins, cashews, lemon juice, chick peas, or peas, and salt. Stir until well blended. Slowly add in coconut milk and lemon juice and cook until all heated through.

Chili - Vegetable Cashew or Mexican

Serves 10

No fret, several ways to cook this chili. You can use either the long method with dried beans, a quicker version using can beans, or Mexican chili. The choice is yours. See below for choices.

Ingredients:

1 cup dried kidney beans

1 cup dried pinto beans

1/2 cup dried black beans

1 slice of kombu seaweed, optional

4 cups fresh tomatoes, peeled and cubed

1 medium onion, chopped

1 large green pepper, chopped

2 large carrots, chopped

1/2 cup fresh or frozen corn

2 garlic cloves, minced

1 bay leaf

2 tablespoons chili powder

1/3 cup of fresh parsley, minced

1 teaspoon dried dill weed

1 teaspoon dried basil

1 teaspoon dried oregano

1 teaspoon ground cumin

1 teaspoon ground allspice

1/4 teaspoon ground black pepper

1/2 cup unsalted raw cashews

1 dried chili pepper, finely minced (optional)

1-2 cups rainbow Swiss chard, spinach, or beet greens, thinly sliced (optional)

Tips:

Use fresh herbs if available.

If using dried beans, cover with water and add a piece of kombu to help relieve gas from beans, and soak overnight. Check out the beans and legumes chapter for more info.

If using can beans, drain and rinse beans prior to use.

I grate an organic chocolate bar for the chocolate.

Chili - Vegetable Cashew or Mexican (continued)

Directions:

Sort, wash beans, and place in large bowl of water. Water should be 2" above beans. Add slice of kombu to beans and let soak overnight. Drain beans. Simmer several hours until all beans are tender. Add tomatoes and extra water so there is again 2" of liquid above beans. Add remainder of ingredients, except for cashews, and simmer 1 hour. Add cashews and simmer another 30 minutes. If making Mexican chili, omit cashews, add beer and chocolate, and simmer 30 minutes. See below.

For Quick Chili:

Use 16-ounce cans, 1 can black beans, 1 can red beans, 1 can cannelloni beans, and 32-ounces whole stewed tomatoes and simmer for 1 hour and 30 minutes.

For Mexican Chili:

Add one : 7-ounce bottle of Corona Beer and 1/4 cup grated dark chocolate.

Dal with Greens

Serves 3 - 4

Dal is a staple dish in India served as a soup, or when a thicker consistency it is served as a side dish. There are many different spellings, the most common being Dal or Dahl. It is also called "pulses." The name comes from the Sanskrit word meaning "to split," and this recipe calls for split yellow lentils that when cooked turn a mellow shade of yellow. Dal dishes are usually spicy with good flavor, are easy to digest, high in fiber, and loaded with vitamins. Dal is a good source of protein for vegetarians or anyone that eats little or no meat, and is usually eaten with rice or bread and sometimes yogurt.

Ingredients:

1 cup yellow split lentils

5 1/2 cups water

2 tablespoons fresh ginger, thinly sliced

1 chili pepper, seeded and minced or 1 teaspoon dried chili pepper flakes

1 teaspoon ground turmeric

1/4 teaspoon sea salt

1 teaspoon ground cumin

1 teaspoon ground coriander

1/4 teaspoon ground paprika

2-3 large garlic cloves, finely chopped

8 ounces Swiss chard or spinach, thinly sliced

1/8 teaspoon cayenne pepper, (optional)

1 teaspoon hing (Asafetida Powder) (optional)

Tips:

No pre-soaking of lentils required.

Dal should not be pasty but more like a slightly thick soup.

Directions:

Rinse lentils, check and remove small stones, and set aside. Bring water to a boil, add lentils, ginger, chili pepper or flakes, and reduce heat to medium or lower. Add turmeric and salt. Cook for one hour stirring lentils occasionally. After one hour add cumin, coriander, paprika, cayenne pepper, and hing to lentils. Continue cooking for about another 45 minutes, stirring occasionally. Wash chard or spinach. Add greens and garlic and continue cooking another 15 minutes or until Dal has thickened and lentils are completely soft. Serve over rice or quinoa.

Grandma's Potato Latkes with a Modern Twist

Makes 12

Growing up, potato latkes were a staple in our family. They were usually made from a mix and served with apple sauce that came in a jar. Remembering these comfort foods, I wanted to make latkes from scratch and serve them with homemade applesauce. Hence, the following version emerged that is healthier, tastier, and fills our home with wonderful aromas reminding me of my childhood.

Ingredients:

1 cup beet greens or baby spinach, thinly sliced

2 1/2 cups potatoes, grated (about 2 large russet)

2 large eggs, beaten

1/2 cup onions, finely chopped

3 cloves garlic, chopped or to personal preference

1/4 teaspoon black pepper

3 tablespoons matzo meal, ground crackers, or spelt flour

2 tablespoons butter

sea salt to taste (optional)

Tips:

Not a fan of greens, substitute with grated carrots. I use traditional matzo meal but recipe also works well with spelt flour or crush your favorite crackers. Other alternative flours can be used, but I do not recommend rice flour due to its grainy texture.

Serving Suggestion:

Serve with homemade applesauce.

Directions:

Lightly steam greens, drain, and squeeze out any liquid. After grating potatoes, squeeze out most of liquid. Mix together eggs, beet greens, onion, garlic, pepper, and matzo meal or flour and add to potatoes stirring until well blended. Heat a little butter in cast iron skillet or fry pan. Drop mixture into pan, pat into a circle, and cook on both sides until brown. Add additional butter as needed.

Laura's Zucchini Pie

Serves 4 - 6

Filling Ingredients:

4 cups unpeeled zucchini, thinly sliced
1 cup onion, coarsely chopped
1/4 cup butter
1/2 cup fresh parsley, chopped or 2 tablespoons parsley flakes
1/2 teaspoon salt
1/2 teaspoon black pepper
1/4 teaspoon garlic powder
1/4 teaspoon dried sweet basil
1/4 teaspoon dried oregano
2 extra large eggs, well beaten
2 cups (8 ounces) cheese, shredded (mozzarella, jack, cheddar or a combination)
biscuit dough recipe, see below

Pie Filling Directions:

Preheat oven to 375 degrees. Cook zucchini and onions in butter until tender, about 15-20 minutes. Drain well. Stir in parsley and seasonings, adjusting seasonings to personal taste. In large bowl blend eggs and cheese. Stir in vegetable mixture and place in prepared biscuit crust. Bake for 30-45 minutes. Check pie edges near end of baking to make sure crust isn't getting too brown. If browning too rapidly, cover crust edges with tin foil and continue baking until center of pie is firm and crust is nicely browned.

Biscuit Dough Ingredients:

1/4 cup unsalted butter
1 1/2 teaspoons baking powder
1/2 teaspoon salt
1 cup white spelt flour or flour of choice
3/8 cup milk, adjust for right consistency

Biscuit Dough Directions:

Cut shortening into flour, add baking powder and salt and blend until mixture resembles fine crumbs. Add milk, stirring until dough leaves sides of bowl and is soft and sticky. Place dough onto lightly floured surface and roll out until large enough to fit into a 9" or 10" pie plate.

Submitted by:

Laura Melisi, Flautist

Lentil Rice Burgers

Makes 4

Ingredients:

1/2 cup brown lentils

1/4 cup red lentils

1/4 cup white rice

2 cups water

1 tablespoon cider vinegar

1/4 cup walnuts, ground

1/4 teaspoon sea salt

1/4 teaspoon black pepper or to taste

1/4 teaspoon ground wasabi

2 tablespoons extra virgin olive oil

1 medium onion, chopped

3-5 garlic cloves, minced

1 tablespoon butter

cheese (optional)

Tip:

Instead of frying burgers, eliminate butter and oil and broil burgers for about 5 minutes on each side. Melt a slice of cheese on top or serve with your favorite sauce for extra zing.

Directions:

Place lentils, rice, and water in saucepan. Bring to boil, lower heat, cover, and simmer for about 30 minutes or until lentils are soft and liquid has cooked away. Mix together vinegar, walnuts, salt, pepper, wasabi, and lentil-rice combination, until well blended. Heat 1 tablespoon oil in a skillet, add onions, and sauté until almost caramelized. Add garlic and stir a few more minutes. Combine onion-garlic mixture with lentil-rice mixture and refrigerate for about 1 hour. Form into patties and fry in remaining oil and butter until heated through.

Lentil Tortilla Bake

Serves 6

Ingredients:

3/4 cup brown lentils

1 small onion, chopped

1 medium carrot, chopped

2 cups water

1/2 teaspoon sea salt

pepper to taste

1 cup salsa or tomatillo sauce

8 or 9 corn tortillas cut in 4 equal strips

3/4 cup Monteray Jack or cheddar cheese, shredded

1/4 cup fresh coriander, chopped (optional)

> **Note:**
>
> For salsa, see Appetizer and Snack Chapter, and for tomatillo sauce, see This and That Chapter or buy already prepared.

Directions:

Preheat oven to 350 degrees. Boil lentils, onion, and carrot until lentils are soft and all water is absorbed. Season with salt and pepper to taste. Place a thin layer of salsa on bottom of an 8" x 8" pan. Cover salsa with corn tortilla strips and place 1/2 lentil mixture on top of tortillas. Place 1/2 of remaining salsa on tortillas, cover with a second layer of tortillas, and spread remaining lentil mix on tortillas. Top with remaining sauce, remaining tortilla strips, and sprinkle shredded cheese evenly over top. Finish with coriander on top if using. Bake covered 20 minutes.

Submitted by:

Emily Loghmani, Registered Dietitian

Mac 'N' Quiche

Serves 6

Not sure if you want macaroni and cheese or a quiche, this recipe will satisfy your hunger for either. Paired with a fresh salad you will have a complete and satisfying meal.

Ingredients:

1-1 1/4 cups dry fusilli brown rice macaroni (yields 2 cups cooked)

1 cup onions, chopped

1/4 cup chicken stock

1 cup feta cheese, crumbled

4 large eggs, beaten

2 tablespoons coconut milk, whole milk, or white wine

2 garlic cloves, finely chopped

1/2 teaspoon dried basil

dash ground nutmeg

1 pound mustard greens, spinach, or arugula, chopped and steamed (or a combination)

2 tablespoons panko bread crumbs, ground flax seeds, or crumbs of choice

paprika, few shakes

1 orange, thinly sliced for garnish

6 fresh parsley sprigs, finely chopped for garnish

Directions:

Cook pasta according to directions. While pasta cooks, cook onions slowly in stock in pan until translucent and tender. In large mixing bowl combine cheese, eggs, milk or wine, and spices. Add greens, macaroni, and onions, and stir until well blended. Transfer mixture to a 10" pie plate or tart pan that has been lightly oiled. Sprinkle with bread crumbs or flax seeds and finish with a sprinkle of paprika on top. Preheat oven to 350 degrees and bake about 40 minutes. Let sit a few minutes before cutting into wedges. Garnish each wedge with a slice of orange and some parsley.

Parsnip Burgers

Makes 6

Burgers are tasty on their own or for an added treat, serve with kohlrabi sauce for a very natural sweet sauce that has a slightly spicy bite.

Ingredients:

1 pound parsnips, peeled and chopped

2 tablespoons butter

1/2 cup onion, finely chopped

sea salt to taste

red and black pepper to taste

2 tablespoons quinoa flour

1/2 cup breadcrumbs

1/4 cup fresh parsley, chopped

extra virgin olive oil

2 cups kohlrabi, chopped (for sauce)

1/4 teaspoon ground nutmeg

Directions:

Place parsnips in large pot with enough water to cover. Bring to boil and cook about 10 minutes until tender. Drain parsnips and mash, reserving the broth. Melt 1 tablespoon butter in pan over medium heat, add onions, and cook about 5 minutes until onions are almost soft. Stir in salt and pepper, and cook another 2 minutes. Add flour, breadcrumbs, and parsley to the onion mixture, stirring until well mixed. Add mixture and 1 tablespoon of parsnip broth to the mashed parsnips, mixing until desired consistency to form into patties. Lightly coat cast iron skillet with olive oil, then add remaining butter. When butter is melted, add patties and cook about 7 minutes on each side until lightly browned. Drain on paper towels. Serve warm with kohlrabi sauce (see Millet Patties in Side Dishes - Grains and Legumes Chapter) or your favorite sauce.

Rice and Beans with Pineapple Salsa

Serves 4 - 6

Ingredients for Rice and Beans:

1/2 red onion, chopped

1 small red pepper, chopped

extra virgin olive oil to prepare pan

1 14-1/2 ounce can fire roasted tomatoes with chilies or use fresh tomatoes and a chili pepper, chopped

1 tablespoon cilantro, minced

1/2 orange, freshly squeezed

2 cups black beans, 1 can or cooked dry beans

2 cups pinto beans, 1 can or cooked dry beans

2 garlic cloves, finely chopped

1 cup uncooked rice of choice, prepare according to directions

> **Tip:**
> See grains and legumes chapter for cooking dry beans.

Directions for Beans:

Sauté onion and red pepper in a little oil until tender. Add tomatoes with chili peppers, cilantro, and orange juice. Simmer 15 minutes. Rinse beans if using canned and add to tomato mixture. Add garlic and stir until ingredients are well blended. Let simmer another 15 minutes.

Ingredients for Salsa:

2 cups fresh pineapple, chopped small

2 garlic cloves, finely chopped

2 tablespoons red onion, finely chopped

1 tablespoon fresh mint, minced

1 tablespoon fresh cilantro, minced

1 tablespoon lime juice, freshly squeezed

1/2 tablespoon lemon juice, freshly squeezed

1 tablespoon orange juice, freshly squeezed

1/4 teaspoon ground cumin

5 shakes cayenne pepper or to taste

> **To Serve:**
> Place rice on plate, top with bean and tomato mixture, and place a scoop of salsa on top of beans. Surround rice with some nacho chips.

Directions for Salsa:

Place pineapple, garlic, onion, mint, and cilantro in bowl. Add lime, lemon, and orange juices to pineapple mixture. Add spices and stir until blended. Allow to sit at room temperature for at least 30 minutes to blend flavors. Makes about 2 cups.

Stuffed Zucchini and Summer Squash Boats

Makes 6 boats

Ingredients:

3 zucchini squashes

3 summer squashes

2 tablespoons extra virgin olive oil

1 large onion, chopped

1/2 cup mushrooms, thinly sliced

2 garlic cloves, minced

3/4 cup long grain rice, cooked

1 jalapeno pepper, seeded and finely chopped

1/4 cup fresh parsley, finely chopped

1/4 cup fresh oregano, finely chopped

1 teaspoon ground cumin

1 teaspoon ground cinnamon

1/4 cup pine nuts

1/3 cup raisins

1/4 cup Parmesan cheese, shredded

1 1/2 cups fresh tomatoes, chopped

1/2 cup water

1 cup Monterey Jack or cheddar cheese, shredded

sea salt and pepper to taste

1/4 teaspoon red pepper (optional)

> **Note:**
> Serving size depends on size of squashes.

Directions:

Preheat oven to 400 degrees. Cook rice according to package directions. Wash squash, cut off ends, slice lengthwise in half and carefully scoop out squash pulp so you do not cut through bottom of squash. Heat oil in skillet and sauté onions, mushrooms, and garlic for 5 minutes. Add squash pulp and rice to sautééd vegetables. Stir in jalapeno, pine nuts, raisins, and Parmesan cheese until well mixed. Use this mixture to stuff the squash. For sauce, stir together tomatoes and spices with water, and place half on bottom of a large glass baking pan. Place stuffed squash boats on top of tomatoes in baking pan. Cover squash with remaining tomato mixture. Cover pan loosely with a piece of parchment paper, and bake 30 minutes. Remove parchment paper and baste squash with tomatoes. Sprinkle cheese over each squash boat and return uncovered to oven to bake for another 10 minutes.

Sweet and Spicy Beans and Vegetables

Serves 2 - 3

The sweet and spicy flavors blend nicely with the delicate flavor of couscous.

Ingredients:

2 tablespoons extra virgin olive oil

2 carrots, chopped in small chunks

1 zucchini, chopped in small chunks

1 sweet potato, chopped in small chunks

1 cup vegetable broth

1 large onion, diced

1 16-ounce can pinto beans

3/4 cup fresh mushrooms, thinly sliced

2 garlic cloves, chopped

3/4 teaspoon ground cinnamon

1/2 teaspoon ground turmeric

1/8 teaspoon ground red pepper

fresh parsley, minced for garnish

Serving Suggestion:

Serve beans in a bowl, place a few tablespoons of whole wheat couscous on beans, top with some fresh parsley, and serve.

Directions:

Heat oil on medium high heat. Sauté onion, carrots, sweet potato, zucchini, and half the garlic, turning often, about 15 minutes until almost soft. Add vegetable broth and let mixture come to boil. Add pinto beans and spices and reduce to simmer. Continue cooking until vegetables are tender and beans are hot.

Vegetable Cutlets

Serves 3

Ingredients:

1 cup onion, chopped

1/2 cup red pepper, chopped

1 cup carrots, peeled and grated

2 small garlic cloves, chopped

1/2 cup fresh green beans, coarsely chopped

3 large eggs

1 teaspoon sea salt

1/2 teaspoon black pepper

4 tablespoons matzo meal, organic rice crispies, crushed or bread crumbs

2 tablespoons coconut oil or oil of choice

2 tablespoons butter

> **Note:**
> Serve with a mushroom or marinara sauce and a salad.

Directions:

Sauté onions, red pepper, and carrots in 1 tablespoon butter for about 10 minutes. Add garlic. While vegetables cook, steam green beans until almost tender, drain, and set aside. Beat eggs with salt and pepper. Add matzo meal, rice crispies or bread crumbs to vegetables and stir until all mixed. Heat oil and remaining butter in cast iron pan. Shape mixture into cutlets and cook until browned on each side. A little extra oil or butter may need to be added to pan. Place cutlets on paper towels to absorb any excess oil, and serve.

Zucchini Spaghetti

Serves 4

This is a yummy, healthy faux pasta - a great substitute for the real thing. It is also good served with regular pasta in a half and half combo. As this is a light dish, it is best served with a light tomato sauce. Cook recommends using a sauce made from fresh tomatoes or canned diced tomatoes.

Ingredients:

6-8 medium or large zucchini, unpeeled and cut into 1/4 inch strips, like wide shoe laces

3 large garlic cloves, chopped

olive oil to coat pan

salt and pepper to taste

sauce of choice, with or without meat (Cook's choice - a light sauce)

Parmesan cheese, freshly grated

> **Tip:**
> Cut the zucchini strips wide and thick enough, so they do not disintegrate or become mushy while sautéing.

Directions:

Heat oil at medium heat in a frying pan. Add garlic and zucchini strips and saute until just cooked, a dente. Add salt and pepper to taste. Remove from pan to plate and add sauce on top. Top with cheese.

Submitted by:

Toni McFarland

Zucchini Rice Pizza - Spicy Style

Serves 6

Although not a traditional pizza with a hard crunchy crust, this dish gives the effect of a pizza. Recipe eliminates the need for flour, as crust has been replaced with a soft rice bottom so the dish looks like a slice of pizza when cut.

Ingredients:

1 cup white rice

3 zucchini's, quartered lengthwise and thinly sliced

2 onions, chopped

2 tablespoons butter

2 cups fresh tomatoes, chopped or 1 16-ounce can

1 tablespoon fresh basil, chopped or 1 teaspoon basil

2 tablespoons fresh oregano, chopped or 2 teaspoons dried

1/4 teaspoon sea salt

1/4 teaspoon ground black pepper

5 garlic cloves, chopped

1-1 1/4 cups cheese, grated - Monterey Jack, Colby,
or cheddar (*Cook's choice* - combination of all 3)

1 jalapeno pepper, minced (optional)

Directions:

Preheat oven to 350 degrees. Prepare rice according to directions. While rice cooks, sauté zucchini and onions in butter until tender and most liquid has evaporated. Mix together tomatoes with their juice, spices, and garlic. Place rice on bottom of a buttered 8" x 11" glass baking dish. Spoon zucchini and onions over rice. Top with tomato mixture. Sprinkle cheese on top. Bake for about 20 minutes or until cheese on top is bubbly.

Medicinal Support

Recipes in this section can be used to help
specific health projects

Better Than Fried Dough

Fermented Cucumbers

Healthy Green and Fruity Drink

Immune Boost Chicken Soup with Astragalus Root

Lemonade

Miso Soup

Sweet & Nutty Treats

Vegan and Soy Free Cheese - Dairy Free

Better Than Fried Dough

This healthy choice reminds me of the unhealthy fried dough I ate at the carnivals I visited as a child. This version is a healthier trio of butter, cinnamon, and honey. So simple, delicious, nutritious that I believe it will become a favorite of everyone in the family. Honey is widely accepted by scientists as an effective medicine for all kinds of disease. In the January 17, 1995 issue of Weekly World News, the Canadian magazine published a list of diseases and conditions that can be significantly helped with regular use of honey and cinnamon. A few include supporting the immune system to minimize colds and flu, fatigue, indigestion, arthritis and more.

Ingredients:

bread, organic - whole wheat, sourdough, millet, or your choice

butter, organic, local, or raw

honey, organic raw

ground cinnamon, organic

Tips:

No toaster? Lightly toast both sides of bread in the oven.

You can use honey that isn't raw, but since it has been processed it won't have the same benefits.

Very important - honey is not recommended for babies or children under age 1!

Directions:

Toast bread or lightly grill in a cast iron skillet. If toasting spread a thin layer of butter over toast while still warm. Alternatively if using a skillet, lightly prepare pan with butter or oil, lightly butter one side of bread, and grill. When the first side is done, spread a light layer of butter on the other side, and grill to desired doneness. Spread a thin layer of honey over one side of bread and generously sprinkle cinnamon over honey. Yum!!!

Song: Better Than Fried Dough - Disc 2 - Song 4 - Jazz Waltz - Fast Tempo
This song was inspired by the wonder of riding a carousel at a fair.

Fermented Cukes

Fills 1 Mason Jar

Fermenting raw foods is a method used to preserve vegetables meant to be eaten in small amounts and served as a condiment. Fermented foods are good for the immune system, and rich in vitamins, minerals, fiber, and contain enzymes that support digestion and increase nutrients.

Ingredients:

5 pickling cucumbers, peeled and thinly sliced

2 garlic cloves, thinly sliced

1 tablespoon plus a teaspoon Celtic sea salt or whey

1 tablespoon mustard seeds

2 tablespoons fresh dill, minced

1 1/2 cups filtered water

1/2 cup onion, thinly sliced (optional)

Tips:

If your home is warm, two days will be enough time to let sit before placing in refrigerator or cool area. If your home is very cold, best to let sit for three days before moving.

Once moved to the refrigerator the cucumbers can be kept for several months and the flavors increase in time.

Directions:

Place cucumbers, onions, and garlic in a wide mouth quart size mason jar. Cover vegetables with water. Add salt, mustard seed, and dill. Shake well and add more water if needed, making sure there is at least one inch room between cucumbers and top of jar to allow for expansion. Cover jar tightly and keep at room temperature out of direct sunlight for two to three days. Then store in refrigerator or a dark, cold area like a root cellar with a temperature no higher than 40 degrees.

Song: Cool as a Garlic Cuke - Disc 2 - Song 8 - Funk Shuffle - Medium Tempo

Marilynn was going to make beet cavass, and I was going to write a tune called "Beat Cavass," but beet cavass can get moldy, since it's raw, whereas the cuke's don't mold. Cool!

Healthy Green and Fruity Drink

Serves 2

You will need a juicer for this drink. It doesn't need to be fancy or expensive. Juicing raw kale provides many benefits as this green vegetable is plentiful in iron, calcium, and vitamins K, C, and A. As kale can be bitter, it works well juiced with some sweeter fruits. A raw clove of garlic added to the drink also helps to balance out the flavors of bitter and sweet.

Ingredients:

1 bunch kale, organic
(*Cook's choice* – dinosaur kale)

1 apple, organic (*Cook's choice* - cortland)

1 pear, organic and fairly firm
(*Cook's choice* – Asian)

1 medium clove fresh garlic

1 radish (optional)

> **Tip:**
>
> It is best to drink fresh juice within 15 minutes of juicing to retain all the healthy benefits from the drink.

Directions:

Quarter apple and pear, remove seeds, and okay to leave the peel on. Remove garlic casing. Juice one leaf of kale at a time, add garlic, radish, and alternate pear and apple quarters ending with apple.

Immune Boost Chicken Soup with Astragalus Root

Serves 6

I first became introduced to the benefits of astragalus root by a friend who was a Chinese acupuncturist. One winter she sent me a holiday card with a very simple chicken soup recipe using this root which is widely known for its immune boosting properties. As I love lots of ingredients in my chicken soup, I started experimenting with the root until the following healthy soup version emerged.

Ingredients:

6 cups water

1 1/2-2 pounds organic chicken breasts or legs

1 1/2 teaspoons cider vinegar

1 onion, chopped

3 carrots, peeled and sliced

2-3 large garlic cloves, minced

3 small bok choy or baby spinach, thinly sliced - yields about 2 cups

1 tablespoon dried wakame or arame seaweed

1 bay leaf

3 large whole astragalus roots or 9-12 if small roots

1/4 teaspoon dried oregano

1/4 teaspoon sea salt or to taste

1/4 teaspoon black pepper or to taste

1/2 cup mushrooms, chopped your choice of variety (optional)

> **Tip:**
>
> For a more hearty soup, add soup matzo balls located in "This and That Chapter".

Directions:

Put water in a soup pot, rinse chicken, and add all ingredients except for greens. Cook for at least 2 hours. Add greens and cook for another 1 hour or longer. Take chicken off bone in chunks, discard bones, and return chicken to soup for another 10 minutes.

Lemonade

Yields 4 cups

This is a very refreshing drink to be enjoyed in summer or consumed during Spring and Fall as part of a cleansing program. Many similar versions of this recipe can be found and it has also been referred to as the "Lemonade diet" or the "Master Cleanser". As lemons are astringent, they contract and tighten the intestines which helps to loosen and clear toxins from tissues and organs, support the liver, and purify the blood. Cayenne pepper is a natural stimulant that helps the body keep warm, help clear the blood, eliminate toxins, and mucus. Maple syrup is a natural sugar, and is full of wonderful energy that keeps the body energized and happy. When drinking lemonade as part of a cleansing program, one should drink at least 6 glasses a day. A simple and safe fast would be to only drink lemonade one day a week for three weeks. When fasting, double recipe so you have enough to drink throughout the day to keep your energy up for the 24 hours. It is highly recommended that you seek the advice and guidance of a doctor if you anticipate beginning any cleansing program that lasts longer than one day.

Ingredients:

8 tablespoons lemon juice, freshly squeezed

32-ounces water, filtered or spring

1/4 teaspoon cayenne pepper, adjust to taste

4 tablespoons organic or raw maple syrup or adjust to taste (optional)

> **Tip:**
> If drinking as part of a fast, I suggest using some maple syrup to keep your energy up and keep you satisfied.

Directions:

Squeeze lemons into water, add cayenne, and maple syrup. Stir and enjoy this deliciously refreshing, healthy drink.

Miso Vegetable Soup

Serves 3

This is a nourishing soup that is light, simple, and quick to make. Served at the beginning of a meal, it stimulates the appetite and relaxes the body. A traditional dish of Japan, it is considered the staff of life used as a strengthening body tonic and believed to improve resistance to illness.

Ingredients:

3 cups water or combination of 1/2 water and 1/2 green tea

1 carrot, thinly sliced into 1" long pieces

2 cups spinach, finely sliced

1 tablespoon nori seaweed

3-4 teaspoons organic miso paste
or to taste

1/4 cup uncooked white rice or mochi

3 scallions, parsley, chives, or watercress, finely chopped for garnish

garlic, minced (optional)

Directions:

Bring water or water and tea to boil, and add carrot, spinach, and white rice or mochi. Simmer until rice is almost done. While rice and vegetables simmer, soak seaweed in 1/4 cup water for 10 minutes. Drain water from seaweed, add to soup, and simmer 10 minutes. If using garlic, add just prior to removing pot from heat. Gradually stir in enough miso paste to enhance but not overpower the soup's flavor. Make sure paste is well blended. Cover pot and let sit for 10-15 minutes to continue to blend flavors. Spoon into bowls, sprinkle on some sliced scallions or garnish of choice, and serve.

Tip:

Do not boil miso since healthy enzymes are destroyed by intense heat during cooking.

Add miso after removing pot from heat. Generally use 1 teaspoon miso to 1 cup boiled water.

In Summer when weather is hot, use more greens or vegetables in season and less miso. In Winter when weather is cooler, use more root vegetables and more miso.

Option:

Pieces of mochi, is made from a glutinous rice and mugwort herb and can be used to thicken soup instead of rice.

Sweet and Nutty Treats

This recipe is really easy. I usually just throw all of the ingredients in by the handful until the consistency is how I like it.

Ingredients:

6-8 pitted dates, soaked in just enough warm water to cover dates

1 cup nut butter (peanut, almond, cashew, macadamia, sunflower, or any combination)

1 cup chopped nuts (almonds, walnuts, cashews, or your favorites)

I cup dried cranberries, raisins, or dried fruit combo of your choice

1/2 teaspoon ground cinnamon

1/4 teaspoon ground cardamom

1/4 teaspoon ground fennel

ground almonds or coconut to roll treats in

1/3-1/2 shredded coconut (optional)

Directions:

Put soaked dates with their water into a blender or processor and blend until a paste is formed. In a separate bowl, blend chopped nuts, cranberries, coconut, and spices. Add date puree and nut butter. Mix well until pliable enough to roll into balls. If mixture is too dry and crumbly, add a bit more nut butter. If it is too wet, add a bit more cranberries, coconut, and or ground nuts. Roll into small 1" balls. Roll the balls in ground coconut or ground nuts of your choice to coat completely. Then enjoy right away or chill and enjoy later.

Herbal Additions:

Add 1-2 teaspoons spirulina for a super green food boost (yes your nutty treats will turn green too).

Add 1/8-1/4 teaspoon ground lavender flowers to aid relaxation and protect your kids from too much of a sugar high!

Add 1/2 teaspoon ground rose petals for a little boost of the emotional heart. It may sound strange, but it is delicious!

Add 1-2 teaspoons Ashwaghanda powder to give your adrenals a boost and support immune function.

Submitted by:

Amanda Komisarek, CHP, CRMT - Dover, NH

Lion's Tooth Wellness | www.lionstoothwellness.com

Vegan and Soy Free Cheese

So many of our traditional culinary herbs are also incredibly therapeutic for our bodies. Rosemary, thyme, sage, and garlic are only some of the many herbs which properties are antimicrobial, antiviral, and are packed with antioxidants that fight free radicals and toxins in our bodies. I recommend using herbs in your cooking whenever you can! They taste great and are so good for you!

Ingredients:

1 cup macadamia nuts

1/2 teaspoon non-bleached sea salt

1/4-1/2 cup water

Cheese cloth

> **Serving Suggestions:**
> This soft cheese is great in omelets and scrambles, on toast, on top of salads, in quesadillas, with fruit, in sandwiches... use your imagination!

Options:

You may want to consider adding optional flavorings to your cheese as follows:

Chopped sun dried tomatoes

Chopped olives

Delicious culinary and therapeutic herbs such as garlic, dill, chives, scallions, rosemary, sage, thyme, cilantro, or parsley

Cranberries, citrus rind, cinnamon, or cardamom for a sweet more desert like cheese

Directions:

Place macadamia nuts and salt into a blender. Add enough water to cover the nuts. Puree until nuts reach as smooth a consistency as your blender will allow. Have a medium sized bowl and mesh strainer ready. Drape 2-3 layers of the cheese cloth over the strainer and pour the nut mixture into the cheese cloth. Press out as much liquid and moisture as possible. Wrap the cheese cloth around the puree so it is covered completely and place in a clean bowl. Place a heavy object on top of the covered nut puree to allow further drainage of any remaining liquid. I use a large mason jar filled with water, but any clean, heavy object will do. Find a safe warm place for your "science experiment" to sit for 1-2 days depending on your taste. The puree will naturally begin to ferment and will slowly start to change its flavor. Sample a little cheese after 24 hours to see if it is tangy enough for your taste. If you want more goat cheese flavor, wait another day and taste again. The fermentation will continue to sour and flavor the cheese. Once it is to your liking, remove the cheese cloth, and wrap the cheese in saran wrap or Tupperware container for up to 1 week.

" How can I describe it? Good food is like music you can taste, color you can smell. There is excellence all around you. You need only to be aware to stop and savor it."

– Gusteau (Character) from *Ratatouille*

VEGETABLE AND HERB STUFFED SHELLS - page 177

Pasta

Angel Hair Pasta with Broccoli and Mushrooms

Crab Mac and Cheese

Harvest Pumpkin Pasta with Brown Butter Sauce

Penne Pasta, Spinach and Chick Peas

Ravioli with Sauteed Vegetables

Stellar Mac n' Cheese

Tuna Pasta Casserole

Vegetable and Herb Stuffed Shells

Angel Hair Pasta with Broccoli and Mushrooms

Serves 3 - 4

Ingredients:

1 1/2 tablespoons extra virgin olive oil

3 cups broccoli florets

1 cup mushrooms, sliced

1/2 lemon, freshly squeezed

1/4 cup onion, sliced

2 garlic cloves, minced

1/4 cup dry white wine, vegetable or chicken broth

1 cup heavy cream

1/2 teaspoon sea salt

1/4 teaspoon chili flakes or black pepper to taste (optional)

1 8-ounce box angel hair pasta, cooked

Tips:

Cook recommends using De Boles organic Jerusalem artichoke flour angel hair pasta.

Spinach can be substituted for broccoli.

Directions:

Heat oil in skillet, add onions, one clove garlic, mushrooms, and saute a few minutes. Add broccoli to pan and continue to cook until onions and garlic are slightly brown and broccoli is desired tenderness. Stir in wine and lemon juice until well blended. Add cream and cook over medium heat until mixture comes to a boil. Reduce heat and cook about 15 minutes. Stir in second garlic clove, salt, and pepper if desired, and add pasta to cream mixture. Cook over low heat until pasta is coated with sauce.

Submitted by:

Janet Bryant

Crab Mac and Cheese

Serves 5 - 6

Versatile dish that is fancy enough for company and enjoyed by children.

Ingredients:

8 ounces brown rice fusilli pasta or pasta of choice
2 cups cheese, grated (equal parts of Fontina, Jarlsberg and Monterey Jack)
1/4 cup butter
1/4 cup spelt flour or flour of choice
1 3/4 cups organic whole milk (*Cook's choice* - organic, raw and local)
1/4 cup organic whipping cream
1/2 teaspoon sea salt
1/4 teaspoon black pepper
8 ounces wild fresh crabmeat
1/4 cup fresh chives, thinly sliced
1/4 cup shallots, finely chopped
1 garlic clove, chopped
Paprika

Directions:

Cook pasta according to directions on package. While pasta cooks, grate cheese and make sauce. Melt butter in saucepan and when melted remove from heat, add flour and stir until well blended and smooth. Return to heat and gradually stir in milk, cream, salt, and pepper. Continue stirring until sauce comes to a boil, reduce heat, and cook one more minute before removing from heat. Mix pasta, crab, chives, shallots, and garlic all together. Place half in a casserole dish, top with 1/3 of cheese, and half the sauce. Add remaining pasta crab mixture, 1/3 of cheese, and remaining sauce. Sprinkle top with remaining cheese and sprinkle lightly with paprika. Bake in a 350 degree oven for 15 to 20 minutes or until cheese is melted and top is lightly brown.

Harvest Pumpkin Pasta with Brown Butter Sauce

Serves 4 - 6

Knowing that I love pumpkin, my mom found this great pasta and bought me a package to try. I thought about what tastes best with pumpkin, and came up with this recipe. My husband and I both loved it, so I made it again for a pumpkin pot-luck at work. The dish was a hit and many people asked for the recipe.

Ingredients:

1 package pumpkin/ginger rice noodles or plain rice noodles

2 tablespoons extra virgin olive oil

1 pound boneless chicken breast (optional)

1 small pumpkin or butternut squash

sea salt and cracked pepper

2 garlic cloves, minced

2 tablespoons butter

1 teaspoon ground cinnamon

2 teaspoons honey

10 tablespoons butter
(1 stick plus 2 tablespoons)

1/2 teaspoon sea salt

1 tablespoon fresh sage, chopped

2 tablespoons cream or milk

1/3 cup Parmesan cheese

Tip:

Look for noodles in the Asian section.

Note:

Using rice noodles makes this recipe Gluten Free!

Directions:

Remove skin from squash or pumpkin and cut in small chunks. Lay chunks in baking pan and toss with 1 tablespoon oil. Sprinkle with sea salt, pepper, garlic, and dot with 2 tablespoons butter. Bake at 400 degrees for approximately 20 minutes or until squash is soft, tender, and starting to brown slightly. Remove from oven, add cinnamon, and honey, and mix gently to combine. If using chicken, cut into chunks, and saute in frying pan with remaining oil, and salt, and pepper to taste, until cooked through and slightly browned. Cook noodles per package directions, drain, and rinse with cold water. For sauce, melt 8 tablespoons butter in pan with 1/2 teaspoon salt, sage, and stir frequently until butter starts to brown. Add milk or cream and Parmesan cheese to pan, stir and continue to cook until well blended. Combine noodles with cooked chicken, squash, and brown butter sauce, and toss to mix.

Submitted by:

Sheri Santo | www.sherisanto.com

Penne Pasta, Spinach and Chickpeas

Serves 4

Ingredients:

1 10-ounce package, fresh baby spinach or 10-ounce package, frozen chopped spinach

1 pound penne rice pasta

1/3 cup extra virgin olive oil

6 garlic cloves, minced

1/2 teaspoon crushed red pepper flakes or to taste

2 medium tomatoes, seeded and diced

2 cups fresh cooked chickpeas or 1 15-ounce can rinsed and drained

1 15-ounce can chicken broth

1/4 cup Parmesan cheese, freshly grated

1/4 teaspoon sea salt (optional)

1/4 cup white wine (optional)

Alternate Ingredient Substitutions:

Use pinto beans instead of chickpeas, arugula or swiss chard instead of spinach or pasta of your choice.

Tip:

You might want to add a little less chicken broth, especially if you use some wine and if you like lots of sauce you might want to use less cooked pasta.

Directions:

Wash spinach, discard stems, place in large skillet with just the water that clings to it, and cook covered over medium heat about 5 minutes or until wilted. Drain, cool, and squeeze out excess liquid from fresh or frozen spinach. Set aside. Bring a large pot of water to a boil, add pasta, and cook al dente according to package directions. To prepare sauce, heat olive oil in large skillet over medium heat, add garlic, and red pepper flakes, and cook about 2 minutes. Add tomatoes and chick peas, and cook 2 minutes. Stir in spinach, salt, chicken broth, and wine, and cook about 3 minutes. If more liquid is needed, add 1/4 cup of boiling water from the pasta. Drain pasta and place in large serving bowl. Spoon sauce over pasta and stir until well blended. Sprinkle on Parmesan cheese, stir, and serve. Pass a small bowl of Parmesan cheese for final touch.

Ravioli with Sautéed Vegetables

Serves 2

Ingredients:

8 ounce organic ravioli (*Cook's Choice* - basil, asiago, and pine nut pesto)
1/2 orange pepper, thinly sliced
1/2 yellow pepper, thinly sliced
3 petite tomatoes, thinly sliced
1 tablespoon extra virgin olive oil
1 tablespoon butter
1-2 garlic cloves, minced
1/4 cup dry white wine
sea salt and pepper to taste
Parmesan cheese
1/2 cup scallions, chopped

Tip:
Garlic retains its flavor and health properties best when not overcooked, so I add it towards the end of the cooking process, after the other vegetables have been sautéed.

Directions:

Cook ravioli per directions. While ravioli cooks, wash and slice peppers and tomatoes. Place oil, peppers, and tomatoes in frying pan, and toss vegetables until lightly coated. Sauté 5 minutes, add butter, half the scallions, and continue to sauté a few more minutes. Add garlic and sauté a minute or so. Add wine. Stir and sauté until all vegetables are well blended and are of desired tenderness. Add salt and pepper to taste. Place vegetables in center of plate, arrange ravioli around vegetables, sprinkle grated Parmesan cheese over all, and finish by sprinkling remaining scallions on top.

Stellar Mac n' Cheese

Serves 4 - 6

So yummy, even children love this dish.

Ingredients:

8 ounces small brown rice shells or macaroni

2 cups fresh spinach, Swiss chard or beet greens, minced

2 cups sharp cheddar cheese (about 1/2 pound), grated
(*Cook's Choice* - raw organic)

1/4 cup butter

1/4 cup spelt flour or flour of choice

2 cups whole milk (*Cook's Choice* - raw organic)

1/2 teaspoon sea salt

1/4 teaspoon black pepper

1 tablespoon flaxseeds, ground

few shakes of red pepper

paprika

1/2 teaspoon garlic granules (optional)

Directions:

Preheat oven to 350 degrees. Cook pasta according to package directions. Tear greens into small pieces and steam until tender. Mix pasta and greens together, place half in a 1 1/2 quart baking dish, top with half the cheese and then with remainder of pasta and greens and set aside. For sauce, melt butter in saucepan and remove from heat to blend in flour. Once blended, gradually stir in milk, seasonings, and flaxseed and cook over medium heat. Stirring off and on, bring sauce to a rolling boil. Continue to stir and cook for one more minute. Pour sauce over casserole mixture. Sprinkle remaining cheese over top and shake on some paprika. Bake 15 to 20 minutes or until cheese is melted and browned.

Song: Stellar Mac 'n' Cheese - Disc 2 - Song 10 - Swing Style - Medium Tempo

Marilynn's Stellar Mac and Cheese inspired me to create a riff on the jazz standard "Stella By Starlight."

Tuna Pasta Casserole

Serves 6

This casserole pairs tuna and seaweed from the ocean to balance each other. Sadly the fish industry has been widely affected today due to toxins and farming. For this reason, this recipe uses only a small amount of sustainably caught wild tuna and includes seaweed which helps pull heavy metals out of the body.

Ingredients:

2 1/2 cups dry brown rice fusilli or shells (Cook's choice - Pasta Joy)

1 tablespoon wakame seaweed

5 tablespoons butter

1/4 cup bread crumbs, finely ground

1/4 cup onion, chopped

1/4 cup celery, chopped

3/4 cup mushrooms, sliced

1/4 cup oat flour, freshly ground or spelt flour

3/4 cup cheddar cheese, shredded (Cook's choice - organic raw cheese) or asiago

2 1/2 cups organic whole milk (Cook's choice - raw if available)

1/4 teaspoon black pepper

1 teaspoon sea salt

3/4 cup green frozen peas, thawed

1 can wild albacore tuna, drained (pole/troll hand line caught)

2 garlic cloves, finely chopped

paprika

3 shakes cayenne pepper (optional)

Directions:

Preheat oven to 375 degrees. Cook pasta according to package directions, drain and set aside. While pasta cooks, put seaweed in small bowl and cover with water for 4-5 minutes. When seaweed has doubled in volume drain the water. Melt 1 tablespoon butter, mix in breadcrumbs, and set aside. Sauté onions, celery, and mushrooms in 1 tablespoon butter until soft and golden. In saucepan, melt remaining butter and remove from heat. Add flour to melted butter and stir until smooth. Return pan to medium heat, gradually add milk, and stir until well blended and mixture comes to a boil. Reduce heat, add cheese, and cook until cheese is melted. Pour sauce over pasta, add peas, tuna, garlic, seaweed, and spices and stir until well blended. Spread buttered bread crumbs over casserole, and sprinkle with paprika. Bake 20 minutes or until top is lightly golden and casserole is bubbling.

Vegetable and Herb Stuffed Shells

Serves 3 - 4

Ingredients:

1 box brown rice shells

1 small onion, chopped

3 large garlic cloves, minced

1 bunch fresh spinach or 1 bag, chopped, or 2 cups fresh zucchini, thinly sliced

1 tablespoon extra virgin olive oil

1 12-ounce container ricotta cheese

8 ounces mozzarella or Monterey Jack cheese, freshly grated

1 large egg, beaten

3 cups fresh tomatoes, chopped or 1 26-ounce box (*Cook's choice* - Pomi)

1 tablespoon basil, freshly minced or 1 teaspoon dried

1 tablespoon oregano, freshly minced or 1 teaspoon dried

1 shake red pepper

sea salt and pepper to taste

fresh parsley for garnish

Directions:

Preheat oven to 350 degrees. Boil 4 quarts of water with a dash of oil. Cook shells per package directions. While shells cook, sauté onion with 2 garlic cloves until lightly brown. Add spinach or zucchini to onion mixture, and cook until wilted and flavors are blended. In another pan simmer tomatoes with basil, oregano, red pepper, salt, and pepper for 20 minutes. While vegetables cook, and light tomato sauce simmers, stuff shells. In a bowl add the filling ingredients: egg, ricotta cheese, 6 ounces grated cheese, sautéed onions, garlic, and spinach or zucchini, and stir to mix all together. Stuff each shell with filling mixture. Pour a thin layer of tomato sauce in bottom of an 8" x 11" pan. Place shells on top of sauce, sprinkle on remaining garlic, and top with remaining tomato sauce. Cover with parchment paper and bake 40 minutes. Remove parchment paper, sprinkle remaining cheese on top of shells, and cook until cheese is melted. Garnish with parsley before serving.

" Some people like to paint pictures, or do gardening, or build a boat in the basement. Other people get a tremendous pleasure out of the kitchen, because cooking is just as creative and imaginative an activity as drawing, or wood carving, or music."

– Julia Child

SPINACH, AVOCADO, TOMATO SALAD - page 186

Salads

3 Bean Salad

Chicken Salad

Egg Salad with Mexican Flair

Fruit Salad with a Surprise

Mexicali Corn Salad

Pasta Gioia Salad

Spinach, Avocado, Tomato Salad

Sprout Salad

Summer Arugula Salad with Honey Mustard Vinaigrette

Tangy Potato Salad

Toni's Famous Salada

Wild Crabmeat Salad

3 Bean Salad

Serves 6 - 8

This is a quick and simple salad as is, but if you prefer more sweetness or less spice, I encourage you to adjust the mustard and maple syrup for your own preference.

Ingredients:

2 cups fresh green beans, chopped

1/2 cup orange pepper, chopped

1/4 cup red onion, chopped

1/2 cup scallions, thinly sliced

2-3 garlic cloves, minced

1 can red kidney beans

1 can garbanzo beans

3 teaspoons spicy mustard

2 teaspoons ume plum vinegar or apple cider vinegar

1 1/2 tablespoons maple syrup or honey

1 tablespoon fresh dill weed or 1 teaspoon dried

1/4 teaspoon black pepper

> **Tip:**
> Try making your own mustard using powdered mustard or some wasabi to give salad more of a kick.

Directions:

Wash green beans, cut off ends, chop into 1/2 inch pieces, and steam until tender. Place in a bowl with peppers, onions, scallions, and garlic. Rinse garbanzo and kidney beans, and add to bowl. Place mustard, vinegar, maple syrup or honey, dill, and pepper in a separate bowl. Whisk until well blended, pour over bean mixture, and stir. Let ingredients sit on counter for 30 minutes to meld flavors, then place in refrigerator to chill.

Chicken Salad

Serves 4 - 6

Inspired by Nana's mom who was born in 1903 in Nova Scotia and later moved to Arlington, MA. She lived up in the heights area of Arlington during the depression in the early 1940's. During these challenging times, she raised chickens in a coop in her back yard. Raising a family in those days was costly and one of the many ways mom made her money last longer was to use the chicken, home grown herbs, and vegetables in various recipes. This family recipe has become a favorite of her grand children.

Ingredients:

3 1/2 cups cooked chicken, cut into chunks

1 cup mayonnaise

1 teaspoon fresh thyme

1 teaspoon fresh lemon thyme

1/2 teaspoon dried lemon pepper

1/2 teaspoon fresh dill or 1/4 teaspoon dried dill weed

1/4 teaspoon sweet dried basil

1/4 teaspoon dried oregano, (*Cook's choice* - Turkish)

1/4 teaspoon fresh chives, sliced

1/4 teaspoon fresh cilantro, minced

salt and pepper to taste

Tip:

Using 2 very large chicken breasts yields approximately 3 1/2 cups chopped chicken. Mixing chicken warm with other ingredients will help absorb all the flavors.

Note:

See Chicken Fricassee recipe by Nana in "Main Dish - Poultry" chapter for specific instructions for cooking chicken.

Directions:

While still warm, remove chicken from bones of each breast and chop into 1/2" pieces. Place chicken chunks in a bowl, add mayonnaise, all the herbs, and stir until well blended. Refrigerate.

Submitted by:

Nana of 5 hungry boys

Egg Salad with a Mexican Flair

Serves 2 - 3

An easy salad that takes no time to prepare. Due to the combination of spices, it is a bit perkier than a traditional salad but feel free to adjust for personal preference. A great take along salad for a summer picnic, and as no mayonnaise is used, no fret it won't spoil on warm days.

Ingredients:

4 hard boiled eggs

1 ripe avocado

1/2 lime, freshly squeezed

1/4 teaspoon chili powder

1/8 teaspoon ground cumin

3 grinds of black pepper

2 dashes red pepper

dash sea salt (optional)

Directions:

Boil eggs until hard boiled, peel, and process in a food blender. Peel and puree avocado. Squeeze lime juice over avocado, blend together, and add to blended egg. Season with chili powder, cumin, peppers and salt. Enjoy!

Fruit Salad with a Surprise

Serves 4 - 6

Simple summer salad with added surprise of triple sec or substitute with your favorite freshly squeezed citrus. Cook's choice is a blood orange when available.

Ingredients:

3/4 quart fresh strawberries, sliced

1/2 small honeydew melon, cubed

1 kiwi, peeled and sliced

1 orange, peeled and sliced

1 teaspoon sugar

1/2 teaspoon maple syrup

1 1/2 tablespoons triple sec

> **Tip:**
> Fresh orange or clementine juice can be substituted for triple sec.

Directions:

Wash and slice strawberries. Sprinkle sugar over berries and stir to coat. Set aside for 15 minutes to soften strawberries and produce some liquid. While strawberries sit, peel melon, remove seeds, and cube. Peel and slice kiwi and orange and cut each slice into quarters. Add to strawberries with the maple syrup and triple sec. Stir to coat all and let marinate for at least 20 minutes at room temperature.

Mexicali Corn Salad

Serves 6 - 7

Fresh corn always makes me think of bright summer days, cookouts, picnics, and visits to the beach. Makes a great side salad to take anywhere or enjoy at home.

Ingredients:

3 cups fresh corn (about 4 ears) or frozen corn

1/2 cup zucchini, shredded

1/2 cup red pepper, finely chopped

1/2 cup scallions, thinly sliced

2 garlic cloves, minced

1 jalapeno pepper, finely chopped

2 limes, freshly squeezed

2 tablespoons extra virgin olive oil

1/2 teaspoon cumin

1/4 teaspoon sea salt

Directions:

Remove husks from fresh corn, cut off kernels, and add to a saucepan with a little water. Bring to a boil, reduce heat and simmer for 8-10 minutes until corn is tender or use frozen corn and follow package directions. Drain water and place corn in a bowl. Shred zucchini using food processor or large holes on a hand shredder. Add zucchini, red pepper, scallions, garlic, and jalapeno to corn, and stir until well blended. Squeeze limes into a small bowl, add oil, spices, and whisk. Pour over vegetables and stir until well mixed. Cover bowl and chill for several hours.

Pasta Gioia Salad

Serves 6 - 8

My husband consented to be my official new recipe taster. He also agreed to lend his expertise in creatively naming some of the recipes he samples, hence this one which in Italian means "Pasta Joy!" We wish you joyful eating!

Ingredients:

12 ounces artichoke shell pasta

1/4 cup shallots, finely chopped

1/3 cup pickling cucumbers, finely chopped

2 garlic cloves, finely chopped

1 cup green peas, frozen or fresh

3 teaspoons extra virgin olive oil

3 teaspoons umboshi plum vinegar

3 teaspoons balsamic vinegar

1/4 teaspoon black pepper

Note:

No salt is needed as umboshi vinegar is very salty. If on a salt restricted diet, you may want to substitute brown rice vinegar, apple cider vinegar, or freshly squeezed lemon juice instead of the umboshi.

Directions:

Cook pasta according to directions. Let peas defrost or shell fresh peas and lightly steam. Add shallots, cucumber, and garlic to pasta with the peas and toss. Whisk together vinegars and oil, add to pasta, and stir all until well blended. If needed, adjust vinegars and pepper to personal preference.

Spinach, Avocado, Tomato Salad

Serves 4

This is a colorful, nutritious, and very simple salad to prepare that is chock full of antioxidants, omega 3's, and vitamins A and C.

Ingredients:

Fresh spinach, about half a bag

1 red onion, sliced into thin rings

2 large tomatoes or 3 plum tomatoes, thinly sliced

2 tablespoons pine nuts

1 or 2 avocados, sliced

1/2 cup feta cheese, crumbled

1/2 lemon, freshly squeezed

1 tablespoon lime juice, freshly squeezed

3 tablespoons extra virgin olive oil

1/4 teaspoon sea salt

1/4 teaspoon black pepper

few shakes cayenne (optional)

Directions:

Wash spinach, dry well, and place in serving bowl. Place onions, tomatoes, and pine nuts in a separate bowl and mix together with wooden spoon. Add avocado and feta cheese to tomato mixture, lightly blend, and combine all with spinach. In another bowl squeeze together lemon and lime juices, whisk with oil, salt, and peppers and pour over salad. Let sit a few minutes to allow flavors to meld. If needed, adjust salt and pepper to taste. Give one final toss before serving.

Sprout Salad

Ingredients:

1 cup mung bean sprouts

1 cup alfalfa or radish sprouts

1/2 cup each daikon and carrots, cut into match sticks or grated, mixed with a pinch of salt

1 bunch watercress or arugula, washed and chopped

2 tablespoons tahini

1 tablespoon umeboshi paste

2 tablespoons lemon juice, freshly squeezed

1 tablespoon mellow white miso

Directions:

Prepare carrots and daikon with salt and let sit while preparing rest of ingredients. Wash sprouts well. In separate bowl make dressing by combining tahini, umeboshi paste, lemon juice, and miso whisking until well blended. Add dressing to vegetables and serve.

Tangy Potato Salad

As mayonnaise has been eliminated, no fret about this recipe going bad in the warm weather.

Ingredients:

2-3 pounds potatoes, peeled and chopped

1/4 cup scallions, thinly chopped

2 tablespoons fresh chives, finely chopped

1 tablespoon extra virgin olive oil

2 tablespoon apple cider vinegar

1 tablespoon balsamic vinegar

1/4 teaspoon sea salt

1/2 teaspoon black pepper

garlic granules, few shakes (optional)

Directions:

Place potatoes in large saucepan with enough water to cover. Bring to boil, reduce heat, cover, and simmer about 30 minutes until potatoes are fork tender. Remove potatoes, allow to cool and place in a large bowl with scallions and chives. Place oil, vinegars, salt, pepper, and garlic granules into a glass jar. Cover and shake until blended. Pour seasoned oil over potatoes and toss until well blended. Serve warm at room temperature or refrigerate to meld flavors further.

Summer Arugula Salad with Honey Mustard Vinaigrette

Serves 4

Yellow watermelons are small with few seeds. They can be hard to find due to their short growing season during July and August, but they are so delicious they are worth the hunt. These melons are sweeter than the red ones and blend well with the arugula and mint. Substituting a small red watermelon is almost as good.

Salad Ingredients:

2 cups arugula, coarsely chopped

1 small pickling cucumber, peeled and finely chopped

2 tablespoons fresh mint, finely minced

1 cup yellow watermelon, cut in small chunks with rind and seeds removed

1 1/2 tablespoons pine nuts

1/4 cup feta cheese

> **Tip:**
> Depending on personal preference, add more of your favorite ingredients and less of your least favorites.

Directions:

Wash arugula and place in bowl. Add cucumber, mint, watermelon, and pine nuts to arugula.

Make dressing below. Pour some dressing over salad and stir until evenly coated. Sprinkle cheese over salad ingredients and quickly toss. Serve remaining vinaigrette on the side.

Vinaigrette Ingredients:

1/4 cup Balsamic vinegar

1/4 extra virgin organic olive oil

1/4 teaspoon sea salt

1/4 teaspoon black pepper

1 teaspoon powdered mustard

1 tablespoon honey (Cook's choice - raw)

2 drops Tabasco sauce (optional or to taste)

Vinaigrette Directions:

Place all ingredients in a glass jar, cover, and shake until well blended.

Toni's Famous Salada

Serves 2, or double for 4

This is a delicious fresh tasting salad! The only down side of this recipe is - it ruins your taste for store bought dressings.

Ingredients:

1/2 head lettuce, broken or cut up

1-2 fresh garlic cloves, chopped
(depending on taste and size of clove)

extra virgin olive oil to coat

lemon juice, several squirts to taste

salt to taste

1 or 2 tomatoes, chopped
(amount to personal preference)

4-6 pitted black olives (optional)

mint to taste, minced (optional)

feta cheese (optional)

Tip:
The cook suggests adding tomatoes to salads towards the end, so juice from the tomatoes doesn't separate and compromise the taste of the dressing combination.

Directions:

Put lettuce and chopped garlic in a big bowl and coat lightly with olive oil, then squeeze on a little lemon juice to taste (important to coat with the oil before adding the lemon juice). Add a little salt to taste. Add tomatoes, olives, mint, and cheese, and lightly toss all ingredients.

Submitted by:

Toni McFarland

Wild Crabmeat Salad

Serves 2

This simple, fresh, elegant dish creates a beautiful and colorful presentation. Serve for lunch or dinner accompanied with some breadsticks or whole wheat bread. It can easily be doubled to serve 4.

Ingredients:

8 ounces wild Dungeness crabmeat, tear into pieces

1 tablespoon fresh cilantro, finely chopped

2 tablespoons mashed avocado or mayonnaise

1 tablespoon lemon juice, freshly squeezed

3 twists of black peppercorns

6 leaves of Boston bib lettuce

5 organic grape tomatoes, thinly sliced

18 slices fermented cucumbers (recipe in medicinal section) or plain pickling cucumbers

1 teaspoon powdered wasabi (optional)

fresh dill (optional)

Tip:

For an extra kick, add some powdered wasabi to avocado or mayonnaise. Mix up a little oil, vinegar, and spices of your choice and drizzle over the lettuce leaves and serve.

Directions:

Mix together crabmeat, cilantro, avocado or mayonnaise, and lemon juice until well blended. Twist black peppercorns over crabmeat mixture and stir until well blended. Wash lettuce and arrange 3 leaves on each plate. Place half the salad in center of each plate where leaves meet. Place half the cherry tomatoes around crabmeat on each plate with one slice in center on top of crabmeat. Place 3 cucumber slices on each lettuce leaf. If using fermented cucumbers, drizzle a teaspoon of pickling juices from the jar on top of each lettuce leaf. If using plain cucumbers, sprinkle a little snipped fresh dill over salad.

" Life is a lot like jazz... it's best when you improvise..."

– George Gershwin

VEGETABLE FRIED RICE - page 202

Side Dishes – Grains and Legumes

Buckwheat Groats known as Kasha

Citrus Lentils

Millet Patties

Quinoa Stir fry with Spinach and Walnuts

Quinoa Tabouli

Self Mashing Lentils

Vegetable Fried Rice

Veggies n Fruit Couscous

Buckwheat Groats

Serves 4 - 6

Also known as Kasha. This traditional grain has been enjoyed by our family over the years and is often combined with some bow tie pasta for a heartier dish.

Ingredients:

1 teaspoon butter

1 medium onion, chopped

3 garlic cloves, finely chopped

1/2 cup fresh mushrooms, chopped

1 large egg

1 1/2 cups buckwheat groats, medium or coarse

2 1/2 cups boiling water

1/2 teaspoon sea salt or to taste

1/4 teaspoon black pepper or to taste

fresh parsley, finely minced

bow tie pasta (optional)

Tips:

To prevent garlic from losing its medicinal healing qualities and its flavor during cooking, chop and allow it to sit for 15 minutes and add near end of cooking.

For even greater benefit, sprinkle half of the chopped raw garlic over kasha and pasta, stir and serve.

Directions:

Melt butter in small skillet and sauté onions, half the garlic, and mushrooms. Beat egg in small bowl and mix in buckwheat groats. Place groats in large skillet and cook over low heat until grains are separated. Add water, sautéed vegetables, salt, and pepper. Cover pan and cook until all water is absorbed. Just prior to serving, stir in remainder of fresh garlic. Garnish with some fresh parsley. If using bow tie pasta, cook per package directions. When done stir into kasha until all mixed together and add garnish.

Citrus Lentils

Serves 4 - 6

Ingredients:

1 cup green lentils

1/2 cup onion, diced

1/2 cup celery, diced

1 tablespoon extra virgin olive oil

1 1/2 cups water

1/4 teaspoon Himalayan salt

5 shakes cayenne pepper

1/2 lemon, cut into 4-5 slices

few thin slices orange rind

1 cup baby spinach, thinly sliced

1/4 cup orange juice, freshly squeezed (*Cook's choice* - minneola orange)

Directions:

Wash lentils. Sauté onions and celery in oil until lightly browned. Bring water to a boil with spices, lemon slices, and orange rind. Lower heat to simmer, cover pan, and cook 30 minutes. Add spinach and orange juice and cook another 30 minutes or until lentils are desired consistency.

Submitted by:

Carol Ehlen, Jin Shin Jyutsu Practitioner

Millet Patties with Kohlrabi Sauce

Yields 8 patties

This is a vegetarian, gluten-free, and dairy-free recipe that contains no animal products. Although many steps, recipe is simple and worth the time. So settle in with the music and know the end result will be a healthy, nutritious meal for the family.

Ingredients for Patties:

1 cup cooked millet

2 cups water

1 tablespoon flax seed, ground

1/4 cup water

1/4 cup shallots or red onions, finely minced

1/4 cup carrots, peeled and finely shredded

2 tablespoons colored peppers or 1 jalapeno

1 garlic clove, minced

1/2 teaspoon ground cumin

1/2 cup frozen green peas

1/2 teaspoon ground turmeric

7 twists black pepper

1/4-1/2 teaspoon sea salt or to taste

1/8 teaspoon red pepper if no jalapeno

1 tablespoon coconut oil

1 tablespoon butter

Tips:

Enjoy as a sandwich on a bun or as a main dish with additional sides.

Patties can be wrapped in parchment paper, frozen, and saved for another meal.

Directions for Patties:

Wash millet, remove any stones, add 2 cups water, and simmer 20-30 minutes until grains are cooked and water has evaporated. Add 1/4 cup water to flax seeds, stir, and set aside to thicken a bit. Add shallots, carrots, peppers, garlic, green peas, and all spices to millet. Stir flax seed mixture into millet and vegetable mixture and stir well. Divide mixture into 8 balls and flatten each into a patty. Heat a cast iron skillet to medium and add coconut oil and butter. When hot, add patties. Cook each side until lightly brown and heated through.

Millet Patties with Kohlrabi Sauce (continued)

Kohlrabi Sauce:

Kohlrabi (German for cabbage/turnip) are sputnik-shaped vegetables that taste like broccoli stems and are related to cabbage and cauliflower. If you cannot find kohlrabi, substitute with cauliflower or turnip or a combination of both.

Ingredients for Kohlrabi Sauce:

3 cups kohlrabi, peeled and chopped into small pieces

2 tablespoons butter, melted

1 5.46-ounce can coconut cream, full fat (Cook's choice - Thai Kitchen)

1/4 teaspoon ground nutmeg

1/4 teaspoon garlic powder

7 twists black peppercorns

1/4 teaspoon sea salt or to taste

Directions for Sauce

Simmer kohlrabi approximately 30-60 minutes until tender. Add butter, coconut cream, and spices and gently bring to a boil. Put half the kohlrabi in a blender with half the butter-coconut mixture and blend. Add remaining kohlrabi and butter-coconut mixture and blend well until smooth and creamy. Serve this light sauce with the millet patties.

Quinoa Spinach and Walnut Stir-Fry

Serves 4 - 6

As this dish tastes great warm or cold, leftovers can be enjoyed as a cold salad or for a light lunch.

Ingredients:

1 cup quinoa

1 6-ounce bag fresh baby spinach

1/2 cup walnut pieces

2 tablespoons extra virgin olive oil

1 teaspoon garlic, minced

1 cup grape or cherry tomatoes

1/2 cup Parmesan, freshly grated or feta cheese, crumbled

1/4 teaspoon fresh ground pepper

1/2 teaspoon sea salt

fresh basil leaves for garnish, minced

scallions, sliced (optional)

olives, sliced (optional)

Directions:

Place quinoa in small bowl, add water to cover, and swirl to rinse. Pour into a fine mesh strainer and drain well. Rinse and strain 2-3 times. Add a little salt to 2 cups water and heat to boiling. Reduce heat and add quinoa. Cover and cook at medium low heat until water is absorbed, about 15 minutes. Set aside. While quinoa cooks, spread walnuts in a small skillet and stir over medium low heat about 5 minutes until lightly toasted. Heat oil in a medium skillet, add spinach and tomatoes, and stir fry until spinach is almost wilted and tomatoes are warm. Stir spinach, tomatoes, walnuts, and cheese into cooked quinoa. Add scallions and olives if using. Stir everything until well mixed. Garnish with basil. Serve warm.

Quinoa Tabouli

Serves 6 - 8

This delicious, light, nutritious dish can be served at room temperature or chilled. It makes a great side dish, lunch, or light supper.

Ingredients:

1 cup quinoa

1 3/4 cup water

1 red pepper, cut in half

1 zucchini, sliced lengthwise into 4-5 slices

1-1 1/2 cups pickling cucumbers, chopped

1/2-1 cup red onion, chopped

2 cups watercress leaves or arugula, chopped

1/4 cup lemon juice, freshly squeezed

1/4 cup extra virgin olive oil

1-2 teaspoons garlic, finely minced

1/2 teaspoon sea salt

1/4-1/2 cup feta cheese, crumbled (optional)

1 tomato, chopped (optional)

Note:

Do not stir quinoa during cooking so the grain cooks consistently.

Serving Suggestion:

Tabouli is great on its own but for an added treat try mixing in the optional ingredients of feta cheese and fresh tomatoes.

Directions:

Place quinoa in a mesh strainer to wash off natural coating. This may take 2-3 washings until water is clear. Place quinoa, water, and a pinch of salt in a 3-quart pan. Bring to boil, reduce heat, cover, and simmer 15 minutes. Turn off heat and let sit for 10 minutes. Fluff with fork and cool to room temperature. Brush pepper and zucchini slices with a light layer of oil, and place on broiler rack. Broil vegetables turning once or twice until pepper skin is black and zucchini is roasted. While vegetables roast, chop cucumbers, onion, and watercress, and add to quinoa. Remove blackened pepper skin. Slice pepper and zucchini into thin strips. Add to quinoa and stir until well mixed. In small bowl whisk together lemon juice, oil, garlic, and salt. Pour over quinoa and vegetables, stirring gently until all ingredients are combined. Add feta and tomatoes if using and give one final stir.

Self Mashing Lentils

My husband used to play in a jazz duo with his friend Danny at this fabulous restaurant. Food was always fresh and delicious. On occasion John, another sax player, would fill in for Danny. On these evenings his wife, Laura, would come hear the guys play and we would all have dinner together. One evening we got a chance to talk with the chef, and told him how much we enjoyed the lentils. He said it was easy and gave us a few tips. Hence we both tried making a lentil side dish. With some input from Laura, I eventually came up with this recipe which pleased my husband who has never been a fan of lentils. With only a few quick stirs during cooking, lentils will have a nice creamy texture without the need for extra ingredients or additional mashing. A simple, nutritious side that is a nice change from the usual mashed potatoes or rice.

Ingredients:

1 medium shallot, chopped

2 garlic cloves, minced

1/4 teaspoon red pepper flakes or to taste

1 cup dried red lentils, washed and drained

1 1/2-2 cups vegetable broth

1 tablespoon extra virgin olive oil

1/4 teaspoon Himalayan salt

black pepper to taste (optional)

Tips:

Rinse lentils, drain, and discard any stones.

Experiment with whatever vegetables you have in the refrigerator to make your own vegetable broth or if in a hurry, use an organic store bought broth.

Directions:

Sauté shallots and garlic in oil until soft. Add vegetable broth, salt, pepper, and pepper flakes, and bring to a boil. Stir in lentils, cover, and simmer 40-50 minutes until cooked and thick. Lentils should be stirred a few times while cooking. A nice side to accompany any meal.

Continued on next page...

Self Mashing Lentils (continued)

Homemade Broth Ingredients:

1 1/2 cups parsnips, chopped

1 1/2 cups sweet potatoes, chopped

1 1/2 cups tart apples, chopped

Homemade Broth Directions:

In medium saucepan, simmer parsnips and sweet potatoes in water for 10 minutes, then add apples, and simmer another 10-15 minutes or until desired consistency. Strain broth from vegetables and use to cook lentils. Potatoes, parnips, and apples can be set aside to use another time or use to stuff a squash, see Fall Medley recipe in Side Dish - Vegetable Chapter.

Inspired by:

Steve, Chef

Plum Island Grill, Newbury, MA

Formerly at Pow Wow River Grill, Amesbury, MA

Vegetable Fried Rice

Serves 4 - 6

Ingredients:

1 cup Sushi rice, white rice or
rice of choice

1 teaspoon dried wakame seaweed

2 carrots, chopped

1/2 cup onions, chopped

4 ounces fresh mushrooms, sliced

1/2 cup daikon radish, thinly sliced

1 8-ounce can Chinese baby corn,
cut each in 4 slices

1 7-ounce package bean sprouts

1 1/2 tablespoons toasted sesame oil

2 large eggs, beaten

1 cup frozen green peas

1/2 teaspoon ground ginger

4 shakes red pepper or to taste

3 tablespoons coconut amino acids or tamari sauce

1/2 cup scallions, thinly sliced

3 garlic cloves, minced

> **Tips:**
>
> Sushi rice can be starchy, so I recommend rinsing before cooking.
>
> I usually make rice earlier in the day so it is nicely chilled when needed.

Directions:

Cook together rice and seaweed, according to rice package directions. When all water has evaporated put rice in refrigerator to cool. While rice cools stir fry carrots, onions, mushrooms, and daikon, in a lightly oiled wok. When vegetables are brown and tender, add rice, baby corn, and bean sprouts, and stir until all heated through and lightly browned. Place eggs in a small bowl and whisk until mixed. Slowly add to rice and vegetables and stir until eggs are cooked and look like little yellow threads. Add peas, ginger, red pepper, coconut aminos or tamari, half the scallions, and half the garlic. Cook and stir until everything is well blended and hot. Sprinkle remaining scallions and raw garlic over rice before serving.

Veggies n Fruit Couscous

Serves 4

A simple, quick, dish that combines colorful vegetables rich in antioxidants and lots of fiber. Since recipe can easily be adapted for a variety of vegetables, fruits, and spices, you might want to try substituting the fruit for raisins with curry, or be adventuresome and try what you have in your cupboards adjusting for personal preference.

Ingredients:

1 cup whole wheat couscous

3 teaspoons extra virgin olive oil

1 cup Vidalia or other sweet onion, thinly sliced

1/2 sweet red pepper, thinly sliced

1/2 yellow pepper, thinly sliced

2 cups zucchini, thinly sliced

1 tablespoon fresh ginger, minced or 1 teaspoon ground ginger

2 teaspoons coconut aminos, Braggs aminos, or tamari sauce

1 cup water

1/4 cup dried cranberries or cherries, chopped

1/4 cup orange juice, freshly squeezed with pulp if using cranberries

2 tablespoons lemon juice if using cherries

1/4 cup almonds, thinly sliced

few shakes red pepper (optional)

Directions:

Warm 2 teaspoons oil in a large frying or cast iron pan over medium-high heat. Add onions and cook stirring frequently for 2 minutes. Add peppers, zucchini, ginger, and aminos or tamari and cook stirring frequently for 6 to 7 minutes or until vegetables are just tender. Place water, juice, and cherries or cranberries into a 2-quart saucepan and bring to a boil. Remove from heat and stir in dry couscous and remaining oil. Cover pan and let stand for 5 minutes or until couscous is soft. Fluff couscous with a fork and place in a large bowl. Add vegetables and toss well. Couscous can be made a day ahead and served cold, if you wish.

" If more of us valued food and cheer and song above hoarded gold, it would be a merrier world."

– J. R. R. Tolkien

PARSNIP OVEN FRIES - page 214

Side Dishes – Vegetables

Asian Beets

Basic Cabbage Stir Fry

Cabbage Fruit Hash

Carrot Parsnip Mash

Creamed Peas and Onions

Delicata Pinwheels

Fall Medley Stuffed Squash

Garlicky Beet Greens

Margarita Carrots

Parsnip Oven Fries

Rutabaga for a Change

Spinach Casserole

Sweet Potato Vegetable Combo

Swiss Chard

The Great Asparagus Caper

Asian Beets

Ingredients:

3 red beets

2 tablespoons brown rice vinegar

1 tablespoon maple syrup

1 teaspoon wasabi powder

1/4 cup scallions, thinly sliced

Directions:

Wash beets, cover with water, bring to boil, reduce heat, and simmer for about 45 minutes or until beets are tender when pierced. Allow to cool, cut off ends, and slip off skin. Chop beets into 1/2" pieces and place in bowl. In separate small bowl add vinegar, maple syrup, and wasabi, and whisk until well blended. Add this to beets with scallions, and stir until vegetables are evenly coated. Refrigerate for at least an hour. Stir again before serving.

Basic Cabbage Stir-fry

Serves 6 - 8

Ingredients:

8 cups cabbage, chopped

1 bunch green onions, chopped

2-3 garlic cloves

2 tablespoons extra virgin olive oil

1/2-1 teaspoon turmeric

2 medium carrots, cut lengthwise into 1"
pieces

1 large green pepper, cut lengthwise into 1" pieces

2 tablespoons soy sauce

1/2 teaspoon salt

1 teaspoon powdered ginger

2 cups bean sprouts (optional)

1/2 teaspoon crushed red pepper (optional)

> **Serving Suggestion:**
> Serve with brown rice. For more protein, serve with lentil burgers, sauteed chicken strips, or tofu.

Directions:

Sauté onions and garlic in oil until just beginning to soften. Add turmeric, carrots and green peppers and sauté all together until al dente. Add cabbage, soy sauce, and remaining spices. A little water, about 1/4 cup, may need to be added. Cover and cook until cabbage is soft. Add bean sprouts and crushed red pepper.

Submitted by:

Emily Loghmani, Registered Dietitian

Cabbage-Fruit Hash

Serves 2

This is a surprisingly yummy dish that is full of fresh flavors you'll want to have again and again.

Ingredients:

2 cups green cabbage, thinly sliced

1 orange, freshly squeezed

1/4 cup fresh cranberries, chopped

1 teaspoon fresh ginger, chopped

1 apple, chopped

Directions:

Place cabbage in skillet, pour orange juice over cabbage, add cranberries, and simmer covered for 20 minutes. Add ginger and apple to mixture, and continue simmering until cabbage is tender and all flavors are blended together.

Carrot Parsnip Mash

Serves 2 -3

This makes a great side dish that is so simplistic but so scrumptious!

Ingredients:

1/2 pound carrots, sliced

1/2 pound parsnips. sliced

1 tablespoon butter

sea salt and pepper to taste

> **Serving Suggestion:**
> Serve with pan seared scallops and arugula with quinoa.

Directions:

Cut ends off carrots and parsnips, peel, and slice into 1/2" slices. Add water to cover vegetables and simmer until tender. Discard cooking liquid. Add butter, salt, and pepper to carrots and parsnips, and mash with a fork. Mixture should be a bit chunky.

Creamed Peas and Onions

Serves 4

This makes a delicious side for Thanksgiving dinner. The recipe can easily be doubled.

Ingredients:

1 15-ounce package frozen green peas

8–10 shallots or about 12-15 tiny onions

3 tablespoons butter

3 heaping tablespoons flour

1 cup milk, or less

salt and pepper to taste

heavy whipping cream, to taste (optional)

Tip:
Some similar recipes suggest adding a dash of nutmeg. If you like a little spice, this is nice.

Directions:

Place peas in colander and run cold water over them to separate and remove any freezer ice. Peel shallots or onions, place in boiling water on stove, and cook until just al dente and before they begin to separate, about 5 minutes or less. Remove from heat and drain. In a separate pan slowly melt butter on medium heat. Gradually add flour and stir to make paste. Turn heat to low or remove pan from heat. Gradually add milk until desired thickness. Sauce should be thick but not pasty. A little cream can be added for extra richness if desired. Yum! Season with salt and pepper. Add shallots and peas to sauce and stir gently.

Submitted by:

Toni McFarland

Delicata Pinwheels

These little pinwheels look difficult but are so easy to prepare. Delicata squash has a creamy delicious flavor, similar to corn and sweet potato. Due to the sweetness of the squash, it pairs nicely with slightly bitter greens. Also, the addition of spices may not be necessary and depends on personal taste. Serve as a side with your favorite main course for a beautiful presentation.

Ingredients:

delicata squash, about 7" long

1 bunch beet greens, chopped yields about 4 cups

1 tablespoon butter, melted

1/4 cup feta or Parmesan cheese

1 tablespoon pine nuts

sea salt and pepper to taste

Tips:

Squash size varies from 5 to 10 inches in length. Although available year-round, are best from late summer through early fall. Dumpling squash can be used instead of delicata with the same results, but a different presentation. Cook squash as above, cut in half, remove seeds, and fibers, and fill. Other greens can be substituted.

Directions:

Preheat oven to 400 degrees. Wash squash, use a fork to poke 3 or 4 holes in the squash, and place in a baking pan. No need to butter or oil pan. Bake in oven, rotating a few times until squash skin has darkened and is soft to touch. Wash, chop, and steam greens to desired tenderness. Drain all cooking liquid. Remove squash from oven and allow to cool a bit, then carefully cut into 4-6 slices depending on size of squash. Lay each slice on a cutting board and scoop out seeds and pulp making sure to leave the squash and skin intact. Place greens, melted butter, cheese, pine nuts, and seasoning if using into a small bowl, and stir until completely mixed. Spoon a little filling into each squash round. Use a spatula to transfer squash filled pinwheel to a plate.

Fall Medley Stuffed Squash

Serves 4

Ingredients:

1 1/2 cups sweet potatoes, chopped

1 1/2 cup parsnips, chopped

1 1/2 cup apples, chopped

3/4 teaspoon ground cinnamon

2 acorn or delicata squash

1 tablespoon butter, melted

ground ginger, to taste (optional)

2 cups water

> **Tip:**
> Drained liquid from vegetables can be frozen or refrigerated to use another time.

Directions:

Preheat oven to 400 degrees. Wash squash, pierce skin a few times with a fork, and place in roaster pan. Bake in oven about 45 minutes, turning squash periodically. Exact cooking time depends on size of squash. While squash cooks, peel and chop sweet potato and parsnips and place in a saucepan. Cover with water and simmer 10 minutes. Add apple and cook another 10-15 minutes until tender. Drain liquid and set aside to use another time. Mash potatoes, parsnips, and apples, add cinnamon, and mix until well blended. When squash is thoroughly cooked, cut in half and remove seeds. Brush tops and inside cavity with warm melted butter and fill squash with the mashed mixture. Return squash to oven for 5 minutes until heated.

Garlicky Beet Greens

Serves 2

Ingredients:

1 pound beet greens, well washed

1/4 cup chicken broth

3 garlic cloves, thinly sliced

1 tablespoon butter

2 tablespoons extra virgin olive oil

sea salt to taste

cracked pepper to taste

Directions:

In a large skillet, bring broth to a rolling boil. Drop in beet greens. Add garlic to broth and greens. Stir often to ensure greens cook evenly. As greens begin to wilt and water evaporates slightly, add butter. Reduce heat and cook for only 5 minutes after greens have wilted and most of liquid has cooked away. Stir in oil and season to taste with salt and pepper.

Submitted by:

Sheri Santo | www.sherisanto.com

Margarita Carrots

These carrots take no time to make and are so delicious!

Ingredients:

1 bunch fresh baby carrots,
(*Cook's choice* - organic)

2 tablespoons butter

1 lime, freshly squeezed

1 tablespoon tequila

2 teaspoons sugar

Tip:

If you cannot find fresh baby carrots, do not buy precut packaged baby carrots but substitute with whole carrots and cut in 2" lengths.

Serving Suggestion:

Serve with jalapeno, scallion polenta.

Directions:

Peel and boil carrots whole until almost tender. While carrots cook, melt butter and add lime juice, tequila, and sugar. Stir to blend. Bring glaze to boil, turn heat down to medium and cook sauce until reduced by half. Place cooked carrots into sauce, stirring so carrots are completely covered with sauce. Continue to cook carrots in sauce until only a little sauce remains and carrots are nicely glazed.

Parsnip Oven Fries

Serves 3 - 4

A parsnip is a root vegetable that looks similar to a carrot but is larger and white in color. It is a bit sweet and tastes somewhere between a carrot and a potato. For those who love their potatoes, this is a nice variation that includes both the sweetness and the spice of life.

Ingredients:

1 pound parsnips

1 tablespoon extra virgin olive oil

1/4 teaspoon sea salt

1/4 teaspoon garlic granules

1/8 teaspoon black pepper

1/4 teaspoon ground cardamon

1/2 teaspoon cumin

1/4 teaspoon ground turmeric or curry powder

1/8 teaspoon red pepper flakes (optional)

parchment paper

Tip:
These have a nice spicy flavor, but if you don't like spice just eliminate red pepper.

Directions:

Preheat oven to 425 degrees. Cut off both ends of parsnips, peel and cut in half. Depending on thickness of parsnips, cut in half again or in quarters. Pieces should be about 2" long and about 1/2" thick. Try to cut pieces close to same size so parsnips cook evenly. Place parsnips in a bowl and toss with oil until well coated. In small dish add all spices and stir until completely blended. Add spices to parsnips and stir until parsnips are evenly coated. Cut a piece of parchment paper to cover bottom of baking sheet. Place parsnips on top of parchment paper in a single layer. Make sure slices do not touch each other. Bake for 15 minutes. Turn parsnips over and continue cooking another 15 minutes or until all are nicely browned.

Rutabaga for a Change

Serves 3 - 4

A root vegetable which is a bit spicy with a sweet flavor that is enhanced when cooked. With less carbs and calories, and more vitamins and minerals than potatoes, they make a nice change from the usual mashed potatoes in Fall and Winter.

Ingredients:

1 rutabaga, 4 cups chopped
2 tablespoons butter
1/4 teaspoon Himalayan salt
1/4 teaspoon black pepper
2 garlic cloves, minced
1/4 cup Parmesan cheese
1/3 cup sliced scallions

Tips:

As rutabagas are quite hard, use caution when chopping.

It is a very fibrous vegetable that is not as smooth as mashed potatoes but has a really nice texture consistency.

Directions:

Wash, peel, and chop rutabaga into small chunks. Place in medium size saucepan, cover with water, add a little salt to the water, and cook covered for 40-45 minutes until desired tenderness. Remove to a bowl and mash with butter, salt, and pepper. When desired consistency, stir in garlic, Parmesan cheese, and scallions. Stir and place in a glass or ceramic casserole baking pan and bake in a 400 degree oven for 20 minutes.

Spinach Casserole (Houston Chronicle Recipe of the Week)

Serves 4

This recipe came to me as I gazed into a nearly empty fridge, wondering what on earth to cook for dinner. Necessity being the mother of invention, I threw together a bunch of leftovers – cooked rice, chopped spinach, and white sauce. The concoction turned out surprisingly delicious, so I refined it to eventually become this award winning, easy and inexpensive dish. Put spinach on the table!

Ingredients:

2 10-ounce packages frozen spinach, chopped

5-6 tablespoon butter (total amount used for spinach, sauce, and rice)

1/2 cup uncooked long-grain rice

2 cups homemade white sauce (recipe follows)

1 6-8 ounce package Monterey Jack cheese, thinly sliced or grated

4 tablespoons flour

1 1/2–2 cups milk

pinch of sugar

salt and pepper to taste

nutmeg, small pinch to taste (optional)

Continued on next page...

Tips:

This is a delicate tasting dish.

You will not need to use all the cooked rice, as rice layers should be the thinner layers so as not to overwhelm the spinach.

Cheese layers should also be thin, to not overwhelm other flavors.

Using 3 packages of spinach will stretch the recipe to serve 6, maybe more.

Serving suggestions:

Dish can be assembled in advance, and refrigerated until time to heat. It is perfection served with a simple baked or broiled fish, a light pasta dish with seafood, meatloaf, or roast.

Spinach Casserole (continued)

Directions:

Preheat oven to 350 degrees. Cook spinach and squeeze out all liquid. Add 1 tablespoon butter, salt and pepper to taste. Remove from stove. Cook rice according to package directions. (You will not need to use all the cooked rice.) Remove from stove. Make white sauce (directions below). In a 9" X 9" greased glass baking pan, layer half the spinach; cover with a thin layer of rice so spinach is the thicker layer; half the white sauce to cover rice; and half the cheese to lightly cover sauce. Repeat layers, ending with cheese lightly covering top. Bake covered about 20 minutes until heated through. Remove cover and cook another 10 minutes or until cheese browns a little.

White Sauce Directions:

Melt 4 tablespoons butter in small saucepan over low heat. Slowly add flour, stirring until smooth. Slowly add milk, stirring constantly until smooth. Add sugar, salt, and pepper to taste. Add nutmeg to taste if desired. Remove sauce from stove when consistency is thick, without tasting floury.

Submitted by:

Toni McFarland

Sweet Potato Vegetable Combo

Serves 3

No matter how these delectable sweet potatoes are prepared they are one of my all-time favorite foods to eat! These beautiful root vegetables are rich in antioxidants, have a high fiber content, and are full of vitamins A and C.

Ingredients:

2 cups sweet potato, cut into small cubes

1 1/2 tablespoons extra virgin olive oil

1/4 teaspoon Himalayan salt

1/2 teaspoon cayenne pepper

1/2 teaspoon garlic granules

1/4 cup red onion, chopped

1/4 cup red pepper, chopped

1/4 cup sweet corn, frozen or fresh

2 tablespoons scallions, finely sliced

Directions:

Preheat oven to 400 degrees. Place sweet potato cubes in 8" x 8" pan. Add olive oil and stir until all are coated. Add all spices. Cook 15 minutes, then add onion, pepper, and corn and stir until evenly mixed. Cook 30 minutes or until vegetables are tender and are a bit glazed. Garnish with some fresh scallions and serve.

Swiss Chard

Serves 3

Ingredients:

1 bunch Swiss chard

grapeseed oil or extra virgin olive oil

1 shallot or any sweet onion, chopped

1 garlic clove, minced

Himalayan pink salt or sea salt (*Cook's choice* – Himalayan pink salt)

Directions:

Rinse chard, cut rib out, and chop remaining leaf into bite size pieces. Place chard in a pot of boiling water. Reduce heat and simmer 3 minutes. While simmering, pour grapeseed oil in pan and warm. Add shallot and garlic, and sauté until tender, about 5 to 8 minutes. Drain chard, add to onions and garlic, and cook for another 6 to 8 minutes. Add salt to taste.

The Great Asparagus Caper

Serves 4 - 6

One night, we made roasted asparagus at our daughter, Sheri's house and she said sometimes she adds other ingredients. I asked her for the recipe to include in the cookbook and she said there is no recipe! So my good friend Beth and I have this routine where we take a Zumba class together; then go to Philbrick's Fresh Market, our favorite organic grocery store to buy food to make for dinner; and while cooking my favorite musician plays music for us to cook by, and the following recipe emerged. But then we needed a title. Beth suggested caper but I said the main ingredient is asparagus. We thought a bit, but it was my husband, Steve, who came up with the title. These evenings have turned out to be super fun starting with exercise, followed by good food, fabulous music, and great company. Maybe this will become a favorite tradition of yours too!

Ingredients:

2 pounds asparagus

1/2 lemon

1 tablespoon capers

1/2 cup tomatoes, chopped

1/4 cup green stuffed olives or olives of choice, sliced

2 tablespoons extra virgin olive oil

1/4 teaspoon Himalayan salt

1/4 teaspoon black pepper

1/4 teaspoon garlic powder

1/2 cup feta cheese

Tips:

To cook this much asparagus, it is best to use two cookie sheets so asparagus gets nice and roasted. But, if you'd rather asparagus to be more steamed, then one cookie sheet is fine.

Directions:

Wash asparagus, snap off ends, and put on a cookie sheet. Add capers, tomatoes, and olives to asparagus. Squeeze lemon juice over all and drizzle with oil. Sprinkle on spices. Toss all ingredients together with your hands. Bake in a 400 degree oven for 15 to 20 minutes or until asparagus is nicely roasted. Sprinkle on cheese and heat another 5 minutes or until cheese is warm and asparagus is desired tenderness.

Song: The Great Asparagus Caper - Disc 1 - Song 11 - Rock Style - Medium Tempo

The unique combination of aspargus and capers in this dish suggested the name for the recipe, and the tune. The double-meaning of caper made me think of a spy or adventure movie, which lead me to feature the bongos.

Smoothies and Drinks

Banana-Macadamia-Carob Shake

Carrots and Friends

Chakra Juice

Festive and Fruity Mulled White Wine

Fresh Orange-Grapefruit Juice

Frothy Cantaloupe Drink

Healthy Wassail

Sunshine Citrus Smoothie

Tropical Shake

Watermelon Cooler

Banana, Macadamia, Carob Shake

Serves 2

Due to the delicious combination of ingredients, this shake is bound to become a favorite of children and adults.

Ingredients:

2 bananas, frozen and sliced

1/4 cup Macadamia nuts, ground

1 cup water, milk, plain yogurt, or plain kefir

2 tablespoons carob powder

1-2 teaspoons flaxseeds, ground

2 scoops protein powder of your choice (optional)

Tips:

Whole milk can be used instead of making nut milk.

Decide whether you prefer a thick or thin shake. Using frozen bananas will yield a thick shake. For a lighter drink, do not freeze bananas. If not using frozen bananas, you might want to add some ice cubes to chill drink a bit.

Directions:

Grind nuts in blender and add water, yoghurt or kefir. Bingo - you have a yummy, light nut milk. Add all other ingredients and blend together. If too thick, add more liquid.

Carrots and Friends

Serves 2

You will need a juicer for this recipe. We absorb more nutrients when vegetables and fruits are juiced. To ensure full benefit of nutrients, it is best to drink fresh juice within 15 minutes of juicing. This is one of the most delicious, nutritious drinks full of antioxidants, and healthy benefits. I highly recommend using organic vegetables and fruits in this drink.

Ingredients:

1 pound carrots

3 celery stalks

1 beet

1 apple or firm pear

1 garlic clove, small

1 handful of parsley

1 or 2 radishes (optional)

Tips:
If vegetables and fruits are not organic, I recommend peeling fruit and vegetables prior to juicing.

Directions:

Wash all ingredients. Cut ends off carrots, celery, and beet. Quarter apples and remove seeds. If using a firm pear, cut in half and remove stem and seeds. Peel garlic. Place ingredients one at a time in a juicer, and continue to add vegetables, fruit, parsley, and garlic until all are blended. Pour into glasses, stir and enjoy!

Chakra Juice

Serves 3 - 4

Some of you may be wondering, what is a Chakra? A Chakra is a spinning wheel of light, an energy center in the body. There are 7 main chakras and each is associated with a particular color. When we eat foods of a particular color we nourish, stimulate, and strengthen certain parts of the body. As this drink contains all the colors of the rainbow, a glass of chakra juice will support the whole body.

Ingredients:

1-1 1/4 cups apple juice, organic

1/2 cup strawberries, fresh or frozen

1/4 cup papaya, fresh or frozen

1/4 cup mango, fresh or frozen

1/2 cup pineapple, fresh or frozen

1/2 cup honeydew melon

1/3 cup blueberries, fresh or frozen

2 tablespoons organic grape juice

mint springs for garnish

Tip:
This is a thick and frothy drink which looks very festive served in a martini or other special glass.

Directions:

Combine in a blender apple juice, strawberries, papaya, mango, pineapple, honeydew, blueberries, and grape juice, and blend until thoroughly mixed. Pour into glasses, garnish with a sprig of mint and serve.

Song: Chakra Juice - Disc 2 - Song 9 - Rock Style - Slow Tempo

The seven sections of this tune represents the seven Chakras. Each Chakra is related to a note of the seven-note scale (C-D-E-F-G-A-B), so this song moves musically and energetically up through the seven Chakra keys.

Festive and Fruity Mulled White Wine

This delicious mulled wine is great for winter gatherings.

Ingredients:

1 bottle dry white wine
(*Cook's choice* - Savignon Blanc)

2 1/4 cups water (as needed)

1 tablespoon fresh ginger or
2 teaspoons dried ginger

peel from 1/2 lemon, cut in small strips

1/2 lemon

1 small apple, sliced

2 teaspoons whole allspice

2 teaspoons whole cloves

4 cinnamon sticks

6-8 whole star anise

1/4 cup sugar or more to taste

Tip:

Wine can be kept on low heat for 1-2 hours, but spices need to be removed with slotted spoon or through mesh strainer to prevent wine from becoming bitter.

Optional additions:

2 tablespoons dried cranberries, orange peel, or 1 pear, sliced.

Choosing wine:

It need not be expensive, but do use something that is drinkable.

Directions:

Add 1 1/4 cups water to saucepan. Add ginger and lemon peel, reserving some peel for garnish, and simmer over low heat. Squeeze lemon over apple and add to saucepan. Continue to heat 10 more minutes on low. Add wine and remaining spices. Heat another 20 minutes on low, adding remaining water slowly during the cooking as liquid evaporates. Keep heat as low as possible during cooking so wine doesn't boil. When fruit begins to disintegrate, remove it with a slotted spoon. Add sugar near end of cooking. Strain and serve in glass mugs. Garnish with remaining lemon peel.

Method:

Cook's choice - add spices directly to saucepan for best flavor. Spices should be strained before serving. For simplicity, spices can be placed in a small mesh cloth bag but additional spices may be desired because the flavors will not come through as much. With this method there is no need to strain spices, just remove bag and serve.

Submitted by:

Wendy Carter

Fresh Orange-Grapefruit Juice

Serves 2

Juice is thick and foamy with a beautiful light pink color. Once you make your own juice, you will never go back to store bought!

Ingredients:

2 navel oranges

1 large pink grapefruit

> **Tips:**
>
> Pith is the white matter under the peel that contains valuable bioflavonoids and provides anti-cancer benefits.
>
> Juice is best served within 15 minutes to ensure full benefit of nutrients.

Directions:

With a sharp knife, remove peel from oranges and grapefruit being careful to leave as much of the pith as possible. Cut each fruit into 6 wedges and place one at a time into a juicer. Stir and serve immediately after juicing.

Frothy Cantaloupe Drink

Serves 2 - 3

Such a simple treat to make that is delicious as well as nutritious! Drink will be foamy and have a beautiful orange color.

Ingredients:

1 cantaloupe

fresh mint, for garnish

Directions:

Remove skin from cantaloupe, remove seeds, and cut into 1" pieces. Place 1/2 cup of cut fruit into blender and blend until liquefied. Continue adding cantaloupe and blending until well mixed. Pour into fancy glasses and garnish with a sprig or two of fresh mint.

Healthy Wassail (hot mulled drink)

Yields approximately 6 - 7 cups

Wassail refers to several traditions, the most common being an ancient Southern English celebration with the intention to ensure a good crop of cider apples for the next year's harvest. Its name also refers to the salute 'Waes Hail'. The term itself is a contraction of the Middle English phrase 'wæs hæil' which literally means 'good health' or 'be you healthy'. The drink was traditionally enjoyed during the holiday season, and one we now enjoy sharing with friends and family on cold winter evenings to warm the heart and spirit.

Ingredients:

4 cups apple juice or cider
(*Cook's choice* - organic)

1 cup cranberry juice
(*Cook's choice* - organic)

1/3 cup sugar

3 cinnamon sticks

1 teaspoon ground allspice

1 1/2 teaspoon whole cloves,
about 40 or as needed

1 small orange, stud with cloves

3-5 slivers fresh ginger, thinly sliced (optional)

1 lime, thinly sliced and quartered (optional)

3/4 cup rum (optional)

> **Tips:**
>
> Recipe is appropriate for small crockpot. If you have a large crockpot, double recipe.
>
> No crockpot? Simply place all ingredients in a large pot. Bring to boil, then lower heat and gently simmer for 2-4 hours.

Directions:

For this recipe I use a crock pot. If you don't have a crock pot, see directions for stove top in tip box above. Place juices, sugar, cinnamon sticks, allspice, orange that has been studded with cloves, ginger, and rum into crock pot. Cover and cook on low setting 2-8 hours. About one hour prior to serving add lime slices so they have a chance to soften, add extra flavor, and color when served. While wassail slowly cooks all day, your home will be filled with its wonderful aromas. Fill mugs and add a bit of the fresh fruit. Here's to your health!

Sunshine Fruit Smoothie

Serves 3

A refreshingly light in color and texture smoothie to enjoy in Springtime as the weather begins to turn warmer and we are welcomed with the gift of more sunshine. The colorful combination of fruits provide a powerhouse of nutrients. This delicious drink is a rich source of vitamin C, flavonoids and phytochemicals which help protect the body. You also receive an abundant supply of potassium, phosphorus, and fiber from the oranges and bananas.

Ingredients:

3 ripe bananas, cut into chunks

1 cup fresh pineapple, cut into chunks

1 orange, freshly squeezed

1/2 lemon, freshly squeezed

1/2 lime, freshly squeezed

1 cup plain yogurt, whole fat (Cook's choice - Greek Gods)

fresh mint sprigs for garnish (optional)

Directions:

Combine all ingredients in blender and blend until smooth. Serve at once in tall glasses and garnish with a sprig of fresh mint.

Tropical Shake

Serves 2

I try to always keep some bananas on hand in the freezer to be used in shakes. So, if you have bananas getting too ripe, just peel, slice, wrap, and place in freezer for future smoothies. Bananas should keep in freezer for about 2 weeks. You can also store pineapple, mango, and papaya in the freezer to be used whenever you crave a yummy drink.

Ingredients:

1 mango

2 bananas

1 cup pineapple

1 tablespoon flax seed or coconut flour

1 cup water, plain yogurt, or kefir

2 scoops protein powder of your choice (optional)

Tips:
Adjust fruits for personal preference. Add some ice cubes for a colder, thicker shake. However, if you use some frozen bananas and frozen pineapple, there is no need for ice.

Directions:

Peel and slice mango. Peel and slice bananas into chunks. Cut rind off pineapple and cut into chunks. Pour water, yogurt, or kefir, whichever is your preference, into blender. Add all fruit and flax seed or coconut flour. If using protein powder, add last to not over blend.

Song: Tropical Shake - Disc 1 - Song 10 - Samba Style - Fast Tempo
This song uses Latin American rhythms with a splash of jazz. It just might make you want to get up and shake something!

Watermelon Cooler

Serves 2 - 3

Once blended, the cooler takes on a beautiful pale pink color with a wonderful frothy texture that is refreshingly light making this the perfect drink for hot Summer evenings.

Ingredients:

4 cups watermelon chunks, remove seeds and rind

1/4 cup mint tea, cool to room temperature and chill

5 large mint leaves

mint for garnish (optional)

Tips:

Great non-alcoholic drink, and versatile enough to be used at an evening cocktail party by simply adding your favorite alcohol to create a watermelon martini cooler.

Directions:

Place watermelon chunks in a blender. Add tea and mint leaves. Blend well until completely smooth. Pour into fancy glasses and garnish with a sprig of mint if desired.

Soups and Stews

Aunt Marilyn's Zucchini Soup

Butternut Squash Soup Enhanced with Sweet Potato

Carrot-Parsnip Soup

Cauliflower and Potato Soup

Corn Vegetable Chowder

Cream of Pumpkin Soup

Dairy Free Cream of Asparagus Soup

Gazpacho Cold Soup

Hearty Minestrone Soup

Lentil Stew

Light Vegetable Fish Chowder

Madagascar Stew

Potato-Broccoli-Leek Soup

Spicy Creole Fish Stew

Split Pea Soup

Sweet and Spicy Cod Stew

Aunt Marilyn's Zucchini Soup

Ingredients:

4 cups zucchini, chopped (about 2 pounds)

2 onions, chopped

5 garlic cloves, chopped

extra virgin olive oil

2 cups chicken broth

2 teaspoons curry powder

1/2 teaspoon black pepper

dash red pepper

1 teaspoon salt (optional)

Directions:

Sauté zucchini, onions, and garlic in a little olive oil until transparent. Let cool. Add to a blender and blend well. Transfer mixture to saucepan and add chicken broth, curry, pepper, and salt. Simmer for one hour. Adjust spices to taste.

Submitted by:

Laura Melisi's Aunt Marilyn

Butternut Squash Soup Enhanced with Sweet Potato

Serves 4

Ingredients:

3 tablespoons extra virgin olive oil

3-4 garlic cloves, chopped

1 large onion, chopped

4 cups butternut squash, peeled and chopped

1 cup sweet potato, peeled and chopped

3 cups chicken broth

2-3 tablespoons fresh ginger, chopped

1/2 teaspoon ground coriander

1/2 teaspoon ground cinnamon

freshly ground peppercorns, to taste

fresh cilantro, parsley, or chives for garnish

Directions:

Heat oil in soup pot. Add onions and cook over medium heat until soft and almost caramelized. Add garlic and cook another minute or so. Add squash and sweet potato and continue to cook for another 5-10 minutes, stirring occasionally until everything is well blended. Add chicken broth, ginger, coriander, cinnamon, and peppercorns. Stir, cover pot, reduce heat, and simmer for about 45 minutes. When squash and sweet potatoes are soft, remove from pot, place in a blender or food processor and blend until smooth. Return to pot with chicken broth, stir until well blended, and heat for a few more minutes. Serve with garnished herbs if desired.

Carrot-Parsnip Soup

Serves 6 - 8

A delicious, creamy soup without the need for any thickener or cream. Also a dairy-free version when olive oil is substituted for butter.

Ingredients:

1 1/2 pounds carrots

1/2 pound parsnips or sweet potatoes

1 tablespoon butter or extra virgin olive oil

1 1/4 cups onion, chopped

2-3 garlic cloves, minced

4 cups water or chicken broth

1-1 1/2 tablespoons ginger, freshly grated or 1/2-1 teaspoon ground

1/4 teaspoon ground cumin

1/4 teaspoon ground allspice

1/2 teaspoon ground cinnamon

1/8 teaspoon ground coriander

1/8 teaspoon cayenne pepper or to taste

1/4 teaspoon sea salt

1/2 cup raw cashews, toasted

fresh cilantro or parsley, chopped for garnish

Tips:

Add a little extra water or chicken broth if you prefer a thinner soup.

Soup freezes very well.

Directions:

Peel carrots and parsnips or sweet potatoes and cut into 1" pieces. Heat butter or oil in soup pot, add onions and sauté over medium heat for about 5 minutes. Add half the garlic and spices. Turn heat to low and sauté for another 8-10 minutes until onions are very soft. Add carrots, parsnips or sweet potatoes, and water or chicken broth to onions and spices, and bring to a boil. While vegetables and broth come to a boil, toast cashews in small pan until lightly brown or add to pot without toasting. Lower heat and simmer until vegetables are tender about 20 minutes depending on size of pieces. Use a blender to puree everything together in small batches. After blending, return to pot, stir in remaining chopped garlic, and gently warm. Garnish with some chopped fresh cilantro or parsley.

Cauliflower and Potato Soup

Serves 4

Ingredients:
1 onion, chopped

1 teaspoon extra virgin olive oil

1 head cauliflower, chopped

4 white potatoes, peeled and cubed

4 cups chicken broth, vegetable broth, or water

1/4 teaspoon black pepper

4 garlic cloves, chopped

3 scallions, sliced for garnish

Directions:
Saute onion in oil. Cook cauliflower and potatoes in broth or water until soft. Add cooked onions, black pepper, 2 garlic cloves, and cook a few minutes. Set aside about 1 cup of vegetables. Blend remaining vegetables in small batches in a blender until thick. Return blended mixture to pot, add unblended vegetables, remaining garlic, and stir. Warm soup for another 10 minutes or until desired temperature. Serve with some scallions on top.

Corn Vegetable Chowder

Serves 4 as a main course

Some of the inspiration for this recipe came from my much treasured Moosewood Cookbook and another of my favorite books, Vegetarian Pleasures as well as my personal preferences that resulted in the blending of farm fresh vegetables and fresh herbs to create a healthy, hearty Fall and Winter soup.

Ingredients:

3 fresh corn cobs or 1 1/2-2 cups frozen corn
(*Cook's choice* - white, local grown)

1 tablespoon butter

2 tablespoons extra virgin olive oil

2 medium onions, chopped

2 stalks celery, chopped

2 carrots, chopped

4-6 garlic cloves, minced

1 teaspoon paprika

4 1/2 cups water

2 large potatoes, peeled and diced (about 2 1/2 cups)

1 1/2 cups broccoli, chopped

1 cup cauliflower, chopped

1 bay leaf

1/4 cup fresh cilantro or parsley, minced

1/2 teaspoon dried thyme

1/2 teaspoon Himalayan salt

few dashes cayenne pepper

black pepper, freshly ground to taste

2 scallions, thinly sliced

2 small slices of Astragalus root (optional)

extra cilantro, for garnish (optional)

1/4 cup light cream, (optional)

1 scallion, thinly sliced for garnish

Continued on next page...

Corn Vegetable Chowder (continued)

Directions:

If using fresh corn, shuck husks and remove silk. In a large pot add water and cook corn until tender. Remove corn from its cooking liquid but do not discard cooking liquid as this is the base for the soup. Allow corn cobs to cool a bit before slicing niblets off the cob. In a large skillet add butter, oil, onions, celery, carrots, and half the garlic, and sauté over medium heat about 10 minutes or until onions are tender but not brown. Sprinkle on paprika, stir, and cook 1 minute. Add this mixture to pot of water the corn cooked in and add potatoes, broccoli, cauliflower, corn, bay leaf, cilantro, thyme, salt, and pepper. Cover pot and cook about 15 minutes or until vegetables are tender. Stir in two scallions and cook 2 more minutes. Remove bay leaf and Astragalus root. Depending on how chunky you like your chowder, scoop out 3-4 cups of chowder, puree, and return to pot. Stir in remaining garlic and cayenne. Heat for another 5 minutes. Ladle chowder into a bowl and garnish with scallions and cilantro or parsley.

Tip:

The use of Astragalus root gives a nice boost to the immune system. As it is woody, you will want to remove it before blending. Soup is nice and creamy without the addition of cream, but can be added for a richer version.

Cream of Pumpkin Soup

Ingredients:

3 tablespoons butter

1 cup yellow sweet onion, chopped

1 32-ounce box chicken broth, organic

1 15-ounce can pumpkin

1/2 cup whole milk, organic

1 1/2 teaspoon sea salt

1/2 teaspoon ground cinnamon

1/2 teaspoon ground ginger

1/4 teaspoon ground nutmeg

1/8 teaspoon ground black pepper

5 tablespoons brown sugar

1 1/2 tablespoons raw honey

Cracked black pepper (12 turns of pepper mill)

> **Serving Suggestion:**
> Serve in mini pumpkins. Cut tops off pumpkins, hollow out removing seeds and strings, and scrape inside with a spoon to smooth.

Directions:

Sauté onion in butter in saucepan until tender. Add half the chicken broth and bring to a boil. Reduce the heat and simmer 15 minutes. Add remaining half of chicken broth, pumpkin, and milk. Mix together and transfer mixture to blender. Blend until smooth. Return mixture to stove top. Add spices, and brown sugar. Heat on medium high until mixture just begins to bubble. Reduce heat and simmer 10 minutes. Turn heat off, add honey and stir until well blended.

Submitted by:

Sheri Santo | www.sherisanto.com

Dairy Free Cream of Asparagus Soup

Serves 6

This light, flavorful soup is a dairy-free alternative to a traditional creamed soup. Potatoes, the secret ingredient, are used as a thickener, flavor enhancer, and replace the need for cream to achieve a velvety, creamy texture.

Ingredients:

2 pounds fresh asparagus

5 1/2 cups water

3 tablespoons butter

1 large onion, chopped

2-3 large garlic cloves, minced

2 cups red potatoes

1/2 teaspoon Himalayan salt

1/4 teaspoon black pepper

1 tablespoon fresh dill (optional)

sprigs of dill for garnish (optional)

cayenne pepper, to taste (optional)

1/2 teaspoon kuzu, arrowroot or cornstarch (optional)

Tip:

For a nice presentation, drizzle a bit of puree made from the potato, onion, garlic mixture (that was set aside) on top of soup prior to serving. Adding a sprig of fresh dill or sprinkle some minced dill on top is nice too. Soup can be made without potatoes but you will want to add a thickener of your choice. Prior to serving, mix kuzu or arrowroot with some cold water or cooled asparagus broth and stir until well blended. Add a bit at a time to soup and stir until desired consistency. Any leftover asparagus cooking liquid can be frozen to be used in the future in another recipe.

Directions:

Snap ends off asparagus, wash and snap or cut into 1 inch pieces. Bring 4 cups water to a boil, add asparagus, and simmer until fork tender. In a separate pot, melt butter, onion, and half the garlic, and sauté until onions are soft and a bit caramelized. Peel potatoes and chop into small pieces. In another pot, bring 1 1/2 cups water to a boil, add potatoes, and simmer until soft. Remove potatoes and set aside potato water. Add potatoes to sautéed onion garlic mixture with 1 cup potato cooking liquid and blend until nice and creamy. Put pureed potato mixture in a large pot but set aside 1/4 cup of mixture to drizzle on top prior to serving. Blend half the asparagus, about 2 cups, with some of the cooking liquid and add to pot with potato mixture. Blend remaining asparagus, remaining potato cooking liquid, and some cooking liquid from asparagus and add to pot. Stir in dill if using, remaining garlic, salt, and pepper and gently heat a few minutes. Adjust spices as needed. Pour into bowls and drizzle a little of the blended potato mixture over the top of the soup. Add a little dill or few twists of black pepper.

Gazpacho

Yields 3 Cups

During Summer there is an abundance of fresh vegetables and herbs, so this recipe can easily be doubled or tripled.

Ingredients:
6 fresh tomatoes, chopped
1/2 cup cucumber, chopped small
1/2 cup green pepper, chopped small
1/4 of a lemon, freshly squeezed
1/2 of a lime, freshly squeezed
1 tablespoon extra virgin olive oil
1 tablespoon parsley, finely minced
1 teaspoon cilantro, finely minced
1 jalapeno or anaheim pepper, finely chopped or 1/8 teaspoon tabasco
1/2 teaspoon ume plum vinegar or red wine vinegar
3 garlic cloves, chopped
fresh basil, chopped for garnish
1/8 teaspoon ground red pepper (optional)

Directions:
Wash tomatoes and remove skin. To more easily remove skin, boil some water, place tomatoes in hot water, remove from heat and leave in hot water for 5 minutes. Carefully remove tomatoes from hot water, hold under running cold water to cool a bit. Skins should then be easy to remove. Depending on how chunky you like your gazpacho, chop 1 or 2 tomatoes into small chunks. Cut remaining tomatoes into quarters and place in a blender. Peel cucumber, remove seeds, mince, and place in blender with tomatoes, reserving about 1/2 of chopped cucumber to add later. Wash pepper, remove seeds and ribs, chop, add to blender, and set aside about 1/2 of the pepper to add later. Squeeze lemon and lime juice into blender. Add oil, spices, pepper or tabasco, vinegar, and garlic to tomatoes and vegetables in blender and whirl until well blended. Add reserved chopped veggies, about 1 cup to blended ingredients. Chill one hour, stir, pour into bowls, and garnish with chopped basil.

Hearty Minestrone Soup

Serves 4 or more

Ingredients:

4 cups water

1 onion, chopped

3 large carrots, peeled and chopped

2 cups fresh green beans, snip off ends and chop

1 cup fresh mushrooms, sliced

3 cups fresh tomatoes, chopped or 1 24-ounce can

1/2 cup fresh basil chopped or 2 tablespoons dried

1 tablespoon fresh oregano, chopped or 1 teaspoon dried

4-6 garlic cloves, chopped

1/3 cup uncooked organic white rice

2 cups kidney beans, canned or dry cooked per package instructions

> **Tip:**
> For directions for cooking dry beans, see Grains and Legumes chapter.

Directions:

In large soup pot combine water, onion, carrots, green beans, mushrooms, tomatoes, basil, oregano, and half the garlic. Bring to boil. Reduce heat, cover and simmer 45 minutes. Add rice and kidney beans and cook another 30 minutes or until vegetables are tender. Add remainder of garlic 15 minutes before done.

Lentil-Vegetable Stew

Serves 6 - 7

One Summer I bought an organic tomato plant to grow in a planter on our porch. As the plant started growing, it was evident it was not a tomato plant at all but a jalapeno plant! Fortunately, we love hot peppers because this plant produced many. At season's end, I brought the plant inside and over the winter it gave us 3 more peppers. The next Summer was fabulous weather for vegetables so, back outside on the porch the plant went. To my surprise, again it continued to produce the hottest and most delicious peppers so we named it "the plant that keeps on giving." This makes for a very sweet and spicy stew. Also, you wouldn't even know there are lentils in it unless someone told you so its great for children or people who think they don't like lentils.

Ingredients:

6 cups water

1 cup red lentils

3 medium carrots, peeled and chopped

1 large sweet red pepper, chopped

1 small onion, chopped

1 small zucchini or 1 1/2 cups green beans, chopped

2 cups cauliflower

1/4 teaspoon dried oregano

1/4 teaspoon dried thyme

2 pieces kombu, about 5" long

1 tablespoon arame seaweed, break into 1" pieces or wakame

1 1/2 cups fresh tomatoes or 1, 14-ounce can tomatoes

3 garlic cloves, chopped

1/4 teaspoon Himalayan salt or to taste

1 cup arugula, chopped (optional)

1 small hot pepper, finely minced (optional)

fresh basil, minced for garnish (optional)

Tips:

Check your jalapeno pepper for heat. If pepper is very hot you can set aside the seeds to dry and save to use another time. Discard the thin membrane as it is very hot. You may also want to wear gloves while cutting hot pepper or hold with a paper towel to protect your fingers from the pepper's heat. No need for additional pepper if you use a jalapeno and little salt is needed if you use seaweed. For anyone not into lots of spice, just eliminate the hot pepper and add black pepper to taste.

Directions:

Place water and lentils in a large soup pot and bring to a boil. Add vegetables but not tomatoes, spices, kombu and arame to pot. Reduce heat, cover pot, and simmer for 45 minutes. Add tomatoes and garlic, and continue to simmer for another 30-45 minutes or until vegetables are desired tenderness.

Light Fish-Vegetable Chowder

Serves 7

A nice light soup that is dairy-free without the need for any cream or added thickeners. If you prefer a chowder that is bit thicker, remove one cup or less of chowder once fully cooked, and whirl in a blender until creamy. Slowly add back into soup stirring until all mixed.

Ingredients:

1 tablespoon butter

1 cup onion, remove skin and chop

2 green onions, sliced

2 carrots, peel and chop

4 cups organic chicken broth or vegetable broth

1 cup water

3 cups potatoes, peel and cube

2 cups broccoli, chopped

3/4 cup fresh mushrooms, sliced

2 tablespoons uncooked long-grain rice

1/2 teaspoon dill weed

1/4 cup fresh parsley, finely chopped

1/8 teaspoon black pepper

1 tablespoon spelt, whole wheat or flour of choice

3 cloves garlic, minced

1/2 pound white fish, cut in chunks (cod, flounder, or turbot)

1/2 cup fresh or frozen corn (optional)

sea salt to taste (optional)

Directions:

In large pot melt butter. Briefly sauté onion, green onions and carrots and cook 10 min. Add chicken broth, water, potatoes, broccoli, mushrooms, corn, rice, and spices. Cover pot and simmer until all ingredients are fully cooked, about 20 minutes. Remove 2 tablespoons of broth from pot, add flour to it and stir until smooth. Add flour mixture to soup a little at a time, stirring until completely blended. Add fish and garlic to soup, stir, and cook about 10 minutes until fish is fully cooked.

Madagascar Stew

Serves 4 - 6

This island stew is filled with a variety of flavors that will leave your mouth enjoying the spices long after your bowl is empty. Serve over some coconut rice (see recipe below), couscous, or kasha to complete the meal. And you will definitely want to check out the song on CD #1 while you cook.

Ingredients:

1 1/2 cups onion, diced

1 1/2 cups carrots, thinly sliced diagonally

2 teaspoons extra virgin olive oil, cold pressed

2 cups water

1/2 teaspoon sea salt

1/2 teaspoon dried thyme

1/2 teaspoon ground allspice

1/2 teaspoon ground cinnamon

1 1/2 teaspoons fresh ginger, finely chopped

2-3 teaspoons fresh lime juice with pulp

2 cups sweet potato, peel and chop

1 14.5-ounce can organic fire roasted diced tomatoes with green chilies (optional)

1 teaspoon Madagascar vanilla

2 cups fresh rainbow chard or spinach, thinly sliced

Coconut Rice, (optional)

Options:

Use fresh tomatoes or roast fresh tomatoes instead of using canned and a chili pepper. Although chili peppers are optional, they do lend incredible flavor to the stew.

Coconut Rice:

To 1 cup of white rice, add 1 cup organic coconut milk (not light) and 1 cup water. Add a little cilantro, shake of cayenne or black pepper and salt. Cook rice according to directions.

Directions:

Sauté together onions and carrots in oil. Add water and spices and bring to boil. Turn heat down, add lime juice, and sweet potato, and simmer 30 minutes. Add tomatoes, vanilla, and greens, and continue simmering for another 30 minutes or until vegetables are desired tenderness.

Song: Madagascar Stew - Disc 1 - Song #8 - African Style - Fast Tempo

This song, like the stew, mixes many flavors, including the free-spirited rhythms of the music of Madagascar, with a dash of jazz.

Potato, Broccoli, Leek Soup

Serves 8

This soup is thick, delicious, and stands on its own as a dairy free recipe. For those that prefer an extra boost of calcium, you have the option to add a bit of milk.

Ingredients:

2 tablespoons butter

1 1/2 cups leeks, chopped

2 tablespoons kamet, spelt, or flour of your choice

4 cups chicken broth

1 cup water

4 cups potatoes, peeled and sliced

3 garlic cloves, chopped

1/4 teaspoon sea salt or to taste

1/4 teaspoon pepper or to taste

3 cups broccoli, chopped

1/2 cup organic milk (optional)

Directions:

In large pot melt butter, add leeks, and cook until leeks are soft. Add flour and stir until well blended. Add a little chicken broth to flour mixture and stir until well blended. Add remaining broth, water, potatoes, 2 garlic cloves, salt, pepper, and bring to boil. Reduce heat and simmer partially covered for about 35 minutes or until potatoes are tender. While potatoes cook, steam broccoli until tender. Add half the broccoli to potato mixture, the third garlic clove, and pour into blender a little at a time. Purée until smooth. If using milk, blend a little at a time to be sure soup doesn't become too thin. Pour soup back into pot, add remaining broccoli, adjust seasoning, stir to blend, and re-warm up a bit. Serve in a bowl or mug with a few twists of fresh ground pepper, if desired.

Split Pea Soup

Serves 6

This one is so easy! Once prep work is done, just leave it to simmer on top of the stove. The delicious aroma will fill your home, as you contemplate the warm and yummy treat soon to come.

Ingredients:

1 1/2 cups dried split peas

6 cups water

1 large onion, chopped

3-4 carrots, peeled and chopped

1/2 cup celery, chopped

3 garlic cloves, chopped

1/3 teaspoon ground pepper

1/4 teaspoon dried thyme

1 teaspoon dried cumin

1 bay leaf

sea salt to taste (optional)

Tip:
You can blend mixture if you prefer but really no need to.

Directions:

Sort and wash peas and put in a large glass covered pan or soup pot. Add water, peas, and remaining ingredients, and bring to a boil. Cover, reduce heat, and simmer 2 1/2-3 hours until peas and carrots are tender. Stir soup, adjust salt and pepper, and blend or just serve.

Spicy Creole Fish Stew

Serves 4 - 6

Ingredients:

1/3 cup canola oil

1/3 cup gluten free all-purpose baking flour

1 cup red onion, chopped

1 jalapeno pepper, chopped

1 cup carrots, chopped

1 cup celery, chopped (about 4 large stalks)

3 garlic cloves, minced

1 teaspoon paprika

1 teaspoon fresh thyme or 1/2 teaspoon dried

1/4 teaspoon cayenne pepper or to taste

1, 14 1/2-ounce can diced tomatoes

1 cup water

2 cups vegetable broth

1/2 cup long grain white rice

sea salt to taste

ground pepper to taste

1 1/2 pounds cod or tilapia fillets, cut into 2" pieces

1 teaspoon Cajun seasoning

1/3 cup green onions, thinly sliced

2 tablespoons chopped fresh parsley, chopped

Directions:

Heat oil over medium heat in a large heavy-bottomed soup pot or Dutch oven. Slowly stir in flour. Cook mixture 10 to 15 minutes, stirring occasionally until it turns the color of milk chocolate. Add onion, jalapeno pepper, carrots, and celery to pot and cook, stirring, 5 to 7 minutes until vegetables are softened. Add garlic, paprika, thyme, and cayenne pepper and cook for two more minutes. Add tomatoes, water, and vegetable broth and bring to a boil. Stir in rice and salt and pepper to taste. Reduce heat to low, cover pot, and simmer for 25 minutes. While simmering, season fish on both sides with Cajun seasoning. Add fish to pot, making sure the pieces are completely submerged in the liquid. Cover and continue to simmer 7 to 10 more minutes, or until fish is cooked through. Stir in sliced green onions and chopped parsley just before serving.

Submitted by:

Sheri Santo | www.sherisanto.com

" The smell of good bread baking, like the sound of lightly flowing water, is indescribable in it's evocation of innocence and delight."

– MFK Fisher

EGGLESS PUMPKIN RICOTTA MUFFINS OR CAKE - page 253

This and That

A little bit of this and a little bit of that makes up this category

Buckwheat Crepes and Fillings

Eggless Pumpkin Ricotta Muffins or Cake

Fra Diavalo - Sauce

Laura's Apple Stuffing

Marinade for Vegetables

Mushroom Sauce

Out of This World Stuffed Sandwich

Play Dough - Not Just for Kids

Sausage Quiche with Home Made French Pastry Crust

Sauteed Apples with a Kick

Soup Matzo Balls

Tomatillo Sauce

Buckwheat Crepes with a Quartet of Fillings

Yields - 6, 8" crepes, depending on pan size

As buckwheat flour is a non gluten flour, it is a great substitute for anyone avoiding wheat. The nuttiness of the flour lends depth and flavor to the crepes and the coconut milk adds a subtle sweetness eliminating the need for any sweetener.

Ingredients:

3 large eggs

1/2 cup buckwheat flour

1/2 cup organic coconut milk (not light) or whole milk

1 cup water

1 tablespoon butter, melted

1 teaspoon sugar, use only if not using coconut milk

> **Note:**
> Batter can be made a day ahead and refrigerated for convenience. Leftover unfilled crepes can be stored in freezer individually wrapped in parchment paper or wax paper and placed in a freezer bag. Thaw crepes and warm covered in a 300 degree oven for about 5 minutes before filling.

Directions:

Measure all ingredients into a bowl and beat until smooth. Batter should be fairly thin and you may need to adjust milk or water depending on the kind of milk you use. Oil or butter skillet. If using an 8" inch skillet, pour in about 1/2 cup of batter or enough to cover the bottom. Tilt pan to evenly coat or use a pastry brush to spread thinly. Use medium heat and cook one crepe at a time until lightly brown and bottom is set. Use a thin spatula to loosen edges and slide spatula under crepe to turn it over. Cook for another minute or until lightly browned. Remove crepe from pan and place on parchment paper on top rack of a slightly warm oven to keep warm. Repeat the process with remaining batter until all crepes have been cooked, adding additional oil or butter as needed so crepes do not stick to pan. Spoon filling of your choice into center of crepe and roll up crepe. Place crepe seam side down on plate and use a garnish or sauce of your choice, which is optional.

Continued on next page...

Buckwheat Crepes with a Quartet of Fillings (continued)

4 Filling Suggestions

Spinach and Goat Cheese Filling Ingredients:

1 7-ounce bag fresh organic spinach, chopped or frozen

1/4 cup red or white onion or shallots, chopped

1 tablespoon butter

1/4 teaspoon sea salt

1/4 teaspoon black pepper

3-ounces goat cheese, crumbled

dash or two cayenne (optional)

tomatoes, sliced (optional)

Parmesan cheese, freshly grated to garnish tomatoes, optional

Spinach and Goat Cheese Directions:

Steam spinach until tender. Drain excess water and set aside. As spinach steams, sauté onions in butter until slightly caramelized. Add spinach, salt, and peppers to onions and continue to sauté a few minutes. Stir in goat cheese until blended and warm. Give a final stir. Place some filling in center of each crepe and roll up. Slice tomatoes, sprinkle with cheese, and broil tomato slices until cheese lightly browns. Place one tomato slice on top of each crepe and serve.

Vegetable Filling Ingredients:

2 cups cabbage, thinly sliced

2 cups bok choy, thinly sliced

1/2 cup mushrooms, thinly sliced

1/4 cup daikon, thinly sliced

1/2 cup red pepper, thinly sliced

1 tablespoon dry white wine

2 tablespoons butter

1/4 teaspoon Himalayan salt

1/4 teaspoon black pepper

1/2 cup cheese, shredded (optional)

Continued on next page...

Buckwheat Crepes with a Quartet of Fillings (continued)

Vegetable Filling Directions:

Slice all vegetables and sauté in butter with spices until close to desired tenderness. Add wine and sauté a bit longer until liquid has reduced. Place some filling in center of each crepe, roll up, sprinkle some cheese over each crepe, and warm until cheese melts.

Strawberries with Orange Raspberry Cream Filling Ingredients:

1 quart organic strawberries, thinly sliced

3/4 cup powdered sugar

1 cup organic whipping cream

1 tablespoon triple sec or orange juice

1 tablespoon Chambord Liqueur Royale or natural raspberry flavoring

Strawberries with Orange Raspberry Cream Filling Directions:

Place a metal bowl and beaters in freezer until well chilled. Meanwhile slice strawberries and sprinkle sugar over them. Stir until well blended. Set aside for 30 minutes for sugar to break down and create juice from strawberries. Set aside about 1/2 cup of strawberries and juice. Once bowl and beaters are well chilled, add whipping cream and beat until cream begins to thicken, then slowly add in triple sec or orange juice, and Chambord or raspberry flavoring and beat until thick. Gently fold in strawberries until well blended. Fill crepes, roll up, and drizzle a little of the reserved strawberries and juice over each crepe.

Southwest Scrambled Eggs Ingredients:

2 cups fresh spinach, chopped or frozen

1/4 cup onions, chopped

1 tablespoon extra virgin olive oil

4 large eggs

1 garlic clove, chopped

4 tablespoons water

sea salt and pepper to taste

salsa (optional)

Southwest Scrambled Egg Filling Directions:

Lightly oil skillet and sauté spinach and onions together until onions are soft and spinach is wilted. While vegetables sauté, beat eggs with water, salt, and pepper. Add eggs and spices to vegetables and stir until well blended and eggs are almost set. Stir in garlic and continue to cook until eggs are cooked to personal preference. Spoon cooked egg and vegetable mixture into center of each crepe and roll up. Top each crepe with some salsa and serve.

Eggless Pumpkin Ricotta Muffins or Cake

Yields 12 to 14 muffins or a cake

Maybe you ran out of eggs or have an allergy to them, no fret you can still enjoy the bounty from your Fall pumpkin with this incredibly delicious and light recipe without the need for any eggs. Fall has always been a fun time for our family to enjoy our favorite family outings of apple picking and hunting for the perfect pumpkins which usually took a bit of time. After the girls and I would cook together using our bounty and my husband, Steve would play our favorite music blending it with the delicious cooking aromas.

Ingredients:

1 1/2 cups spelt flour or flour of choice
1/3 cup sugar
1 teaspoon baking soda
1 teaspoon baking powder
1/4 teaspoon sea salt
1/2 teaspoon ground cinnamon
1/4 teaspoon ground ginger
few shakes of ground cloves
3/4 cup pumpkin puree, fresh or canned
1/2 cup whole ricotta cheese
1/4 cup walnut or extra virgin olive oil
1 teaspoon Madagascar vanilla
1/2-3/4 cup chocolate chips (optional)
few teaspoons additional sugar (optional)

Tips:

Making pumpkin puree is very simple. Wash pumpkin, use a fork to poke a few times around the pumpkin, place in a dry glass or ceramic baking dish (no need to grease), and bake in oven at 400 degrees until golden brown, approximately 1 hour but time will vary depending on size of pumpkin and your oven. When pumpkin is golden and soft, remove from oven and allow to cool. Cut pumpkin in half, remove seeds and discard (or wash and roast seeds for snacks which is optional), scoop out pumpkin, and mash. Recipe can easily be doubled and cooked in a bundt or springform pan.

Note:

Recipe lends itself well for either dessert or breakfast, so I didn't fret and added it to this section - smiles!

Directions:

Preheat oven to 350 degrees. For muffins use unbleached paper baking cups or grease and lightly flour pan. For cake, grease and flour an 8 x 4 inch loaf pan. Place all dry ingredients in a bowl and stir until well mixed. In a separate bowl combine pumpkin puree, cheese, oil, vanilla, and beat until mixed. Add half the flour mixture to pumpkin cheese mixture and blend on low speed. Best to not over mix batter, so stir in remaining flour mixture, then chocolate if using, and stir just until all ingredients are incorporated into batter. Pour into prepared pans. Finish with a light sprinkle of sugar on top, which is optional, and bake muffins 25-30 minutes, loaf or round pan 45-50 minutes, or bundt or springform pan approximately 60 minutes or until done. I suggest checking prior to finish time to see if cooking time needs to be adjusted.

Fra Diavolo Sauce

Serves 4

The music is written by my husband, Steve Carter, to accompany the recipe Fra Diavolo. You can hear this music on CD# 1.

Ingredients:

2 tablespoons butter

2 tablespoons extra virgin cold pressed olive oil

1/4 cup shallots, chopped

3/4 cup red onions, chopped

4 1/2 cups fresh tomatoes, chopped

3/4 cup Cabernet Sauvignon red wine

1/2 teaspoon Himalayan or sea salt

1/4 teaspoon black pepper

1 teaspoon crushed red pepper flakes

1/2 teaspoon ground chili powder

1/2 teaspoon ground cumin

1/2 teaspoon dried oregano

2-3 large garlic cloves, chopped

2 tablespoons fresh Italian parsley, finely chopped or 2 teaspoons dried

2 tablespoons fresh basil, finely chopped or 2 teaspoons dried

Serving Suggestions:

Serve with DeBoles tomato and basil angel hair pasta made with Jerusalem artichoke flour which is Cook's choice, or use any pasta of your choice, spaghetti squash, rice, or quinoa. Place pasta, squash, or grain in center of plate. Top with seafood, chicken or a combination. Pour sauce over all and enjoy. So delicious!

Optional Add Ons:

Pan seared scallops, shrimp or lobster, or steamed mussels, grilled chicken or a combination.

Directions:

Melt butter in frying pan, add oil and heat on medium. Add shallots and onion and sauté until soft. Add tomatoes, wine, and all spices except for garlic. Simmer sauce for 45 minutes to meld flavors until slightly thickened. Add garlic and continue simmering for about 5 minutes or until garlic softens a bit.

Song: Fra Diavolo - Disc 1 - Song #4 - African - Medium-slow Tempo

"Fra Diavolo" is Italian for "Brother Devil." In this song I tried to capture the smoldering smokiness of the sauce. I used an Afro-Cuban drumbeat, featuring marimba and flute to suggest the smoldering fire, with the guitar and flute adding spiciness.

Laura's Apple Stuffing

Ingredients:

1 1/2 cups celery, chopped

3/4 cup onion, chopped

3/4 cup butter, cubed

9 cups day old bread, cubed (use 1/2 cinnamon loaf and 1/2 multi-grain loaf)

3 cups apples, finely chopped

3/4 cup plump soft organic raisins

1/2 teaspoon sea salt

1 1/2 teaspoon dried thyme

1/2 teaspoon dried rubbed sage

1/4 teaspoon black pepper

Directions:

Preheat oven to 350 degrees. Cube bread and leave out overnight. In a Dutch oven, sauté celery and onion in butter until tender. Remove from heat, stir in bread cubes, apples, raisins, salt, thyme, sage, and pepper. For stuffing a 12-13 pound turkey, use 2 cups of the stuffing; for stuffing a 14-16 pound turkey, use 4 cups of stuffing. Follow turkey baking instructions. Place remaining stuffing in a buttered 2-quart baking dish and refrigerate until ready to bake. Bake stuffing in a covered casserole dish for 20-30 minutes, then uncover and bake 10 minutes longer or until top is lightly browned.

Submitted by:

Laura Melisi, Flautist

Marinade for Grilled Vegetables

Ingredients:

2 1/2 tablespoons cold pressed extra virgin olive oil

1 1/2 tablespoons rice vinegar

1/2 lemon, freshly squeezed

1/4 teaspoon garlic granules

1/4 teaspoon dried basil

1/4 teaspoon dried oregano

1/4 teaspoon sea salt

1/4 teaspoon dried thyme

few shakes cayenne pepper, optional

Tips:

Marinating at room temperature helps vegetables more easily absorb the flavors.

Important to rotate skewers so vegetables cook evenly.

Cook's choice:

A combination of zucchini, mushrooms, onions, peppers, and eggplant go well together and take about the same amount of time to cook.

Directions:

For marinade, measure all ingredients into a bowl and whisk until well blended. Cut vegetables of your choice into chunks and place in marinade. Set the bowl of vegetables on the counter to marinate for 30 minutes. Stir once or twice while marinating. Remove vegetables one at a time and slide onto skewers. Place vegetable skewers on an outside grill and grill, turning skewers a few times to assure vegetables are cooked evenly. If you prefer, skewers can be cooked inside on a broiler pan and broiled in the oven until desired tenderness.

Mushroom Sauce

My husband played music at the Pow Wow River Grill with his long time buddy, Danny Harrington, for many years and during that time we were fortunate to try some fabulous dishes. One of our favorites was a mushroom gravy served with some of their dishes. I told the chef I loved the sauce, and he said it wasn't difficult. He claimed the success of the dish was due to the mushrooms themselves. He gave me a general idea of ingredients used and then I experimented. Although my version may not be as good as his, this recipe does make a delicious sauce that will perk up many a dish.

Ingredients:

1 cup onions, chopped

1 tablespoon butter

1 tablespoon extra virgin olive oil or oil of choice

2-3 garlic cloves, minced

1 cup white wine, pinot grigio or sauvignon blanc

1/4 cup dried porcini mushrooms, approximately 1 ounce

2 cups heavy cream (*Cook's choice - organic*)

1 lemon, freshly squeezed

1 1/2 tablespoons fresh thyme leaves

few pinches of nutmeg or to taste

salt and pepper to taste

Tips:

Dried porcini mushrooms have a very strong flavor and are somewhat expensive, but are delicious in this recipe. You can substitute them with a mixture of dried mushrooms for a lighter flavor.

Serving Suggestion:

Delicious over pumpkin, cranberry ravioli. Use your imagination, the possibilities are endless!

Directions:

Place butter and oil in a saucepan and saute onions and half the garlic until slightly limp and lightly browned. Deglaze pan with wine. Add mushrooms and simmer on low until mushrooms become soft. Add cream, lemon juice, and spices to the mixture and bring to a rolling boil. Reduce heat and simmer until mixture is reduced by about half, approximately one hour. Add remaining garlic to the sauce and heat a few more minutes. If a smoother texture is desired, mixture can be pureed in a blender or food processor.

Inspired by:

Steve, Chef at Plum Island Grille, Newbury, MA
and former Chef at Pow Wow River Grille

Out of this World Stuffed Sandwich

Serves 4 - 6

This is a great make-ahead sandwich perfect for picnics and hiking trips. You can make this many different ways using ingredients you have on hand!

Ingredients:

1 oval loaf of crusty, peasant type bread

oil/spread – any type of spread to mix with some of the following:

olive paste, hummus, pesto, olive oil, cream cheese, goat cheese

add some additional options:

meats/cheese - any type you choose (*Cook's choice* - dill Havarti)

marinated vegetables (*Cook's choice* - red peppers)

any type of lettuce and fresh vegetables (*Cook's choice* - green leaf lettuce and sprouts)

> **Note:**
> Sandwich takes 5 minutes to assemble and 3 hours to refrigerate.

Directions:

Take crusty bread and slice it in half lengthwise. Scoop out inside bread, leaving about 1" inside. Spread oil and choice of spread on both sides of bread - don't be stingy! A great combo is olive paste, goat cheese, and olive oil. Layer the meat and cheese of your choice on top of the oil/spread. Press both sides together and press it down to flatten. Wrap in either wax paper or saran wrap. The goal is to let the oil/spread layer really seep into the bread and meat/cheese layers. Put the sandwich in the refrigerator and weigh it down with a large heavy plate or pan for at least 3 hours. Remove from the refrigerator, remove wrap, and open the sandwich. Layer on the sandwich your choice of marinated and fresh vegetables. If using lettuce, layer it first and then place the other vegetables on top. You can either slice and serve the sandwich immediately or re-wrap it tightly and take it with you to your event. If the sandwich is not chilled, it should be eaten within 2 hours to prevent spoilage.

Submitted by:

Susan Sirois, Owner
Blue Moon Unique Gifts & Fair Trade Imports
www.bluemoondover.com

Play Dough - Not just for kids

Fun for all ages and safe since it is made without any toxic ingredients. Adults as well as children will enjoy kneading this dough. It has a warm, smooth velvety texture that feels wonderful. Making and playing with this dough gives added benefits. Helps exercise arthritic or stiff fingers and helps release any stress or anxiety. And the best benefit of all is, you will have lots of fun with this recipe!

Note:

Several years ago, I was getting ready to teach a Reiki class for children and came across this recipe in the Reiki Times Magazine and thought it would be great to make but it used food coloring. I wanted the recipe to be safe without any artificial coloring, so I tried it with powdered herbs I have on hand that I use in cooking, and was pleasantly surprised at the beautiful colors that can be created.

Ingredients:

1 cup flour

1 cup warm water

2 teaspoons cream of tartar

1 teaspoon vegetable oil

1/4 cup salt

turmeric, curry, mustard, or beet powders provide natural coloring

Directions:

Mix first 5 ingredients together and cook over medium heat. Add desired amount of powdered herb for color desired and cook until all is smoothly blended. Remove from heat and knead until coloring and all ingredients are blended and dough has a nice consistency. Since there are no preservatives in the dough, it is best to store in the refrigerator in a tightly closed plastic bag to retain its soft texture until ready to use again.

Sausage Quiche with Homemade French Pastry Crust

Yields 2 Quiches

Ingredients for Filling:

1 7-ounce package fresh sausage

1 small onion, chopped

1/4 cup cheddar cheese or cheese of choice, grated

4 ounces Swiss or mozzarella cheese, grated

3 large eggs

1 teaspoon salt

3/4 tablespoon real maple syrup

3/4 cup light cream

1/2 cup milk

1 9" pie shell uncooked, see below

> **Tip:**
> For vegetarians use vegetables of your choice.

Filling Directions:

Preheat oven to 375 degrees. Break sausage into small pieces and saute in skillet with onions until caramelized. Drain and place into pastry lined pie plate. Sprinkle cheese over sausage.

Place eggs, salt, maple syrup, light cream, and milk in a bowl and mix until well blended. Pour egg mixture over above ingredients. Bake 40-50 minutes until done. Quiche is done when you insert a knife in the center of the quiche and it comes out clean.

All Purpose French Pastry Pie Crust

Yields 2 pie crusts

Ingredients for Crust:

3 cups all purpose flour

1 teaspoon salt

3 tablespoons white sugar

1 cup shortening, non hydrogenated
(*Cook's choice* - Spectrum organic shortening)

1 egg

1 teaspoon white distilled white vinegar

5 tablespoons cold water

All Purpose French Pastry Pie Crust (continued)

Crust Directions:

In a large mixing bowl combine flour, salt, and sugar. Mix well and cut in shortening until mixture resembles coarse meal. In a small bowl combine egg, vinegar, and 4 tablespoons water. Mix together. Gradually add to flour mixture and stir with a fork. Continue to mix until dough forms a ball. If necessary add one more tablespoon of water. Allow dough to rest in refrigerator 10 minutes before rolling out.

Submitted by:

Janet Bryant

Sautéed Apples with a Kick

Serves 2

Ingredients:

3 apples, Cortland or your favorite

1 tablespoon butter, melted

1 tablespoon maple syrup

1 tablespoon brandy

> **Serving Suggestions:**
>
> Great on top of pancakes and waffles or use to fill crepes. Top with a light dusting of confection sugar or a drizzle of maple syrup.

Directions:

Peel and slice apples and place in skillet. Add butter and stir to coat apples. Cook for about 5 minutes tossing occasionally. Add brandy, stir and cook another 2 minutes. Add maple syrup, stir until all apples are coated, and sauté another 5 minutes or to desired tenderness.

Soup Matzo Balls

Makes about 10

These are light, delicious, easy to make, and are so much better than those made from any store bought mix. This is one of my favorite comfort foods, and reminds me of home cooked meals shared with the family growing up. Try adding them to medicinal chicken soup for a more filling meal.

Ingredients:

4 large eggs

1/4 cup sparkling seltzer water, (*Cook's choice* - Gerolsteiner)

2 tablespoons extra virgin olive oil, sunflower or oil of choice

2 tablespoons butter, melted

1/2 teaspoon sea salt or to taste

1/4 teaspoon black pepper or to taste

1/4 teaspoon garlic powder

1 cup Streit's matzo meal

6 cups water or chicken soup

Tips:

Matzo Meal is ground up crackers made from unleavened bread and can be found at specialty stores or in the international section of your supermarket.

Gerolsteiner seltzer can be found at most supermarkets.

Directions:

Beat eggs. Add seltzer, oil, butter, salt, pepper, and garlic. Mix well. Add matzo meal and stir until well blended. Place in refrigerate for 1 hour. Bring water or soup to boil. Remove mixture from refrigerator and with a tablespoon, scoop mixture into balls about 1 rounded tablespoon each, and drop into boiling water or soup. Reduce heat to low, cover pan and cook for about 30 minutes, turning once while cooking. Balls will float and be lighter in color when done.

Tomatillo Sauce

Yields about 2 cups

This is a green type of salsa. Tomatillos are green tomatoes that are covered with a papery thin skin. They have a refreshing crisp flavor and are rich in vitamin C. Due to the wide variety of climates in Latin America, the fruit can be found year round in some areas. The fruit is best when still green and has not yet burst the husk. The more mature yellowing fruits are often extremely soft and sweet. To store, wrap tomatillos loosely in paper in a single layer or place in a paper bag and store in the coolest section of your refrigerator. Stored this way they will keep for about 3 weeks.

Ingredients:

10-12 Tomatillos

1 1/2 cups water

1 cup onion, chopped

1/2 cup sweet red pepper, finely chopped

3 garlic cloves, minced

1 jalapeno pepper, minced

sea salt to taste (optional)

Tips:

Remove seeds and white membranes from jalapeno pepper unless you prefer very hot food. Once sauce is made, it will keep for several weeks in a tightly sealed jar stored in the refrigerator.

Serving Suggestions:

Sauce is great over mashed parsnips, pasta, ravioli, or served with your favorite Mexican dish and as a dipping sauce for nachos.

Directions:

Remove outer skin surrounding tomatillo. Some tomatoes may be a bit sticky and this is okay, just give them a good wash. Place in a saucepan with water, bring to boil, and simmer until tender. While tomatillos are simmering chop onion, pepper, garlic, and jalapeno. Allow tomatillos to cool a bit and place in a blender with about 3/4 cup tomatillo liquid, and blend until pureed. Puree in small batches, especially if tomatillo mixture is still warm. Add half the chopped pepper, onion, and garlic, and add to tomatillo mixture and puree all together. Pour puree into serving bowl and add remaining chopped pepper, onion, garlic, and salt, and stir to mix. This provides a bit of texture to the sauce.

ALTERNATIVE FLOURS USED

For the sake of variety and in order to not overload my immune system, I often use a variety of flours in my own cooking. My reason for doing so is that if the body gets used to having the same foods day after day, in time one can become allergic to or sensitive to certain foods. Often we can become sensitive to our favorite foods that we eat regularly, and if this happens, the immune system goes into overdrive causing strain and eventually illness. When one eats a wide assortment of foods, eats less potential allergens, and rotates favorite foods eaten on a daily basis, it is a lot easier for the body to maintain good health.

In my recipes, you will see I use different flours, some more often than others. I tend to use spelt flour a lot as it is the easiest to work with and substitutes easily in any recipe that calls for white or wheat flour. Although it does have gluten in it, it isn't used in many commercial foods so many people are able to tolerate it. Also in packaged mixes, you will find combinations of tapioca, sorghum, and potato flours that I have not used yet in my recipes.

Gluten flour is a low-starch, high-protein product made by drying and grinding hard-wheat flour from which the starch has been removed. Maybe you've heard the words gluten-free and have wondered what that means. Gluten refers to a group of proteins found in many grains, especially wheat, rye, and barley. Also found in other forms including wheat starch, wheat bran, wheat germ, cracked wheat, hydrolyzed wheat protein, graham flour, durum, semolina, spelt, couscous, and kamut. Celiac disease is an autoimmune reaction to the ingestion of certain types of gluten. These protein molecules stimulate the immune system and produce antibodies that may attack villi in the small intestine resulting in inflammation, damage, and destruction of the villi. This can impair the body's ability to absorb nutrients from food and can lead to malnutrition and a variety of physical, emotional, and health symptoms. Usually when gluten is removed from the diet, damage is reversed and the condition is controlled. As many people are sensitive to gluten, there are many flours to choose from that do not include gluten. Not all are created equal and some can be a bit finicky, so I suggest you start off with some of my recipes before experimenting more on your own. It is my hope you branch out and try some of the flours listed below, but if you're not ready to do so at this time, you can still enjoy the recipes in this book using your own favorite flours.

Amaranth Flour

A good substitute for anyone sensitive or intolerant to regular flour as it is gluten free. It is high in protein, fiber, iron, some vitamin C, calcium, phytosterols, which help to prevent disease, and the essential amino acid lysine. It has an interesting mild taste that gets stronger when it's old so best to store in refrigerator or freezer. It can be a difficult flour to work with. Best used in pancakes, muffins, cakes, cookies, flat breads, pie crust, and as a crumble topping. If you want to make a yeast bread, you will need to use some flour that has gluten.

Barley Flour

Good substitute for wheat flour with similar consistency with a bland taste. Whole barley flour is a great source of soluble fiber, is high in niacin and iron. Contains gluten.

Brown Rice Flour

Is ground from unhulled rice kernels. It has a grainy texture like cornmeal with a strong, nutty flavor and is naturally gluten-free. When substituting for wheat, does not act exactly the same so may need to experiment unless using a recipe in this book. Good source of fiber, B vitamins, and iron. Use in baked goods, cookies, as a breading, and as a thickener.

Buckwheat Flour

Technically is not a grain or a type of wheat, but an herb derived from the seeds of a fruit related to rhubarb and sorrel. It has triangular-shaped seeds that are milled and then ground into flour. A very nutritious and delicious flour that contains many nutrients including protein, calcium, magnesium, phosphorus, B vitamins, fiber, and iron. The dark flour is a heartier flour and good in pancakes. The light variety is less heavy than the dark flour and is a good wheat substitute. Is gluten-free and may not need added binder as it has a gluten analog that helps dough to stick together. This flour has a strong taste, you may want to combine it with other flours. Use in cookies, muffins, and pancakes.

Coconut Flour

Is made from finely ground dried coconut meat that has most of the moisture and fat removed. It tastes wonderful, has a higher fiber content than other flours, is a good source of protein, and is low in digestible carbohydrate. As it contains no gluten, it is considered hypoallergenic as few people are allergic to it. Due to absorption of liquids, it usually cannot be totally substituted for wheat. For best results substitute up to 25% for wheat when making quick breads and add more liquid as coconut flour will absorb more liquid than wheat flour. Example, if you use 1/4 cup of coconut flour you may need to add 1/4 cup more liquid. This flour tends to clump, not a problem . . . just break up and sift. Also storing in a glass jar in refrigerator or freezer will help keep moisture out. One cup provides 9 grams of fiber and 3 grams of carbohydrates. Add some to smoothies, baked goods, casseroles, or hot cereal.

Corn Flour

Also known as cornstarch or masa. Gluten-free and makes a good substitute for wheat flour. Due to its bland taste, you may want to combine it with other flours. Good source of potassium, manganese, vitamin A, and protein. Use to make corn tortillas, cornbread, and to thicken sauces.

Garbanzo Flour

Also known as chickpea or gram flour is made from ground chickpeas. Has a nutty taste. Loaded with insoluble fiber that benefits your digestive system and is easier to digest than wheat flour. As gluten-free, can be substituted for wheat flour in many recipes. Is high in protein, dietary fiber, and contains a large proportion of carbohydrates. Good source of vitamins A, K, and B vitamins, iron, phosphorous, and manganese. Use in baked goods, breads, muffins, cookies, pastries, to make batters especially tempura, and to thicken sauces.

Kamut Flour

An ancient Egyptian name for wheat, which is an ancient ancestor to modern wheat. It is golden in color with a sweet taste, has more protein and more amino acids than wheat. Some people can tolerate it as it is less allergenic than wheat. No adjustment needed when substituting for wheat flour. Use in cakes, pies, and muffins.

Millet Flour

Is ground from millet seeds. It is gluten-free, easy to digest, and has a buttery, slightly sweet taste that lends itself to not needing much sugar. It can be used alone in pancakes or tortillas, to coat veggies or meat for frying. Use in breads or muffins; needs a binder like xanthan gum or combine it with other flours to a ratio of 1/3 millet to 2/3 whole wheat or corn. Contains about same amount of protein as wheat. Good source of fiber, iron, B vitamins, magnesium, and potassium.

Oat Flour

Flour is made from ground oats. May contain a small amount of gluten. Is sweet, sticky, and requires a binder to rise or hold together. Works best for baking when mixed with other flours. Does not substitute well for other flours. But works well in recipes of oat cakes, fruit crumble, in cookies in this book, and for pancakes, pie crust, and muffins. Good source of fiber. You can easily make your own flour by freshly grinding oats in a coffee grinder, spice mill, or food processor. 1 1/4 cups oats will yield 1 cup of flour.

Quinoa Flour

Pronounced keen-wah and referred to as the "mother grain." When ground into flour, it has a very light and airy texture with a slightly bitter taste that can be improved by adding some cinnamon, cardamon, banana, or apple. It has a higher fat content that helps keep baked products moister. As it is gluten-free, is a nonallergenic option for anyone sensitive to wheat. Good source of zinc, iron, calcium, vitamin B, phosphorus, potassium, magnesium, and manganese. Very versatile, contains more protein than other flours, and can easily be substituted for wheat when making cookies, pancakes, muffins, quick breads and waffles.

Rye Flour

Made from milling rye berries and grains of rye grass. Closely related to wheat flour with a tangy, slightly sour flavor. Flour is high in bran and soluble fiber but low in gluten. As gluten is needed to help bread rise, substitute some wheat flour for some of the rye flour. Most commonly used when making rye and sourdough bread. Whole rye uses the complete grain and is sometimes known as dark rye or pumpernickel, which is much denser. Light rye is made from debranned rye berries, is more powdery, and similar in texture to white flour. You can easily find the dark and light flours in most health food stores, specialty stores, and some supermarkets. For best results when using rye flour, consider substituting 1/3 of the total amount of flour with wheat flour to ensure the bread will rise properly.

Soy Flour

Has a slightly beanlike taste, not related to wheat, but is a common allergen. As I am sensitive to soy and there is much controversy over it, I've chosen not to include it in any of my recipes. Using soy should be your personal choice.

Spelt Flour

A nutritious ancient grain with a deep nutty flavor that is a cousin to wheat. It is very versatile, high in protein, and high in gluten. No adjustment needed when substituting for wheat. Available in whole spelt or white spelt flour. It makes a good wheat substitute that sometimes may be tolerated by wheat sensitive people. Add slightly more baking powder for recipes calling for white flour. Good source of vitamin B2, manganese, niacin, thiamin, and copper. Use in any recipe calling for wheat or white flour.

Teff Flour

Newest of the ancient grains and tiny in size, known as the smallest grain. Its name means "lost" because if you drop some you won't be able to find it. It is high in fiber, nutritious, and higher in protein, iron, minerals, and calcium. Is a distant relative to wheat. White teff has a chestnut-like flavor with darker varieties being more earthy with a slight hazelnut taste. Contains no gluten so a binder is needed. Sometimes can be substituted for wheat flour for anyone gluten and wheat intolerant. However, many people with Celiac disease find they also cannot tolerate this flour. Due to its nutritional content and energy enhancing properties, it has gained favor with athletes. Due to its heavy texture, it makes an excellent pie crust. Good source of calcium, thiamin, and iron. Use in muffins, cookies, and pie crusts.

Whole Wheat Flour

Ground from the whole kernel of wheat and tends to be heavier than traditional white flour. Contains all the nutrients of the whole grain. Good source of fiber, protein, iron, B vitamins, thiamin, magnesium, phosphorous, and zinc. Hard wheat flours usually have more gluten and are best used in baking breads and dinner rolls. Soft wheat flours have less gluten and are better used in pastries and cakes.

TIPS:

1. If you are truly sensitive to gluten, you may want to make sure the flours you use have been processed in a facility that processes only gluten-free grains or look for products that are clearly labeled as Gluten-Free.

2. Organic flour is used in the same way as regular flour. It must follow U.S. Department of Agriculture regulations to be labeled organic. Using this flour is a matter of personal preference.

3. Flours have a limited shelf life. To keep flours fresh, store them in airtight containers in the refrigerator, or freeze them. In this way, your flour is less likely to spoil during warm weather and will last longer, especially if you don't use it very often.

4. Freezing flour for 48 hours before storing will kill any weevil or insect eggs already in the flour. Best not to add new flour to old if flour isn't used regularly.

ABOUT GRAINS AND LEGUMES

Grains provide a foundation for a healthy diet. Use to satisfy hunger, provide energy and endurance, help calm nerves, support sound sleep, promote elimination, and helps memory and clear thinking.

Brown Rice

More nutritious than white. Tan in color with a chewy texture and nutlike flavor. High in B vitamins, which are helpful for the nervous system. Gluten-free, contains no trans-fat or cholesterol and only a little fat and salt. Good source of vitamins and minerals. 100% whole grain food. As rice is susceptible to pests and disease and usually heavily treated with pesticides and fungicides during the growing process, you might want to use organically grown rice, especially if you are chemically sensitive.

Buckwheat Groats

Have a soft, subtle flavor. Cleanse and strengthen the intestines and improve appetite. The roasted variety has a somewhat nutty, earthy flavor and known as Kasha, a traditional European dish. It appears to be a grain but is really a fruit seed related to rhubarb and sorrel. A delicious alternative to rice or porridge that is gluten-free, alkalizing, and high in fiber. Contains eight essential amino acids; many minerals including phosphorus, magnesium, iron, zinc, copper, and manganese. Rich in flavonoids, especially rutin. Found to lower blood pressure, reduce cholesterol, lower glucose levels, and helps manage diabetes.

Corn

Sweet in flavor, this grain is also known throughout the world as maize. Traditionally Native Americans cooked it with lime due to its low niacin content, but when cooked with lime the body is able to absorb more niacin. Fresh corn is best eaten on first day of purchase or up to 3 days if stored in the refrigerator in husks or frozen for later use. A high fiber food, rich in carotenoids, good source of vitamin B1, B5, phosphorus, folate, vitamin C, and manganese. Helpful as a diuretic, nourishes the heart, stimulates appetite, helps regulate digestion, and tones kidneys.

Couscous

It is one of the healthiest grain products similar to a small pasta made from semolina wheat. It is simple and quick to prepare. Is a good source of protein and fiber. Has a much lower glycemic load than pasta and a higher vitamin content than pasta. Compared to pasta, it has twice the amount of niacin, riboflavin, B6, folic acid and contains more thiamine and pantothenic acid.

Millet

Has a sweet and salty flavor. A tiny "grain" that is really a seed. For centuries has been highly prized in China, India, Greece, Egypt, and Africa. It is gluten-free, high in fiber, vitamins and minerals including magnesium, calcium, manganese, tryptophan, phoshorus, B vitamins, antioxidants, and rich in silicon. It cooks like rice but needs more water. Use 3 cups water to 1 cup millet if not soaked prior to cooking. When grain soaked prior to cooking, less water is needed. This is personal preference and depends on how soft you like your grain. Try using 1 cup of millet to 2 or 2 1/2 cups water. Simmer covered for about 30 minutes. When cooked, the yellow grain turns opaque. To prepare grains rinse and remove any stones or unhulled pieces, soak or sprout for 8-24 hours prior to cooking to remove any phytic acid. This process helps the body to more easily assimilate minerals and enzymes and become easier to digest. Strengthens the kidneys, helpful to stomach and spleen, is alkalizing so balances over acid conditions, helps retard bacterial growth in the mouth, and helpful for Candida overgrowth.

Oats

An ancient grain that is naturally sweet, slightly bitter, and harvested in the fall but is available throughout the year. A satisfying and enriching way to begin the day providing lasting energy. The grain has been cultivated for two thousand years in various regions of the world. Before being consumed as a food, was used for medicinal purposes, a practice that is still honored. An excellent source of manganese, vitamin B1, dietary fiber, magnesium, protein, phosphorus, and a powerful source of the antioxidant selenium. Helps renew bones and connective tissues, decrease effects of asthma, strengthens spleen-pancreas, helps lower and remove cholesterol from digestive tract and arteries, stabilizes blood sugar, help with weight control, boosts immune response, strengthens cardiac muscles, and helps build and regulate qi energy. To make hot cereal, add 2 parts water to one part oats to cold water, and simmer until done. For rolled oats cook approximately 15 minutes, steel-cut variety about 30 minutes, and oat groats simmer for approximately 50 minutes but the water should be increased to 3 parts to one part of groats. Use in hot cereal, granola, stuffing, cookies, muffins, and fruit crisps.

Quinoa

Pronounced keen-wah. It is an ancient grain recently rediscovered. It was native to South America and once called the gold of the Incas, who recognized its value for increasing stamina of their warriors. Due to its life supporting role, it is now known as the "mother grain." It has a light and fluffy texture with a sweet, nutty flavor that cooks quickly. It is a wonderful alternative for anyone who is wheat gluten sensitive. It is an excellent source of protein, is easy to digest, excellent source of manganese, and a good source of magnesium, iron, copper, and phosphorus. contains vitamins C, E, B complex. It also has more calcium than milk and has a higher fat content than other grains. A very versatile grain that makes a great substitute for rice or cereal. As it needs to be carefully picked by hand, the grain and flour are more expensive than normal gluten products. Also, the grain needs to be triple rinsed in cold water to remove all saponins (the bitter outside coating) prior to cooking. Best way to do this is to soak it in cold water for 5 minutes, then rise in a fine mesh strainer or through cheese cloth until the water is clear and free of any foam. One cup dry quinoa will yield about 4 to 5 cups when cooked.

White Rice

Sweet flavor. Nutrient dense providing many vitamins and minerals. This energy food supplies complex carbohydrates needed for the body and brain to function. Sodium, cholesterol, hypoallergenic and gluten-free. Has only a trace of fat, and no trans fat or saturated fat. There are may varieties with differences in their cooking characteristics, textures, and subtle flavor variations. Nutritionally, they are equal and can be used interchangeably, depending on the recipe.

Basmati and Jasmine are both aromatic long-grain rices with a distinctive aroma and flavor similar to popcorn or roasted nuts. Basmati grains, when cooked, expand lengthwise and result in long, slender, dry, separate, and fluffy rice. Jasmine grains, when cooked, are soft, moist and cling together. Arborio, a large, bold rice with a characteristic white dot at the center of the grain is a medium grain rice mostly used in risotto. Due to its creamy texture around a chewy center, it has exceptional ability to absorb flavors. Sweet rice, short and plump with a chalky white, opaque kernel contains more protein and fat than other rice. When cooked, it loses its shape, becomes very sticky and glutenous. Best used in fried rice and sushi. The Japanese word Gohan means cooked rice and also means meal. In India, rice is the first food a new bride offers her husband and also first food offered a newborn. There is a saying that grains of rice should be like two brothers - close, but not stuck together. Instead of saying "how are you," the Chinese typical greeting is "have you had your rice today?"

Legumes

Although many varieties, nutritionally they are all rich in protein, carbohydrates, vitamins, and minerals, and low in fat. Due to high protein and nutritional content, they have a low glycemic index so are a healthy form of carbohydrates. They provide abundant fiber, are a rich source of potassium, calcium, iron, some B vitamins, and Omega-3 and Omega-6. In Chinese medicine, beans are embraced as helpful food for the kidneys and traditionally are given a healing value according to their 5-element color. Ayurvedic medicine suggests cooking them with oil or lard or add some seaweed with salt for anyone who is thin, frail, or nutrient deficient.

Cooking Tips: For best results, wash and rinse well, then soak legumes for 12 hours or overnight in four cups water to one cup dry legumes. Change water and discard once or twice. Soaking softens skin and helps eliminate phytic acid so more minerals are available, shortens cooking time, and improves digestibility. As salt is a digestive aid, it has been recommended to use 1/4 teaspoon salt for each cup of dry legumes. To improve flavor, digestion, increase nutrition, and cook faster, place some kombu or kelp seaweed (soak prior to adding) in bottom of pot. Bring legumes to boil, spoon off any foam and discard. Boil for about 20 minutes with lid off, then cover pot. Pour a little apple-cider or brown-rice vinegar into the cooking liquid before legumes are done to help eliminate gas. For individual estimated cooking times, see below. Depending on personal preference, additional cooking time may be needed.

Black Beans

Sweet Flavor. Warming thermal nature. Excellent source of the trace mineral molybdenum that helps detoxify sulfites, which are often added to prepared foods. Very good source of fiber, folate, and tryptophan, and a good source of protein, manganese, magnesium, vitamin B1, phosphorus, and iron. Builds blood, diuretic, helps kidneys and reproductive system. As a general rule, use 1 cup dried beans to 2-3 cups of water and simmer 2 1/2 hours. Try cooking with the herbs coriander, cumin, or ginger.

Garbanzo (Chick Peas)

Sweet flavor. Delicious nutlike taste with a buttery texture that is somewhat starchy. Originated in the Middle East and were very popular with ancient Egyptians, Greeks, and Romans. High in iron and a good source of unsaturated fats. High in fiber and protein. At least 2/3 of its fiber is insoluble, meaning it is able to pass unchanged all the way through the digestive tract to the colon to help it stay healthy. Also helps lower LDL-cholesterol, total cholesterol, and triglycerides. An excellent source of molybdenum, and good source of manganese, folate, copper, iron, tryptophan, and phosphorous. Helps pancreas, stomach, digestive system, and heart. As a general rule, use 1 cup dried beans to 3-4 cups of water and simmer 4-5 hours.

Great Northern and Navy Beans

Sweet flavor. These small, white, creamy beans got their current popular name as a staple food for the United States Navy in the early 20th century. High in dietary fiber and protein. Very good source of folate, manganese, tryptophan, and good source of B1 and the minerals phosphorus, magnesium, iron, and copper. Benefit lungs, promote healthy skin, help stabilize blood sugar, help edema and swelling, good for kidneys, and as a diuretic. As a general rule, use 1 cup dried beans for 3 cups of water and simmer 1 - 1 1/2 hours in a partially covered pot. Try adding a slice of kombu to reduce gas and increase digestibility.

Kidney Beans

Sweet flavor. Cooling thermal nature. Shaped like a kidney and red in color. The white variety are known as Cannelloni beans. Rich in soluble and insoluble fiber. An excellent source of molybdenum and folate. A very good source of protein, manganese, and good source of vitamin B1, phosphorous, iron, copper, magnesium, potassium, and vitamin K. Benefits heart, digestive system, edema and swelling. As a general rule, use 1 cup dried beans to 2-3 cups of water and simmer for 2-3 hours. Cook with some fennel or cumin to help prevent gas.

Lentils

Mild flavor. Neutral thermal nature. Believed to have originated in central Asia and eaten since prehistoric times. High in protein and fiber with virtually no fat. The brown and green varieties retain their shape best after cooking. Lentils cook fairly quickly and are easy to digest. Excellent source of molybdenum and folate, very good source of manganese, and a good source of iron, protein, phosphorus, copper, B1, and potassium. Help lower cholesterol, manage blood sugar, benefits heart and circulation, stimulates adrenal system, increases vitality (jing essence) of kidneys. Before cooking spread lentils out in a single layer on a kitchen towel or cutting board, discard any tiny stones or damaged lentils, and rinse in cool water. As a general rule, use 1 cup dried lentils to 1 1/2-2 cups of water and simmer 30 minutes to 1 hour depending on type of lentils and recipe.

Dried Split Peas (green or yellow)

Sweet flavor. Although small in size, nutritionally are a powerful member of legume family. An excellent source of the trace mineral molybdenum, which helps detoxify preservatives known as sulfites from the body. Very good source of soluble and insoluble fiber and tryptophan, and good source of protein, manganese, potassium, folate, B1, and phosphorous. Benefits the heart, harmonizes digestion, mild laxative, helps balance blood sugar, reduces cholesterol and blood pressure. As a general rule, use 3 cups of water for each 1 cup of peas. Bring to a boil, reduce heat, and simmer covered until desired tenderness.

HERBS AND SPICES USED

HERBAL and SPICE GUIDE

Try selecting organically grown herbs and spices, as this will give you more assurance that they have not been irradiated. [Herbs and spices are irradiated to prolong shelf life and destroy microorganisms, bacteria, viruses, or insects that might be present in the food. Irradiation damages food and creates free radicals. The free radicals kill some bacteria, but also damage vitamins, and enzymes, and combine with existing chemicals (like pesticides) in the food to form new chemical toxins (benzene, formaldehyde, lipid peroxides). Depending on dose of irradiation, foods can lose 5%-80% of many vitamins (A, C, E, K and B complex). As scientists have not studied long-term effects of these new chemicals in our diet, we cannot assume they are safe. www.organicconsumers.org/irrad/irradfact.cfm] For storage, most fresh herbs can be carefully wrapped in a damp paper towel and then placed inside a loosely closed plastic bag in the refrigerator. They will keep fresh for several days. Store dried herbs in tightly sealed glass containers in a cool, dark, and dry place. They should stay fresh for at least six months. To extend shelf life, store in refrigerator.

Allspice

Has a strong spicy taste and aroma that resembles a combination of cinnamon, nutmeg, and cloves. Also known as Jamaican pepper or pimento. Christopher Columbus first came upon the aromatic spice on the island of Jamaica on his second voyage to the New World. Some believe it to be a mixture of spices, but it's actually dried fruit of the pimenta dioica, a tree native to West Indies and tropical Central America. The shriveled berries appear similar to brown pepper corns, but contain two seeds unlike peppercorns (which has only one seed). Corns that are heavy, round, and compact can be stored at room temperature for many years. Best ground fresh by hand prior to use. Due to its warming and soothing qualities, allspice is helpful for gas, indigestion, and as a home remedy for arthritis and sore muscles. Good source of iron vitamins A, B6, C, and niacin, potassium, manganese, copper, selenium, and magnesium. Use in Mexican, Caribbean, Jamaican, and Indian dishes, fall vegetables, chicken, fish, meat, fruit, rice, sauces, baked goods; and blends well with chili, clove, coriander, garlic, mustard, and pepper.

Astragalus Root

Has a mild licorice-like taste that comes from a type of bean or legume that is native to China. No known adverse side effects have been noted and the herb can be safely used in conjunction with conventional therapies. Numerous benefits: balance blood sugar levels, protect kidneys and liver, anti-viral, anti-bacterial, and anti-inflammatory properties; decrease fatigue in athletes. Scientific research has found the root appears to work by stimulating the immune system. So if the immune system becomes overloaded due to work or stress, the root can help to increase energy levels, build strength and stamina. Treat for the common cold, flu, and respiratory infection; stimulate the body's natural production of interferon as well as pituitary and adrenal activity. The root has been investigated as a possible treatment for patients whose immune systems have been compromised by chemotherapy or radiation. Use in Chinese soups and in other soups and stews.

Basil, Sweet

Very fragrant with classic taste of mint-clove-thyme. Featured in many cuisines around the world. It was first native to India, Asia, and Africa. In India, noted as a sign of hospitality and in Italy as a symbol of love. Good source of vitamins K, A, and C; iron, calcium, and good source of fiber, manganese, magnesium, and potassium. Use in Italian dishes, pesto, marinara sauce, fish, tomatoes, and salads. Helps freshen the breath, revitalize skin and hair. Use in tea to help combat nausea associated with chemotherapy and radiation treatment.

Bay Leaf

Pleasantly aromatic with an allspice savory tang. Used since ancient times in cooking and medicinally. Highly praised by the Greeks and the Romans, who believed the herb to be a symbol of wisdom, peace, and protection. The legendary bay tree was regarded as a tree of the sun god under the celestial sign of Leo. Medicinally used as an astringent, diuretic, and appetite stimulant and to help insulin break down blood sugar. Good source of vitamins A, C, B-complex, and minerals copper, potassium, calcium, manganese, iron, selenium, zinc, and magnesium. Use in soups, stews, chowders, tomato sauce, vegetables, and more. Bay leaves are natural insect repellents. Place a leaf in flour containers to help protect against insect infections.

Cardamom

Well known spice in India and Middle East with a strong, unique flavor. Green variety usually used in sweet dishes and teas, and black in curries and rice dishes. Black has a somewhat smoky aroma with a coolness similar to mint. A member of the ginger family. Good source of magnesium. Aids digestion, especially of meat and wheat. Helps reduces gas and flatulence, is anti-spasmodic, warms the body, stimulates and improves memory. Also used to neutralize mouth odors. Used traditionally in Chinese medicine to treat stomach-aches, constipation, dysentery, and other digestion problems.

Cayenne aka Capsicum

Hot and spicy adds zip to food and medicinally as a tonic; is pungent and stimulating with many healthy benefits. Provides quick energy and acts as a nonirritating healing agent. Member of the Capsicum family of vegetables, more commonly known as chili peppers. Widely studied for its benefits in reducing pain, cardiovascular health, able to help prevent ulcers, lower cholesterol, antifungal and antibiotic qualities, and opens and drains congested nasal passages. Current studies show promise as an effective treatment for cluster headaches and osteoarthritis, and pain associated with arthritis, psoriasis, and diabetic neuropathy. Helps colds, flu, sore throat, weak circulation, cleans blood, and eliminates impurities, also thins blood to help prevent heart attacks. Good source of vitamin A, B6, C, K, manganese, and fiber. Increases heart action but not blood pressure. Use in spicy sauces, Mexican foods, vegetables, beans, and more.

Chili Powder

Puts fire on your lips and tongue, makes your nose run and eyes tear. Belongs to the family of foods bearing the Latin name Capsicum. To dry, hang fresh peppers upside down in a sunny spot until dried, then crush and store in a tightly sealed jar, away from sunlight. Helps clear congestion, boost immunity, relieve pain, prevent stomach ulcers, and helps in weight loss. Heart benefits of reducing blood cholesterol, triglyceride levels, and platelet aggregation, while increasing the body's ability to dissolve fibrin (a substance integral to the formation of blood clots). Spicing meals with chili peppers may protect fats in your blood from damage by free radicals. Good source of fiber, vitamin A, vitamin C, potassium, and iron. Use in Mexican, Thai, Indian, or any dish for added heat.

Chives

Mild onion flavor, not as pronounced as its cousins garlic and onions. Due to their delicate flavor, they are very versatile. A member of Allium family and have a strong odor due to the sulfur compounds. Wild chives are known as ramps and have a strong, onion flavor and due to the vibrant flavor may not need much salt. Rich in many nutrients especially vitamin A, K, and potassium (which helps strengthen the immune system and improve overall health). Antioxidants present help cancel harmful effects from free radicals and help protect from various diseases, even cancer. Fiber content helps digest fatty foods like cheese. Helps boost energy levels. Diuretic properties help reduce obesity. Reported to have beneficial effects on the circulatory, digestive, and respiratory systems, helps reduce blood cholesterol, and lowers blood pressure. Best to add near end of cooking so the benefits of allicin aren't lost. Use in cornbread, vegetables, potatoes, salmon, rice, chicken, soups, and more.

Cilantro

Leaves and stem have a slightly citrus flavor. Fresh leaves should look vibrantly fresh, with a deep green color, be firm, crisp, and free from yellow or brown spots. Wash just prior to use as it is very fragile. Clean like spinach, by placing in a bowl of cold water and swish it around with your hands to allow any sand or dirt to dislodge. Remove leaves from water, empty bowl, refill it with clean water, and repeat process until no dirt remains in the water. Good source of minerals potassium, calcium, manganese, iron, and magnesium, and vitamins K, A, C, B6, folate, riboflavin, niacin, and beta carotene; has antiseptic and carminative properties. Use in Asian, Indian, Mediterranean, and Mexican cuisine, guacamole, pesto, chicken, fish, meat, vegetables, soups, and sauces. See Coriander for more info.

Cinnamon Powder

Fragrant, sweet and warm flavor that not only tastes delicious but has unique healing abilities. The brown bark of the cinnamon tree is used as both a food and a medicine. Cinnamon is one of the oldest spices known, mentioned in the Bible and used in ancient Egypt as a beverage flavoring and medicine; was so highly treasured it was considered more precious than gold. In traditional Chinese Medicine, it is valued for its warming qualities providing relief at the onset of a cold or flu. As it increases heat in body, it stimulates action of other herbs.

Smelling the sweet spice is known to boost brain activity. Benefits include anti-clotting action, anti-microbial activity, and helps reduce amount of insulin released after eating to help keep blood sugar levels balanced. Traditionally used as a blood purifier, digestive aid, eases menstrual cramps, diarrhea, intestinal gas, and bloating. Helps fight infection. Good source of trace minerals manganese, iron, calcium, and fiber. Use as a spice and flavoring in food and drinks, applesauce, baked apples and pears, pies, muffins, beans, and more. Increased healing benefits when paired with raw honey.

Clove

Warm and sweet with intense flavor. Native to the Moluccas, formerly known as the Spice Islands of Indonesia and consumed in Asia for more than 2,000 years. Dating back to 200 BC, Chinese courtiers kept them in their mouths to freshen their breath when addressing the emperor so as not to offend him. To determine if good quality, place clove in a cup of water. Clove should float vertically, but if it sinks or floats horizontally, it may be stale or of poor quality. Usually local spice stores, ethnic markets, or health food stores carry spices and herbs that are fresher or of superior quality than local supermarkets. Ground cloves will keep for about six months, while whole cloves stay fresh for about one year. Help fight parasites, are a stimulant. Warming, increase heat in body, promote circulation and sweating, ease nausea, helpful for toothache, anti-spasmodic, help balance blood sugar levels, antiseptic and anti-infective. Good source of manganese, fiber, vitamin C, omega-3 fatty acids, calcium, and magnesium. Ground cloves can overpower flavors of other ingredients; best to start with less and adjust. To make your own clove powder, grind whole cloves in a coffee grinder. Use as a spice or flavoring in breads, pies, beans, chili, soups, hot cider, mulled wine, and more.

Coriander

The fruit has a fragrant flavor similar to both citrus peel and sage. It is considered both an herb and a spice since both its leaves and seeds are used as a seasoning condiment. Its fresh coriander leaves are more commonly known as cilantro and bear a strong resemblance to Italian flat leaf parsley. The spice has a reputation for its medicinal healing benefits, and Hippocrates and early physicians used it as an aromatic stimulant. In parts of Europe, referred to as an "anti-diabetic" plant; in parts of India, traditionally used for anti-inflammatory properties; and in the United States, has recently been studied for its cholesterol-lowering effects. Its healing properties are attributed to its exceptional phytonutrient content. Used for anxiety and insomnia. Good source of fiber, manganese, iron, and magnesium. Use in soups, broths, vegetables, fish, hot beverages, or use in a pepper mill to grind at the table

Cumin

Has a nutty peppery flavor with slight citrus overtones. In ancient Egypt, Greece, and Rome, the culinary spice was used for its medicinal and cosmetic properties. It also was a good replacement for black pepper, which was expensive and difficult to find. In certain Middle Eastern countries, the combination of cumin, black pepper, and honey is considered to be an aphrodisiac. Good source of magnesium, manganese, and iron. Benefits immune system, asthma, digestion, and assimilation of nutrients, and enhances liver detoxification. Use to flavor vegetables, rice, chicken, fish, and complement hearty flavors of legumes.

Curry

Has a mild pungent taste with a bright yellow color. Is a blend of spices, herbs, and seeds. Most blends are a varying composition of cumin, coriander, ginger, red and black pepper, dill seed, cardamom, cinnamon, turmeric, and cloves. Blend developed by the British during the days of the Raj as a way to approximate the taste of Indian cuisine at home. Health benefits: stimulate digestion, help cholesterol, protect the brain from Alzheimer's, possible protection from cancer, arthritis, boosts memory. Good source Vit A, K, folate, calcium, magnesium, potassium, phosphorus, omegas 3 and 6. Use in Indian, South Asian, and Caribbean cuisine, curries, sandwiches, dahl, soups, stews, marinade, rub for poultry, meat, and fish. See Turmeric for more.

Dill

Both leaves and seeds are used. Delicate leaves are fragrant with a soft, sweet taste and dried seeds have an aromatic, sweet, citrus and slightly bitter flavor. Its name comes from the old Norse word dilla which means to lull. It was traditionally used to soothe the stomach and to relieve insomnia. Considered a sign of wealth and revered for its many healing properties. Hippocrates, the father of medicine, used it in a recipe for cleaning the mouth. Ancient soldiers applied burnt seeds to their wounds to promote healing. Helps prevent osteoporosis, growth of free radicals, and prevents bacterial overgrowth. Good source of manganese, calcium, iron, and fiber. Use with fish, chicken, sauces, soups, potatoes, green beans, salad dressing, and in pickling. For best flavor, snip the herb with kitchen shears.

Fennel

Has a unique aromatic taste similar to licorice and anise. It is similar to celery, with a crunchy, slightly sweet and striated texture. Commonly used in France and Italy dating back to the earliest times. Greek myths state that it was associated with the Greek god of food and wine and revered by Greeks and Romans for its medicinal and culinary properties. Add to cooking from autumn through early spring when readily available and at its best. Bulb, stalk, leaves, and seeds are all edible. Related to parsley, carrots, dill, and coriander. Rich in phytonutrients, supports immune system, reduces cholesterol, neutralizes free radicals, antimicrobial, and help lower blood pressure. Good source of fiber, Vitamin C, potassium, manganese, folate, molybdenum, niacin, and minerals phosphorus, calcium, magnesium, iron, and copper. Use in Italian, Mediterranean cuisine, fresh vegetables, scallops, salmon, and in salads.

Garlic

Taste is like no other, hot pungency shadowed by a very subtle background sweetness and flavor. A member of the lily or Allium family. One of the oldest cultivated plants in the world, grown for over 5000 years with ancient Egyptians possibly the first to cultivate the plant. They bestowed it with sacred qualities placing in the tomb of Pharaohs, and gave it to slaves that built the pyramids to enhance their endurance and strength. Ancient Greeks and Romans also honored it for its strength-enhancing qualities as athletes ate it before sporting events and soldiers consumed it before going off to war. It has been called "the stinking rose" in light of its numerous therapeutic benefits. Considered a natural antibiotic and used in World War I and II as an antiseptic, became known as "Russian penicillin." Does not destroy the body's normal flora. Known for its many health building and medicinal qualities as an anti-fungal; kills parasites, stimulates lymphatic system, expectorant, for infection, colds, flu, cough, sore throat, bronchitis, pneumonia, asthma, psoriasis, boils, TB, cancer prevention, diabetes, high blood pressure, and high cholesterol; dissolves cholesterol and is a blood thinner. Good source of manganese, selenium, vitamins B and C. Suggest adding near end of cooking process for maximum flavor and to retain healing benefit of the sulfur compound allicin. How to use: To separate individual cloves, place bulb on cutting board and gently, but firmly, apply pressure with palm of your hand at an angle which causes layers of the skin holding bulb together to separate. Peel garlic with knife or separate skin from individual cloves by placing clove smooth side down on cutting board, gently tap it with flat side of a wide knife and remove skin with fingers or a small knife. If there is a green sprout in center of clove, remove and discard as it is difficult to digest. To retain healing benefits, cook no more than 5-15 minutes. Too much heat for too long will reduce healthy benefits. Use in Italian dishes, soups, hummus, fish, salsa, spinach, and more.

Ginger

Aromatic, pungent, and spicy. Stimulant, warms the body on cold damp days, increases circulation, promotes healthy sweating for detoxification, and helps fight off infections. Folk remedy used for headaches, reduces congestion, for upset stomach, indigestion, and gas. Removes mucus and toxins from the body, opens up stuffy nose due to allergies, sinus, or colds. Excellent remedy for morning or motion sickness, vertigo, and dizziness. Helps move food through the large intestines, cleanses the bowels. Tea is excellent to ease nausea and diarrhea associated with the flu or 24-hour virus. Has anti-inflammatory, antioxidant, and anti-ulcer effects. Fresh ginger can help reduce high blood pressure. Unpeeled fresh ginger can be stored in the refrigerator for up to three weeks or in freezer up to six months. Good source of potassium, magnesium, copper, manganese, and vitamin B-6. Use in tea, sauces, curries, Asian dishes, rice, vegetables, fruits, cakes, cookies, and more.

Hot Pepper

Actually are fruits. Jalapeno has a moist texture and a hot, tangy flavor. Serranos are thinner than Jalapenos, about 1" in length with a dry texture, and hot and spicy flavor. Anaheim, thin, dark green with moist texture and hot, sweet flavor. Haberneros, the hottest peppers. The longer cooked, the hotter food becomes, so recommend adding near end of cooking. Help arthritis, cluster headaches, digestion, and stimulate flow of saliva to stimulate stomach juices. Most of the heat is contained in the ribs and seeds and depending on your heat preference, you may want to discard or use sparingly. Good source of beta-carotene, vitamin C, B vitamins, potassium, and magnesium. Use fresh or dried in chili, dips, Mexican dishes, gazpacho, or any dish you want to give a zing.

Mint

Cool, clean, and refreshing flavor. Belongs to a large family with most common members of peppermint and spearmint. Known to have originated in Asia and the Mediterranean region. Many cultures considered it a symbol of hospitality, offering as a sign of welcome and friendship to guests as they arrived. In the Middle East, tea is still served to guests on their arrival, and in ancient Greece, leaves were rubbed onto the dining table as a warm greeting. Good source of vitamin A and C, some B12 and essential minerals manganese, copper, iron, potassium, and calcium. Use medicinally to aid digestion and relieve indigestion, heartburn, irritable bowel syndrome, a powerful antioxidant to protect the body from forming cancer cells, inhibits growth of bacteria and fungus, eases and unblocks breathing and respiratory passages and airways, nasal allergies, relieve cold and flu symptoms, congestion, headaches. Its calming properties act as a mild sedative, freshen the breath, and good blood cleanser. Tends to turn bitter if too much heat used in cooking. Use in sweet and savory dishes, tea, rice, salads, dressings, sauces, meat, carrots, corn, potatoes, tabbouleh, cakes, cold soup, and dips.

Mustard Powder and Seeds

Have a robust, sharp, spicy flavor, and fragrance. Seeds are mentioned in ancient Sanskrit writings dating back about 5,000 years and used for their culinary properties in ancient Greece. Ancient Romans invented a paste from ground seeds, which was probably the ancestor of our modern day mustard condiment. Physicians in Greece and Rome, including Hippocrates, the father of medicine, used seeds medicinally. Helps relieve respiratory congestion, reduce severity of asthma, decrease some symptoms of rheumatoid arthritis, help prevent cancer, help lower high blood pressure, restore normal sleep patterns in women with menopause symptoms, reduce frequency of migraines, and prevent heart attack in patients with atherosclerosis or diabetic heart disease. Good source of selenium, magnesium, calcium, iron, zinc, manganese, protein, niacin, omega-3 fatty acids, and dietary fiber. For added flavor, try adding some to your pepper mill in a ratio of 2 parts pepper corn to 1 part mustard seed with 1 part allspice berry (optional), and grind as usual. Use in marinades, salad dressing, sandwich spreads, and in pickling.

Nutmeg

Rich fragrance, highly prized spice for its aromatic, aphrodisiac, and curative properties. Since ancient times, used in many Chinese and Indian traditional medicines for illnesses related to the nervous and digestive systems. Contains compounds that help stimulate brain function, control heart rate and blood pressure; anti-fungal, anti-depressant, digestion, relieve tooth pain, improve breath, reduce muscular and painful rheumatic joints. Good source of minerals copper, potassium, calcium, manganese, iron, zinc, and magnesium and vitamin C, A, and beta carotene. Use in sauces, soups, pies, muffins, vegetables, marinades, and curries.

Oregano

Warm, balsamic, and aromatic flavor. It's name means mountain joy and Greeks and Romans regarded it as a symbol of joy and happiness. An old tradition for

Greek and Roman brides and grooms to be crowned with a laurel of oregano. Helpful as a digestive aid, improves dyspepsia. Good source of antioxidants, iron, manganese, dietary fiber, calcium, magnesium, vitamin C, A, K, and omega-3 fatty acids. Use in sauces, pizza, soups, salad dressing, salsa, fish, Italian, Mediterranean, and Mexican cuisines. Best added near end of cooking process due to its delicate flavor, which can be lost due to heating.

Paprika

Spices up a dish adding warmth and color. Releases its color and flavor when heated. Most often used to add color and as a garnish. When sprinkled over colorless dishes, it improves appearance of food but doesn't change its flavor. Made from dried, ground up sweet red peppers or chili peppers that range in flavor from sweet, mild, to hot. An antibacterial agent, stimulant and energizer helps with tiredness and lethargy, normalizes blood pressure, improve circulation, increases production of saliva and stomach acids to aid digestion, fends off colds, prevents scurvy, has cardiovascular benefits, and helps the body absorb iron. Good source of vitamins C, A, K, folate, omega 3s and 6s, and minerals potassium, calcium, magnesium, and phosphorous. Use in soups, stews, casseroles, shell fish, rice, salads, chicken, as a garnish for salad, appetizers, and eggs.

Parsley

A delicious green, vibrant taste that is highly nutritious and more than just a garnish. Its name comes from the Greek word meaning rock celery and is a relative of celery. Two varieties, curly parsley and Italian flat leaf (which has a more fragrant and less bitter taste than the curly variety and holds up better to high heat). Cultivated more than 2,000 years ago, ancient Greeks held parsley to be sacred, using it to adorn winners of athletic contests and to decorate tombs of the deceased. Best washed just before using as it is highly fragile. Clean like spinach by placing in a bowl of cold water and swishing it around with your hands to dislodge any sand or dirt. Remove leaves from water, empty the bowl, refill with clean water and repeat process until no dirt remains in the water. Good source of vitamins C, A, K, folate and iron. Use to freshen breath, has mild anti-bacterial action, helps prostate, bladder infections, cleanses and builds, removes gallstones, jaundice, kidney inflammation, urine retention, rheumatoid arthritis. Use to help harmonize, cleanse, and tone the spleen. Use in pesto, sauces, soups, salads, vegetables, fish, poultry, meat, and as a garnish.

Peppermint

Cool, spicy flavor. A hybrid of water mint and spearmint. Used medicinally as a seasoning and medicine for centuries. Soothes upset stomach, soothes stomach lining, improves flow of bile the body uses to digest fats after a fatty meal so food passes quickly through stomach, helps with reflux, absorbs intestinal gas, nausea, stops hiccups, for symptoms of cold, flu, chills, and chest congestion. Also for diarrhea, activates salivary glands, indigestion, heartburn, colic, irritable bowel, ulcers, menstrual cramps, hot flashes, anti-inflammatory, and anti-microbial, stimulates circulation, helps headaches, and for shock. Emotionally uplifting, has a calming and numbing effect helpful in treating headaches, and anxiety associated with depression. Good source of vitamin C, A, and manganese. Use in soups like gazpacho, dips, yogurt, and more.

Rosemary

Has a pine-like fragrance that is balanced by its rich pungency evoking both the smells of the forest and the sea. In ancient Greece, students placed sprigs in their hair when studying for exams, and mourners threw the herb into graves as a symbol of remembering the deceased. In the 16th and 17th centuries, it was popular in apothecaries as a digestive aid. Due to its strong taste, you might want to add some lemon, pinch of cardamon, or some honey in tea. For centuries, the tea was brewed to soothe headaches, nervousness, and digestive issues due to mental strain. The tea works well as a gentle, cleansing hair rinse to promote shiny hair. Has a positive effect on the mind, stimulates immune system, increases circulation, improves digestion, contains anti-inflammatory compounds that may help reduce severity of asthma attacks, increase blood flow to the head and brain, and improve concentration. Good source of fiber, iron, and calcium. Use 2 teaspoons minced fresh leaf in recipes calling for 1 teaspoon of dried herb. Use with chicken, lamb, winter squash, baby new potatoes, green beans, dried beans, marinades, vinaigrettes, soups, bread dip, sauces, and eggs.

Sage

Sweet savory flavor. In 2001, it received the "Herb of the Year" award from the International Herb Association due to its health-promoting properties. Greeks and Romans were said to have highly prized the many healing properties of sage. Romans treated it as sacred and had a special ceremony when gathering it. Greeks and Romans prized its healing properties and used it as a preservative for meat until refrigeration became popular. These cultures knew from experience, that the herb could help reduce spoilage, which now is being confirmed by science, due to the herb's antioxidants. Add herb near the end of the cooking process to retain maximum essence. Good source of Vit A, calcium, and potassium. Use in tomato sauce, omelets, pizza, salads, bruschetta, chicken, and fish.

Thyme

A delicate herb with a penetrating fragrance. Antiseptic. Egyptians used it as an embalming agent to preserve deceased pharaohs. In Greece, used for its aromatic qualities, burned as incense in sacred temples, and was a symbol of courage and admiration with the phrase the smell of thyme a saying that reflected praise. The ritual was associated with bravery in medieval times where in women gave their knights a scarf that had a sprig of thyme placed over an embroidered bee. A general tonic used for chest congestion, coughs, bronchitis, asthma, an antiseptic for tooth decay and gum disease, fungal infections, parasites, digestive disturbance and gas, a sore throat, laryngitis, and tonsillitis, and to remove mucus from sinus passages due to infections and allergies. Best to add small amounts at the last moment to retain flavor and taste. Good source of vitamin K, iron, manganese, and calcium. Use with beans, eggs, fish, lamb, poultry, soups, and sauces.

Turmeric

Has a peppery, warm, bitter flavor with a mild fragrance of orange and ginger similar to its relatives. Its bright yellow-orange color is attributed to the curcumin, a natural phenol, which is greater in quantity than in curry. Used as a component of Indian Ayurvedic medicine since 1900 BC to treat a wide variety of ailments. Also used in Indonesia and Southern India for more than 5,000 years. In China and India, used as an anti-inflammatory agent to treat flatulence, jaundice, menstrual difficulties, bloody urine, hemorrhage, toothache, bruises, chest pain, and colic. Arab traders introduced it to Europe in the 13th century, but only recently has it become popular in Western cultures. Traditionally used for chronic infections, relieves pain and inflammation, anti-septic, supports heart health, decreases cholesterol, helps cells heal, helps rheumatoid arthritis, IBS, cystic fibrosis, helps prevent cancer, as a blood thinner, helps digest fats, reduces gas and bloating, kills parasites and yeast, protects against kidney stones, Alzheimer's, liver and heart disease, lowers cholesterol, use for detox especially after chemotherapy. Good source of iron, manganese, vitamin B6, fiber, and potassium. A natural coloring and flavoring agent used in mustard, pickles, and relishes. High in magnesium. Use in curries, rice, lentils, with cruciferous vegetables, and egg salad.

ABOUT NEW AND OLD ALTERNATIVES

I'm sure there are way more alternatives available today but I've included a little information about each one used in this book so you get to know them a bit before buying and giving them a try.

Apple Cider Vinegar

Made from organic apples, unfiltered and unpasteurized with the mother of vinegar present. Used by Hippocrates, Father of Medicine, for its amazing health benefits. Is rich in enzymes and potassium. Used for immune support, promote good digestion and pH balance, soothes dry throat, and helps remove toxins from body. You can substitute vinegar with lemon juice or if sensitive to citrus, use 1/4 teaspoon of unbuffered, powdered vitamin C with one tablespoon of water for each tablespoon of lemon juice as an alternative to provide a bit of tartness. Stir and add just before serving.

Note: Buffered vitamin C does not have a tart taste.

Brown Rice Vinegar

Made from brown rice with a sweet essence that has been aged 6 to 8 months. This lighter rice vinegar is preferred for making sushi rice and Asian dishes.

Balsamic Vinegar

Aromatic, aged vinegar traditionally produced in provinces of Italy from the concentrated juice, or musk, of white grapes. Very dark brown in color, with a rich, sweet and complex flavor. Due to its acid nature, it is self-preserving with an indefinite shelf life and does not need to be refrigerated. The finest grades are aged for many years. Originally was only available to Italian upper classes, so a cheaper variety became available around the world in the late 20th century. True balsamic vinegar is aged for 12 to 25 years and you can find ones that have been aged for 100 years, but they are usually very expensive. Commercial balsamic sold in supermarkets is usually made from concentrated grape juice mixed with a strong vinegar and laced with caramel and sugar. But no matter how it is produced, it is always made from a grape product. Shelf life is almost indefinite.

Arrowroot

Bland taste. Use as a substitute for flour or cornstarch in recipes to bind dough in baking. Easy to use as a thickening agent for sauces, glazes, and jellies. To substitute as a thickener, use 2 teaspoons of arrowroot for 1 tablespoon of cornstarch, or 1 teaspoon of arrowroot for 1 tablespoon of flour. First mix with some cool liquid prior to heating. Also can be used as a substitute for eggs as a binder to hold dough together. Especially helpful when using gluten-free flour and in baking. Use 1 tablespoon of powder for each 1 cup of gluten-free flour.

Baking Powder, Corn Free

A single acting baking powder is one in which all the rising takes place when liquid ingredients are added to dry ingredients. To make your own powder mix together 4 tablespoons arrowroot, 2 tablespoons baking soda, and 4 tablespoons cream of tarter. Place all 3 ingredients in a glass jar and shake occasionally. If mixture clumps, mash with a spoon. For best results when using this baking powder, mix all dry ingredients together and wet ingredients separately, preheat oven, add liquid and dry ingredients together, but do not over mix.

Braggs Liquid Aminos

A liquid protein concentrate made from certified non-GMO soybeans. Contains both essential and nonessential amino acids. Use in place of tamari or soy sauce. It has a small amount of natural occurring sodium so you may not need additional salt. Is gluten-free, contains no chemicals, artificial colors, or preservatives. Use on salads, vegetables, soups, rice, beans, poultry, meat, and in Oriental dishes.

Buffalo Meat

Is high in iron, protein, and fatty acids. A good substitute for beef, which provides more iron than beef. Naturally delicious rich flavor with a similar taste to beef but with a slight hint of sweetness. Provides less fat, calories, and cholesterol than red meat or chicken. A chemical-free product without added antibiotics, hormones, drug residues, or preservatives. Is considered a nonallergenic product that many people with allergies may be able to eat.

Carob

A tasty nutritional large bean, similar to fruit that grows on tall trees in hot tropical climates. Sometimes called "Saint John's Bread." Is naturally sweet and not bitter like chocolate, so less sweetener may be needed. Contains some protein, vitamins A and B, calcium, phosphorous, iron, and is high in fiber. Contains no fat, no caffeine, is more nutritious and encourages absorption of calcium. Helpful for digestive upset as a mild laxative and has low-allergenic potential. Similar to chocolate in color and texture. Use as a substitute for cocoa, by substituting same amount of carob for cocoa. In recipes calling for 1 ounce of baking chocolate, substitute 3 tablespoons carob powder, 1 tablespoon oil, and 2 tablespoons water.

Coconut Milk

Sweet flavor. Clears effects of summer heat as it quenches thirst. Is high in vitamins A, E, and electrolytes of potassium, chloride, and calcium. Vegan drink that is low in cholesterol. Use as a substitute for dairy and is well tolerated by anyone lactose intolerant. Good for your health, supports fitness, strengthens immune system, helps a sore throat or ulcers, and new research suggests it can lower blood pressure and blood sugar levels. Protects the body with anti-viral, anti-microbial, anti-bacterial, and anti-fungal benefits. Use as substitute for milk, in smoothies, in baking, in sauces, and stews. You can make your own from fresh coconut, use organic creamed coconut that comes in a box (see sources), or canned whole coconut milk.

Coconut Oil

Once considered unhealthy as it is saturated and high in fat, now considered a special and nutritious health food, which differs from other fats due to the medium-chain fatty acids. Rich in fiber, vitamins, and minerals. Classified as a "functional food" because of its many healthy benefits. The oil is traditionally used in medicine in Asian and Pacific populations. The coconut palm is so highly valued as a food source and medicine that it is called "The Tree of Life" and the Pacific Islanders consider the oil to be the cure for all illness. The coconut palm has no negative effects on cholesterol, enhances the immune system, improves heart health, boosts thyroid function, increases metabolism, and helps promote lean body. Can be used topically to benefit the skin.

Flax Seeds

Nutritious. Adds fiber and essential fatty acids. Use to add texture and help bind dough together when baking, especially important if using flour that has no gluten. Boil 1 tablespoon flax seeds in 1 cup of water for 15 minutes. Mixture cooks down to 1/2 or 3/4 of a cup. Cool and use as a substitute for part of liquid ingredients in baked goods. Keeps a few days in the refrigerator. A simpler way to use as a binder is to grind flax seeds as needed and use 1 tablespoon for each cup of gluten-free flour. Flax seeds or meal does not change taste. Helps mucus inflamed conditions, soothes and cleanses kidneys and bladder.

Gomasio

A condiment made from toasted sesame seeds and sea salt also known as sesame salt. It is high in calcium, and vitamins A and B. Purchase or make your own. To make your own, wash and soak sesame seeds with sea salt for about 7 hours. Drain water and roast quickly in a dry skillet over medium heat until they begin to have a nutty aroma, are golden brown, and start to pop. Then grind in a coffee or nut grinder. Use 1/2 cup sesame seeds to 1/2 tablespoon sea salt. Adjust for personal preference. Store in a tightly closed glass jar in cupboard or on counter.

Green Tea (Camellia Sinesis)

Made from unfermented leaves and reported to contain high concentrations of powerful antioxidants called polyphenols that can neutralize free radicals, and may reduce or help prevent some of the damage they cause. It has a somewhat bitter flavor due to the polyphenols. In traditional Chinese and Indian medicine, practitioners used the tea as a stimulant, diuretic, astringent to help heal wounds, and improve heart health. Studies suggest many health benefits including heart disease and cancer, regulates body temperature, prevents diabetes, helps with weight loss, digestion, lower cholesterol, improves the mind and aging process, and calms the nervous system. Sip a cup of tea while cooking or substitute for some liquid in soups, sauces, rice, and with vegetables.

Himalayan Salt

A pure, hand-mined salt harvested from ancient sea salt deposits deep within the pristine Himalayan mountains that has been used for centuries and believed to be the purest form of salt available. Recognized for its beautiful pink color, high mineral content, and therapeutic properties. It includes over 84 minerals and trace elements including calcium, magnesium, potassium, copper, and iron. Crystals range in color from sheer white, and shades of pink to deep reds. Regular consumption provides essential minerals, trace elements, balances electrolytes, supports proper nutrient absorption, eliminates toxins, balances the body's pH, normalizes blood pressure, and increases circulation and conductivity. Also helps with relief from arthritis, skin rashes, psoriasis, herpes, flu and fever symptoms. The salt is used by holistic chefs, spas, and health professionals for its nutritional and therapeutic properties. Use the same as you would use table salt in culinary dishes, baking, pickling, with fish and chicken.

Kudzo

Also called Kuzu, has a bitter flavor. Its roots contain starch so can be used as a thickener instead of cornstarch or arrowroot. Substitute 1 teaspoon for 1 teaspoon cornstarch or arrowroot. Shown to be helpful in treating migraine and cluster headaches, allergies, diarrhea, tinnitus, vertigo, diabetes, cardiovascular disease, and has potential promise treating Alzheimers'. In traditional Chinese medicine it is considered one of the 50 fundamental herbs used traditionally as a remedy for alcoholism and hangover. The root was used to prevent excessive consumption, while the flower was supposed to detoxify the liver and alleviate symptoms. Wikipedia states, "The Harvard Medical School is studying it as a possible way to treat alcoholic cravings, by turning an extracted compound from the herb into a medical drug."

Maple Syrup

An easy to use substitute for sugar, made from sap just inside the bark of sugar maple trees. Contains natural occurring vitamins of zinc, manganese, thiamine, calcium, and antioxidants. I prefer the richer flavor of Grade B but is also sold in Grade A light amber, medium amber, and dark amber. The lighter the color the more subtle the flavor. When substituting for sugar, I use less maple syrup than original recipe calls for. But sweetness is individual, so you may wish to use more than amount of sugar recipe calls for. Use in cream-based dessert, custard, baked goods, muffins, and pancakes. Store in refrigerator, it doesn't thicken when kept cold.

Miso

A savory, very salty paste that is high in protein, rich in vitamins, and minerals. Use as a light seasoning. The enzyme-rich paste aids digestion, assimilation, is alkalizing, strengthens the blood, and helps the body discharge toxins and heavy metals. In Oriental medicine has been used to treat arthritis, diabetes, colitis, hypoglycemia, headache, dizziness, and improve resistance to illness, irritability, and low energy. Use in soups, sauces, and stews. Miso comes in several varieties. Barley (mugi) Miso, can be used in all seasons and is especially healing. White (shiro) Miso, has a slightly sweet, mild flavor, best used in spring and some of summer. Red (aka) Miso is most commonly used in Japan. Brown Rice (genmai) Miso has a slightly sweet flavor similar to white miso and best used in spring, summer, and fall.

Molasses

Name comes from the Latin word melaceres, meaning honey-like. It is a thick dark syrup that is crystallized out of sugar cane or sugar beet juice. Has a strong taste with moderate sweetness. Is nutritious and provides iron, calcium, zinc, copper, chromium. Used in baking breads, pies, and baked goods such as gingerbread cookies and in brewing ale and distillation of rum. Can use as a substitute for maple syrup, honey, and dark corn syrup.

Mochi

A glutinous rice cake with a bland, chewy texture, made from pressed sweet brown rice. It is easy to digest, warming, and strengthening. Traditionally served in Japan at parties to welcome in the New Year. The origin of the word mochi is uncertain, although mochizuki means "full moon," which the Japanese see not a man-in-the-moon in the night sky, but a rabbit tirelessly pounding rice on his mortar. Cut into squares and use in soups, desserts, or add to any cooked savory dish.

Olive Oil, Extra Virgin - Cold Pressed

Olive oil is a natural juice that preserves the taste, aroma, vitamins, and properties of the olive fruit. Considered the best, least processed oil because it is from the first pressing of the olives and is of high quality. The oil that comes from the first "pressing" of the olive, is extracted without using heat (known as a cold press), or chemicals with no "off" flavors. The less olive oil is handled, the closer to its natural state, and the better quality of oil. Oil that meets all this criteria is designated as "extra virgin." It is rich in antioxidants, vitamin E, carotenoids, and essential fats that lubricate organs, cleanse, and support the body. Use in salad dressings, with foods eaten cold, in most baked goods, and for sautéeing. A health benefit is its ability to displace omega-6 fatty acids, while not having any impact on omega-3 fatty acids which, builds a healthier balance between omega-6 fats and omega-3 fats. It also lowers total cholesterol and LDL levels in the blood, lowers blood sugar levels, blood pressure, and reduces oxidative damage to DNA and RNA (which may be a factor in preventing cancer). Recent preliminary research indicates it may possibly be a chemo-preventive agent for peptic ulcer or gastric cancer, but this needs further study to be confirmed. Best stored away from heat and light to protect against spoilage. Over time, oils can deteriorate and become stale or go bad. If oil is over a year old, it is best to use in cooking and not with cold foods.

Panko Bread Crumbs

Flaky bread crumbs used in Japanese cuisine as a crunchy coating made from bread with crust removed. They have a more crispy, airy texture than most traditional breading in Western cuisine. Use in Asian and non-Asian dishes, especially fish and seafood and even with meat.

Raw Coconut Amino Acids

A soy-free seasoning that is organic, gluten-free, dairy-free, and GMO-free. When coconut trees are tapped, a highly nutrient-rich, low-glycemic, raw sap exudes which is abundant in 17 amino acids, good source of minerals and vitamins, and has an almost neutral pH. By comparison, contains 2-14 times the amino acid content of soy. It is aged and blended with sundried, mineral-rich sea salt, and hand gathered from waters near southern islands of the Philippine coast. Use like soy sauce in dressings, marinades, in stir fry, fish, or chicken. Does not have a coconut flavor. Needs to be refrigerated after opening.

Raw Honey

A sweetener known for its healing benefits of being antibacterial, antiviral, and antifungal. Due to its sweetness, only a little is needed. Substitute 1/2 to 2/3 for amount of sugar. As it is not processed, it is a nutritious whole food that is rich in live enzymes, vitamins, and trace minerals. Use in foods already cooked as beneficial healing benefits are lost during heating. Because no bacteria or mold can grow in honey, it is the only food in nature that does not spoil. I found the following facts so fascinating I wanted to pass on the information to anyone who also wasn't aware how fortunate we are to have honeybees in the environment. Since early times, bees have been known as healers, working long hours to produce their glorious gift of honey! Each honeybee will produce only 1/12 of a teaspoon of honey in her six-week life. To make a pound of honey, a colony must visit 2 million flowers traveling a distance of 55,000 miles. I am truly amazed and grateful to each and every honeybee!

Raw Milk

Used exclusively prior to pasteurization in 1890s. Hippocrates, as well as other physicians, used raw milk in the treatment of disease. In the 1920s, Dr. J. E. Crewe of the Mayo Foundation used a diet of raw milk to cure TB, edema, heart failure, high blood pressure, diabetes, chronic disease, and other ailments. Today Germany uses raw milk therapy in some of its hospitals. Some organizations say health benefits are destroyed in the pasteurization process, but this statement is not supported by all research, so using it is a personal decision. Raw milk is simply real fresh full-fat milk right from the farm, with no processing/pasteurizing/heating, and no transporting in big tanker trucks to big factories and big stores. Cows are not confined and are allowed to feed on organic green grass in spring, summer, and fall, and in winter are fed stored dry hay, silage, and root vegetables. They are not fed any grain that may have added fertilizers, chemicals, hormones, or antibiotics. According to Wikipedia, 28 states allow the sale of raw milk. Usually sold at local farms, farmers markets, and some health stores. For the most benefits, consume milk in its raw state. High-speed blending can damage raw milk so best to stir into a smoothie last to retain all benefits. High heat reduces its healthy benefits, but at least you know your source and its purity. Benefits should be retained when using gentle heating as in warming milk as long as you can touch it without burning. Benefits include a good source of protein, beneficial enzymes, immunoglobulins, amino acids, vitamins A, D, and minerals calcium, phosphorous, and trace minerals.

Seaweeds

Have a salty flavor. Are cooling foods. Varieties used include arame, dulse, kelp, kombu, nori, and wakame. High in vitamins E and A and rich in calcium, phosphorous, potassium, iron, iodine, and trace minerals. Strengthens and stimulates skin, hair, and nails, and nourishes the thyroid and adrenal glands, and strengthens the nervous system. Helps detoxify, eliminate phlegm, remove residues of radiation in the body, cleanse lymphatic system, alkalize blood, and help with liver stagnancy. Also helps the body to eliminate radiation and heavy metals. An excellent source of calcium, iodine, iron, and B12. If one is ill physically or spiritually, seaweeds can help heal the body. Does not need to be boiled, just soak prior to eating so can be used in salads or add to soups, stews, chili, rice, and grains.

Arame

Salty flavor, with a very cooling, thermal nature and is fairly versatile. Richest source of iodine, high in iron and calcium. Benefits thyroid, softens hardened areas in body, moistens dryness, helps lower high blood pressure, builds strong bones and teeth, provides a clear and soft complexion, and, when used daily, promotes glossy hair and prevents hair loss. Use with grains, in soup, stuffing, and vegetable dishes.

Dulse

Salty flavor with very cooling thermal nature. Rich in iodine and manganese. Use as a salt substitute, to season foods, in sauces, with mashed potatoes, vegetable burgers, and in soups.

Kelp

Salty flavor. Easy to cook with. Can be roasted. Similar to Kombu, good for winter cooking. Has a high mineral content and is a great salt substitute. A digestive aid that supports kidney and thyroid function, helps balance hormones, and breaks down hardened masses in the body. Use with beans to soften them and increase digestibility. Contains sodium alginate, which binds heavy metals in the digestive tract.

Kombu

Member of kelp family. Salty flavor with a very cooling thermal nature. Due to mineral content, it greatly increases nutritional value of other foods cooked with it. Use with beans to soften them, reduce gas, and increase digestibility. Add to grains, soups, sauces and legumes to increase iodine and iron content.

Nori

Sweet and salty flavor with a very cooling thermal nature. Has a high protein content and easiest to digest of the seaweeds. Is rich in vitamins A, B1, and niacin. Aids digestion, especially of fried foods. May help lower cholesterol and blood pressure and flush out mucus. Add to soups, stews, sprinkle on grains and salads.

Wakame

Salty flavor with very cooling thermal nature. High in calcium, niacin, and thiamine. Promotes healthy hair and skin. Use in miso soup and to soften beans. Miso soup eaten at beginning of meal helps one relax and prepares the digestive system for more food. Put a small amount of dried wakame in a little hot water for a few minutes prior to adding to recipe.

Tamari Sauce

Naturally aged and fermented from soybeans with wheat, sea salt, and water. Has a high salt content, but a low sodium variety is available. Similar to soy sauce, but a higher quality product. Look for wheat and preservative free. Use in grain dishes, stir fry and with fish or chicken.

Ume Plum Vinegar

The vinegar is a liquid brine byproduct that is left over after pickling umeboshi plums and shiso aka beefsteak leaf. In Japan, it is known as ume su which means plum vinegar. A salty, tangy, ruby red vinegar that is delicious. Sprinkle over cooked vegetables, add zing to salad dressings, marinades, and dips, and great for making pickled or preserved foods. Due to a high salt content when substituting for another vinegar, you will want to reduce or eliminate additional salt in the recipe. Umeboshi plums are valued for their ability to strengthen digestion and traditionally were used to stimulate appetite, help the body maintain proper acid/alkaline balance, and to restore energy.

Wild Salmon

A healthy source of omega-3 fats that is high in protein, essential amino acids, vitamins A, D, B 6, B, E and calcium, iron, zinc, magnesium, and phosphorus. Cook's choice is for wild, opposed to farm raised, to avoid potential contaminants. For specific recipes see appetizer and main dish-fish chapters.

NUT AND SEED VARIETIES USED IN RECIPES
(and how to make nut milk)

Nuts and seeds are both rich in protein, high in fat, and the highest sources of unsaturated fatty acids. Because nuts have a high fat content they can be difficult to digest, best eaten in small quantities. To further protect from rancidity, suggest storing in glass jars in refrigerator or freezer stored 6 months to one year. Best if eaten freshly shelled, cooked, or lightly roasted. A great source of vitamin E, which helps protect nerves and enhance immune function. Help tone the body, add weight, and strength.

Seeds are considered the spark of life, a living and perfect food with all the elements for health. Hulled seeds should be stored in dark glass bottles in the refrigerator as heat and light can cause them to deteriorate and go bad.

Almonds

Sweet flavor. They are the only nut that alkalizes the blood. Good source of magnesium. Almond milk is helpful for lung conditions. It is best to remove skins as they may irritate the lining of the stomach. To remove skins, soak overnight and peel in the morning.

Cashews

Are delicate in flavor with a firm texture that is slightly spongy. They are high in fiber, lower in fat content than most nuts, and have no cholesterol. Are a good source of magnesium, phosphorus, tryptophan, with a high copper content, rich in antioxidants, help body utilize iron, eliminate free radicals. See Recipe: Chili Surprise.

Flax Seeds

Sweet flavor. A rich source of Omega 3s and high in fiber. Strengthens immunity, cleans the heart and arteries, relieves pain, mucus inflamed conditions, soothes and cleanses kidneys and bladder.

Macadamia Nuts

A tree nut with a rich buttery, nutty flavor that is crunchy in texture. Considered one of the finest and most delicious nuts. A high energy food that is full of protein and fiber. High in antioxidants, phytochemicals, vitamins, minerals, and are monosaturated. Eat for snacks, make nut milk, and can be ground to be used as a breading for fish or poultry.

Pecans

High in protein and cholesterol free. Contain more antioxidants than any other nut. A handful supplies vitamin E, calcium, magnesium, potassium, zinc, and fiber. Considered a heart healthy fat. Eating a few, you will feel full quickly.

Pine Nuts

Sweet flavor. Best if roasted or cooked. 3 mg of iron per 1-ounce serving Lubricates lungs and intestines, mild laxative, helpful for dizziness, dry cough, rheumatism, constipation, stimulates hormones, and helps diminish appetite. Has the highest concentration of oleic acid, a mono-unsaturated fat that helps the liver eliminate harmful triglycerides from the body (which helps protect the heart). Iron is a key component of hemoglobin, the oxygen carrying pigment in blood that supplies energy. Rich in magnesium which helps alleviate muscle cramps, tension and fatigue. Note: Do not use Chinese pine nuts.

Sesame Seeds

Sweet flavor. Good source of magnesium. Lubricate intestines, strengthen liver and kidneys. To aid digestion, best eaten ground. Prior to grinding soak overnight, lightly pan roast and then grind.

Walnuts

Sweet flavor. Often considered a brain food because of the wrinkled brain-like appearance of their shells. Good source of important minerals manganese and copper. Contain the antioxidant ellagic acid that helps protect healthy cells from free radical injury and helps with detoxification. High in omega-3 fats. Best if roasted or cooked. Help reduce inflammation, alleviate pain, moisten lungs and intestines, relieve coughing and wheezing, nourish adrenals and the brain. Use in salads, for snacks, and to make nut milk.

How to Make Nut Milk

Milk can be made from your favorite nuts. For each 1 cup of water you will need 1/4 cup nuts of your choice. Soak nuts overnight or in the morning for 4 to 8 hours in enough water to cover them. In morning, drain water from nuts soaking, rinse nuts, and allow them to dry a bit. Place nuts in a blender, blend 30 seconds then add water. Blend until well mixed, foamy and white in color, and you have fresh nut milk. Adjust quantities of nuts and water for the amount of milk you desire.

Tips

Almond skins make milk grainy, so after soaking you will want to remove skins or strain milk through a fine sieve or some cheese cloth. Raw nut milk can be stored in the refrigerator for a few days in a tightly covered glass jar. Milk can be sweetened with a little raw honey, maple syrup, or vanilla if desired.

RECOMMENDED SOURCES FOR PRODUCTS

The following are some of my favorite products that I use often and are always in the cupboard. Some can be found at your local supermarket or health food store, local farm, or will need to be ordered.

Arrowhead Mills

Organic flours | 800-434-4246 | www.arrowheadmills.com

Beyond Gourmet

Unbleached parchment paper | Found in health food stores and some supermarkets

Bob's Red Mill

Flour and oats | 800-349-2173 | www.bobsredmill.com

Braggs Organic Raw Apple Cider Vinegar

800-446-1990 | www.bragg.com

Brookfard Farm

Raw milk, cheese, eggs | 603-742-4084 | www.brookfardfarm.com

Celtic Sea Salt

800-867-7258 | www.celticseasalt.com

HimalaSalt

413-528-5141 | www.Himala.Salt.com

If You Care

Chlorine free baking cups | Found in health food stores and some supermarkets

InJoy Organics

603-286-4696 | www.seashakes.com

Let's Do...Organic

Organic Creamed Coconut | www.edwardandsons.com

Maria and Ricardo's Corn Tortillas

GMO free tortillas | 800-881-7040 | www.habar.com

Mountain Rose Herbs

Organic herbs | 800-879-3337 | www.mountainroseherbs.com

Natural Lifestyle Mail-Order Market

800-752-2775 | www.naturallifestylemarket.com

Philbrick's Fresh Market

Portsmouth, NH 603-422-6758 | North Hampton, NH 603-379-2500

Pomi

Non GMO Italian tomatoes in a box | www.pomi.us.com | Found in supermarkets

Tinkyada, Pasta Joy

Gluten-free pasta | 888-323-2388 | www.ricepasta.com | www.tinkyada.com
Found in health food stores and supermarkets

Raw Coconut Aminos:

888-369-3393 | www.coconutsecret.com

Really Raw Honey

800-732-5729 | www.reallyrawhoney.com

Rumford Baking Powder

Aluminum free, Non-GMO | www.rumfordworld.com

Smart Chicken

888-air-chill | www.smartchicken.com

Spectrum Organic Shortening

800-343-7833 | www.spectrumorganics.com

The Healthy Buffalo

Buffalo and Ostrich meat | 603-369-3611 | www.healthybuffalo.com

Ume Plum Vinegar, Eden Selected

Fermented vinegar | www.edenfoods.com

Wee Bee Honey Naturally Raw Honey

585-652-9592 | www.weebeehoney.net

REFERENCE BOOKS - WEBSITES - MOVIES

In addition to the basic health and interest information I've provided, the following list includes some of my favorite books and movies that can provide even more information.

Books

1. *Staying Healthy with the Seasons*, Elson M. Haas, M.D.

2. *The Good Herb, Recipes and Remedies from Nature*, Judith Benn Hurley

3. *The Complete Food Allergy Cookbook, the Foods You've Always Loved Without the Ingredients You Can't Have*, Marilyn Gioannini with forward by Jacqueline Krohn, MD, Prima Health A Division of Prima Publishing, copyright 1996, 1997

4. *Cooking with Coconut Flour, a Delicious Low-Carb, Gluten-Free Alternative to Wheat*, Bruce Fife, N.D., Piccadilly Books, Ltd, Colorado Springs, CO, 2005.

5. *Nourishing Traditions*, Sally Fallon, New Trends Publishing

6. *Healing With Whole Foods, Asian Traditions and Modern Nutrition*, Paul Pitchford, North Atlantic Books.

Food Websites

www.eatlocalchallenge.com - Encourages eating food that is grown within 100 to 250 miles from home

www.foodcoopinitiative.coop - Helps communities start a local nonprofit co-op

www.localharvest.org - Connects you to CSAs co-ops and farmers' markets in your area

www.ota.com - Information on organic and nonorganic

www.true foodnow.org - A grassroots action network for The Center for Food Safety

www.urbanfarm.org - Advice on how to start an urban farm

www.realmilk.com

www.westinaprice.org

www.organic.org

Movies

Food, Inc.

Food Matters

ACKNOWLEDGEMENTS

So many people have played a part in the completion of this cookbook, and I wish to express my gratitude to each and every one of you for all your help and support.

To my husband, Steve Carter, thank you for your support and encouragement. You were open to trying any recipe I made and giving feedback whether a recipe made it into the book or not. Together we enjoyed many a laugh as we tried to come up with titles that would make us smile and my hope was that if we smiled then maybe anyone using this book would SMILE too! I am so grateful to you for agreeing to create music to cook and dine by to complete my vision for this book! Your creative rhythms and original compositions of music have far exceeded my expectations and you have really made this project come to life! And I look forward to sharing your music with others and our continued adventures!

To Sheri, our older daughter, who has always had a creative and artistic flare. When I mentioned the cookbook to you, I didn't have a clue as to how to set it up. You gave me some guidelines that I incorporated into the book. As you are a new mom and a busy graphic designer, I know how valuable your time is. I mentioned I wasn't sure how to do the finishing format, and you offered without hesitation to format the book. Not to mention all the recipes you contributed for foods that I don't usually cook. Thank you for your creativity and all you do!

To Wendy, our younger daughter, Steve and I both want to thank you for coming up with the perfect title to help pair the music with the cooking. I had been having a difficult time coming up with the right title. I remember your visit when after cooking together and dining, the three of us sat up late tossing around names for the book, and, in no time, you had two that could work and we had a title! Thank you for your encouragement and inspiration!

To Emily, you were my first real friend when I moved to New Hampshire, and I remember telling you about this project. I was just getting started and you offered without hesitation to write a forward for the book. I think that was when the project began to feel real to me. On occasion we would cook together, and, eventually you gave me a few of your recipes to include in the book. As a dietitian, you encouraged me to just be myself in my cooking!

To Jo-el, Steve and I both want to thank you for agreeing to do the cover artwork. I know this was your first book cover and you stretched yourself artistically in creating the cover. As an artist, you listened to what we wanted to convey in the cover, added a bit of whimsy, and did a perfect image of Steve's guitar. Your art really brought forth what the book is about!

To Toni, my cousin who has been like a sister to me, and who upon hearing about the project, offered to read over all the recipes and make edits. I remember how excited I was at such an offer. As grammar and punctuation aren't of interest to me, you had your work cut out for you. And with all the changes and challenges, you always seemed to have fun and we shared many laughs along the way. Thank you for the joy!

To Erika, a published writer (The Little Book of BIG Emotions) and editor of many books: You offered to read the content chapters and edit them for me. This was a huge offer, and I am so grateful for this fortunate, helpful, and synchronous event.

To Diana, a friend and well-respected acupuncturist. When I mentioned the book, you agreed to take a look at a chapter I included on the Seasons to see if I was on the right track relating to the 5-Seasons. I was grateful you agreed to take a look and pleased you fully supported it!

To Beth, my good friend in NH who has been my cheerleader and supporter. Eventually, we became cooking buddies, have had fun shopping for fresh food, cooking to Steve's music, and enjoying our feasts. I treasure these special evenings the three of us have had!

To Janet, a special friend I've known since our girls were small. I knew I could always run thoughts, ideas, and questions by you. Your continual encouragement and support have meant a lot to me!

Also, equally as important are all the people who contributed recipes to this book. Your eagerness to help so I could put out a book that would have something in it for everyone has been so appreciated, and I am grateful to each and every one of you!

This wonderful group of people from 7 different states have contributed some of their favorite recipes to No Fret Cooking. I feel very fortunate to be part of their community, and I would like to share their talents with you. Each contributor is fabulously gifted and has special talents. At the bottom of each contributor recipe, you will find the contributor's name and contact information. It is my hope that you may connect with those you feel drawn to. These awesome people are my family, and my community of friends, and I know you will love them too!

Toni McFarland, Emily Loghmani, Sheri Santo, Wendy Carter, Beth Boynton, Janet Bryant, Debbie Merlin, Laura Melisi, Pat LePore, Amanda Komisarek, Susan Sirois, and Rose Santo.

Thank you everyone for your love, support, guidance, and your individual contributions along this journey to help *No Fret Cooking* become a reality.

In gratitude and love,

Marilynn